# SPORTS VIOLENCE

## The Interaction Between Private Lawmaking and the Criminal Law

**Richard B. Horrow**

Foreword by
James Vorenberg
Associate Dean and Professor of Law
Harvard Law School

Carrollton Press, Incorporated
Arlington & Inverness

**Special Law Series**
**Advisor: J. Myron Jacobstein**
**Law Librarian and Professor of Law**
**Stanford Law School**



Monograph Publishing
Carrollton Press, Inc.
1911 Fort Myer Drive
Arlington, VA 22209

Library of Congress Catalog Number 80-65053
ISBN 978-0-313-27069-7

# FOREWORD

**by James Vorenberg**
**Associate Dean and Professor of Law,**
**Harvard Law School**

Issues relating to excessive violence in sports has received significant attention in recent months. One major aspect involves the relationship of the criminal law to professional sports violence. While most such violence is considered "just part of the game," many exceptionally severe acts are ripe for either criminal prosecution or discipline through the procedure established within each respective league. *Sports Violence: The Interaction Between Private Lawmaking and the Criminal Law* is an attempt to explore this area in detail.

The book is organized to parallel the chronological progression of an exceptionally severe example of sports violence. Chapter One explores the internal pressures which operate to suppress those who wish to pursue a claim against a fellow athlete. With the assistance of responses from surveys sent to 1400 professional athletes on 67 teams in three major sports, the book identifies and examines factors which produce conformity with the generally accepted notion that even severe violence is just part of the game. Chapter Two analyzes the internal league disciplinary mechanisms which purport to deal with violence which is severe enough to overcome pressures to suppress it. In this chapter, relevant procedures of all major professional sports leagues are examined from the perspective of current case law on due process, antitrust, and labor law in order to decide whether they can be, or should be, revised. Chapter Three explores the prosecutorial decision whether to use the criminal justice system to deal with notorious incidents of sports violence. With the help of interviews and responses from surveys sent to 34 county prosecutors in whose jurisdictions the country's major professional teams and their stadiums are located, the book explores the factors which seem to determine whether an athlete is indicted despite the outcome of internal league procedures. Chapter Four details the relevant criminal law that will apply if an athlete is charged and reviews the case law on assault and battery and various defenses such as "consent," "assumption of risk," "provocation," "involuntary reflex," "social utility," and "self defense." A specific instance of an attack during a hockey game is described to illustrate the various levels of how "enforcement" may work in practice. Finally, the book offers a set of recommendations the author believes will lead to fairer and more effective handling of instances of sports violence.

This book is of interest both to sports enthusiasts and those interested in the processes of the law, because of its comprehensive treatment of the specific problems relating to violence in sports—a subject of increasing attention and concern—and because it provides an interesting study of the subtle interrelationsips of traditional legal processes and the privately-conducted systems of law that operate within the professional sports leagues.

# TABLE OF CONTENTS

## SUPPLEMENTAL MATERIAL

The toll on football players is quite severe. The average career of an NFL player is only 4.6 years.[33] More importantly, Dr. Ronnie Sue Stangler, a University of Washington sports psychiatrist, indicates that: "A pro may be trading 20 years of his life for his average $55,171-a-year paycheck. Football is so physically devastating that studies have found a pro's life span is significantly shorter than [that of] most males."[34]

In 1972, the NFL funded the first of two Stanford Research Institute NFL injury studies. An analysis of the 248 pages of classified statistics of Stanford's recommendations on how to curb injuries, and the NFL's subsequent rule changes, reveals pro football's serious problems relating to injuries.[35]

C. BASKETBALL

Since basketball is ostensibly a "non-contact sport," exceptional violence is not as widespread as it appears to be in hockey and football. Nevertheless, potentially litigable incidents do arise. The most notorious of these occurred on December 22, 1977, where an on the court punch by Los Angeles Laker Kermit Washington sent Houston Rocket Rudy Tomjanovich to the intensive care unit of a hospital with a double fracture of the jaw, a

---

33 Trial, supra, at 44.

34 J. Capetta, "The 'Booby' Trap: Does the Violent Nature of Professional Football Vitiate the Doctrine of Due Care in Participant Tort Litigation," 10 Connecticut Law Review 372 (1978).

35 Trial Lawyer's Guide, supra at 401. One judge noted that: "Like coal mining and railroading, professional football is hazardous to the health and welfare of those who are employed as players." Hackbart v. Cincinnati Bengals, 435 F.Supp. at 357.

broken nose, and a concussion.[36]

D. BASEBALL

Though probably the least "violent" of the four sports analyzed, baseball has the capacity for extreme violence that may be directed with criminal intent. The "beanball"--a pitch thrown intentionally at a batter's head--may be "the most dangerous weapon in sports."[37] "It's dangerous every time you step into the batter's box," noted Dave Cash [then] of the Philadelphia Phillies.[38] "Your life is on the line. You're subject to getting killed. I have to put it that way, but how else can you put it?" Being struck by a fastball hurled by a pitcher is extremely painful, and when a batter is hit, retribution can be an effective remedy. Pitchers are often obligated to purposely hit an opposing team's batter to avenge the intentional striking of a teammate. Don Drysdale, retired Dodger pitcher, has stated: "It was two for one. One of our guys, two of theirs."[39]

Criminal law intervention may be required in each of these four sports. However, this paper will concentrate mainly on hockey and football as their

---

36 Nebraska Law Review, supra, at 1128.

37 Criminal Law Quarterly, supra, at 440.

38 Kram, "Their Lives are On the Line," Sports Illustrated 36 (August 18, 1975).

39 Id., at 37. Pitcher Stan Williams of the Dodgers was said to "feel a certain ecstasy at the sight of a sprawled batter." Henry Aaron stated, "He hit me on the head with a 3-and-0 pitch. I was just standing there." Williams later commented to his teammates, "As long as I'm gonna walk him, I might as well hit him."

"violent nature often spawns unnecessary injury."[40] Basketball and baseball will be mentioned wherever appropriate.[41]

---

[40] "Sports, Torts, Courts," 12 _Trial_ 21 (1977).

[41] For example, Chapter II will compare and contrast the internal disciplinary mechanisms of _all_ _four_ sports.

## I) PRESSURES WITHIN PROFESSIONAL SPORTS LEAGUES OPERATING TO SUPPRESS LIGITATION OF POTENTIAL "DURING THE GAME" CRIMINAL LAW VIOLATIONS.

In order to effectively apply the criminal law to any group or organization, the law must be perceived as appropriate and credible as a social control mechanism within that group or organization.[42] Accordingly, this paper explores the mentality of the professional athletic organization from this perspective. It is important to do so for two reasons. First, as will be suggested throughout this paper, it is precisely this "mentality" that mitigates against the effectiveness of the traditional criminal law as a mechanism to control exceptionally severe acts of sports violence. Second, as in more "conventional" areas of "crime", a detailed knowledge of its causes is imperative to the credibility of proposals for its solution.

This inquiry is most appropriately divided into two areas: (A) Pressures which encourage conformity with "generally accepted" "during the game" violence; and (B) Pressures which operate to suppress those who wish to challenge the "generally accepted" norms and practices through the courts.

### A. Pressures Which Encourage Conformity With "Generally Accepted" "During the Game Violence."

For twelve reasons, exceptionally violent sports conduct is viewed either as "not criminal," or as "criminal but necessary."

---

42 Chapter III analyzes how prosecutors view the criminal law in this context.

# PREFACE

This book is a study of criminal violence in professional sports. It examines "during the game" criminal law violations and the forces involved in the litigation process for this legal phenomenon.

There are strong pressures within the various professional leagues to suppress those who wish to challenge "the generally accepted norms and practices" through the courts. The leagues themselves are normally interested in resolving disputes "within the family" and therefore discourage outside court action. In order to vent possible outside legal proceedings, the different leagues have set up internal disciplinary mechanisms which purport to deal with criminal law violations. This study explores the various pressures involved and examines the attitudes and reactions of the leagues and their players.

However, despite the enormous pressure working to keep disputes out of litigation, an increasing number of cases are reaching the courts. Judicial intervention into sports violence cases is carefully discussed and analyzed in this study. Several specific cases are evaluated and the factors which influence a prosecutor's decision to indict are examined. The book has been written at a level that can easily be understood by sport enthusiasts and anyone interested in the process of law. Hopefully, it will contribute to a clearer understanding of this relatively new and important legal phenomenon.

The book has been produced directly from the original research report prepared at the Harvard Law School. The twenty-four appended documents included in the original report are all listed, although some of the documents themselves have been omitted due to confidentiality agreements made with individuals and organizations. It is not believed that these omissions will be at all detrimental to the value of this publication.

I would like to express my great appreciation to Professor James Vorenberg, not only for his help and support in my original research study, but also for his contribution in writing the Foreword for this book.

Richard B. Horrow
Reston, Virginia
January, 1980

Sport is an order of chivalry, a code of ethics and aesthetics, recruiting its members from all classes and all people. Sport is a truce; in an era of antagonisms and conflicts, it is the respite of the gods in which fair competition ends in respect and friendship. Sport is education, the truest kind of education—that of character. Sport is culture because it creates beauty and, above all, for those who usually have the least opportunity to feast upon it.

—Rene Maheu,
General Director, *UNESCO*

At one time in sport, the losing team used to call for three cheers for the winners and the winning team reciprocated with three cheers for the losing team. Do you remember those days? . . . I am sure that you have been appalled, as I have been, while listening to the evidence to hear how sportsmanship has been so lost . . . as to make what once was the sport of hockey something that practically has disappeared from sight . . . .

—From Judge Barry Shapiro's charge to the jury in *Regina v. Smithers*, where 16 year old Paul Smithers was charged and convicted of manslaughter as the result of a death from a fight after a Midget House League game.

## INTRODUCTION

An ancient form of trial was battle by hired champions, in which the substantive rights of the parties turned on the relative fighting and athletic skills of their paid protectors. In contemporary society, just the opposite is the case: the substantive and economic rights of athletic champions depend, in large measure, on the skills of their hired "esquires."[1] In the past few years "sports law" has grown so rapidly as to almost merit its own looseleaf reporter.[2] Behind this growth has been an increased willingness on the part of the courts to attempt to intervene in perplexing sports issues. The sizeable number of recent lawsuits affecting athletes, the expanding scope of congressional inquiry into sports activities, and the increasing body of private commentary[3] indicate the extent of this new trend. It is becoming increasingly difficult for a non-attorney to follow the game.[4]

One significant aspect of the sports law explosion concerns the relationship of the criminal law to professional sports violence. While most "during the game sports violence" is considered "just part of the game," many exceptionally severe acts are ripe for either criminal prosecution or discipline through the mechanism within the respective league. More

---

[1] B. Brody, "The Impact of Litigation on Professional Sports," 14 Trial 35 (1978).

[2] Seven sports articles are listed in the 1964-1967 Index to Legal Periodicals, as contrasted with 61 in the 1973-1976 Index.

[3] J.C. Weistart, "Athletics," 38 Law and Contemporary Problems 2 (1973).

[4] One particularly humorous attempt at legal instruction may be found in Appendix A.

frequently than is generally realized, a player will inflict injury on another player;[5] but such is seldom litigated.[6] In fact, the Michigan Law Review indicates that "because there have been few criminal prosecutions for violence in sports, there are several difficult issues that have received only cursory analysis."[7] Nevertheless, as athletics become more competitive, and as the pressure to succeed becomes stronger, the possibility of violent, unlawful conduct on the playing field increases. Shiela Brooks, Staff Counsel for the National Football League Players Association (hereinafter NFLPA) envisions "a push toward resolving this conduct through the courts in the next decade."[8] It seems clear that the criminal justice system has the power to deal with this conduct through traditional laws prohibiting assault and battery.[9] The seminal argument justifying the criminal justice system's involvement in "during the game sports violence" is advanced by Gary W. Flakne, County Attorney for Hennepin County, Minnesota, and prosecutor in State v. David Forbes,[10] the leading American "sports

---

5 L. Goldstein, "Participants' Liability for Injury to a Fellow Participant in an Organized Athletic Event," 53 Chicago-Kent Law Review 97 (1976).

6 The frequency of professional athletes suing to recover for personal injuries is far less than imagined. Dick Burthelson, Staff Counsel and Assistant Executive Director for the National Football League Players Association estimates that there have only been a total of 10 civil suits involving personal injury. L. Schmidt, "In Football, Its Arbitration," 14 Trial 38 (1978).

7 Note, "Consent in Criminal Law: Violence in Sports," 75 Michigan Law Review 149 (1976).

8 Telephone interview, NFLPA, Washington, D.C. (November 11, 1978).

9 Though other commentators, tangentially refer to this possibility, this is the main conclusion of "Criminal Law: Consent as a Defense of Criminal Battery--the Problem of Athletic Contests," Oklahoma Law Review 845 (1975).

10 Described in detail in Chapter IV.

violence" case:

> The mere act of putting on a uniform and entering the sports arena should not serve as a license to engage in behavior which would constitute a crime if committed elsewhere. If a participant in a sporting event were allowed to feel immune from criminal sanction merely by virtue of his being a participant, the spirit of maiming and serious bodily injury, which at present occurs all too frequently in a sport such as hockey, may well become the order of the day. [11]

Accordingly, this paper will attempt a comprehensive analysis of all aspects of the problem of "during the game sports violence." Initially, the scope of the violence problem will be explored. Then, the chronological progression of a sports violence "case" will be analyzed in four major chapters: (I) Pressures within professional sports leagues operating to suppress litigation of potential "during the game" criminal law violations; (II) Internal league disciplinary mechanisms which purport to deal with "during the game" criminal law violations[12]; (III) Factors which influence a prosecutor's decision concerning whether or not to use the judicial system to deal with "during the game" criminal law violations[13]; (IV) Analysis of legal elements of assault and battery, and the relevant defenses employed in previous sports violence cases.[14] After the analysis of the above concerns, the practical interrelationship of each will be demonstrated through a case study of the Paiement-Polonich hockey stick swinging incident of October 27, 1978, and the subsequent six-week investigation by the Wayne County

---

[11] G. Flakne and A. Caplan, "Sports Violence and the Prosecution, 12 Trial 35 (1977).

[12] Assuming an act is severe enough to get through Chapter I pressures.

[13] Assuming that Chapter II proceedings are not dispositive.

[14] Assuming a case is prosecuted based on the factors in Chapter III.

(Detroit) Prosecuting Attorney's Office. Finally, this paper will propose a number of recommendations intended to remedy certain defects inherent in the current structure of sports violence adjudication.[15]

---

[15] It is important to note that some parts of this paper are less relevant to "the criminal law" than others (antitrust implication of Chapter II internal disciplinary mechanisms, for example). I thought it critical to include all aspects of the problem in hopes of providing a comprehensive perspective. I did, however, develop these "less central" issues in far less detail.

## SCOPE OF THE SPORTS VIOLENCE PROBLEM

### A. HOCKEY

In the 1974-75 hockey season, there were over 44,000 treatments for hockey injuries in U.S. hospital emergency rooms.[16] National Hockey League (hereinafter NHL) penalties that year totalled a record 22,329 minutes, a 25 per cent increase over the 1973-74 season. Also, 8,000 stitches were used to sew up members of the league that year.[17] NHL President Clarence Campbell described the 1974-75 hockey season as the "worst year for sheer violence on the ice."[18] The 1975-76 season was even worse.[19] In fact,

---

16 W. Hechter, "Violence in Sports," 19 Criminal Law Quarterly 431 (1977).

17 See Surface, "Turn Off the Mayhem!," Readers Digest, p.31.

18 See Kennedy, "Wanted: An End to Mayhem," Sports Illustrated 18 (November 17, 1975).

19 See Reed, "Week of Disgrace on the Ice," Sports Illustrated 22 (April 26, 1976). On April 17, 1976, Canadian authorities in Toronto arraigned three National Hockey League (NHL) players on charges of assault and carrying offensive weapons; charges that resulted from hockey "game" involving over 40 penalties. Criminal Law Quarterly, *supra* at 426. The incidents occurred in the third game of the 1976 NHL playoffs between the Philadelphia Flyers and the Toronto Maple Leafs. During the second period Philadelphia Flyer Don Saleski was sent to the penalty box for hooking Jim McKenny of the Toronto Maple Leafs. A Toronto fan taunted Saleski from his seat behind the penalty box, and the player responded by turning towards the fan, and reaching for his hockey stick. An alert guard grabbed the stick, but Saleski wrestled it away. Meanwhile, Flyer defenceman Joe Watson skated to Saleski's rescue and swung his stick over the glass that separates players and spectators striking a constable. Watson later stated: "That was a mistake. I was trying to hit the fan who was bugging Don [Saleski]." Attorney-General McMurtry later charged Don Saleski with assault and carrying an offensive weapon. Teammate Joe Watson was charged with assault, assaulting a police officer, and possession of an offensive weapon (his hockey stick). Later in that same period Flyer Mel Bridgman severely beat Toronto's Borje Salming. Bridgman was subsequently charged with assault and possession of an offensive weapon. That same week, the World Hockey Association (WHA) was embarassed by a Quebec-

"the amount of violence has increased significantly during the past several years."[20]

In one exceptionally severe game,[21] 189 minutes in penalties were assessed, and injuries were received by five players and one team official as a direct result of the fighting and brawling. This incident was the catalyst that produced the first full-scale inquiry into hockey violence. William R. McMurtry, a Toronto private practitioner, was commissioned by the Canadian Minister of Community and Social Services to "explore the implications for...hockey that these violent acts might have."[22] His report has become the definitive work on the causes and prevention of hockey violence.

B. FOOTBALL

As a result of an attempt in 1905 by the entire Pennsylvania football

---

Calgary brawl after which the Quebec Nordiques' team President forced the resignation of Bud Poile, WHA league observer at the game, and the suspensions of Calgary Coach Joe Crozier and team muscleman Rick Jodzio. Jodzio was also charged with assault and intent to maim. Quebec Coach Jean-Guy Gendron was suspended for one game for loss of control over his fighting players. This incident occurred during the second game of the quarter-final round of the World Hockey League playoffs. Following a two-minute stretch in the penalty box, Rick Jodzio skated 80 feet to reach Quebec player Marc Tardif, whom he had been previously intimidating with physical contact. Jodzio hit Tardif full force with a body check, probably knocking him out. Jodzio then jumped on top of him, striking Tardif with both fists. Fight involving both teams erupted and after the ruckus the still unconscious Tardif had to be rushed to the hospital. Jodzio was charged with assault with intent to maim.

[20] Michigan Law Review, *supra*, at 148.

[21] The Hamilton-Bramalea Ontario Hockey Association game of April 16, 1974.

[22] W. McMurtry, *Investigation and Inquiry into Violence in Amateur Hockey* 9 (August 21, 1974).

team to win a game by reducing the Swarthmore star lineman to a bloody pulp, President Theodore Roosevelt threatened to abolish football by executive order unless the game could be made less violent.[23] However, Roosevelt's warning has gone largely unheeded. Jean Fugett, Washington Redskin tight end, stated: "The game is legalized violence, out there you just can't go around beating on somebody's head the way we do. I can go into a game and just literally try to break somebody's neck...It happens all the time."[24] In fact, an increase in violence seems to be the prevalent trend. Professional football player Lynn Swann of the Pittsburgh Steelers, after suffering his fourth concussion and threatening to quit football stated: "Extracurricular violence is increasing and nothing is being done about it."[25]

The seriousness of the violence problem can best be analyzed through injury statistics.[26] From 1969-1974, National Football League (hereinafter NFL) players suffered an estimated 5,110 injuries. A followup study of serious sports injuries reported that serious football injuries[27] in 1974 increased 25 per cent over the previous season.[28] During that year, a

---

[23] Markus, "Sports Safety: On the Offensive," 8 Trial 12 (1972).

[24] Criminal Law Quarterly, supra, at 437.

[25] Note, "A Professional Football Player Assumes the Risk of Receiving a Blow, Delivered Out of Anger and Frustration But Without Specific Intent to Injure," 12 Georgia Law Review 390 (1978).

[26] While there are no specific statistics correlating the number of injuries to violation of the safety rules, commentators suggest that some relationship is plausible given all other indications. P. Schuett, "Tort Liability in Professional Sports: Battle in the Sports Arena," 57 Nebraska Law Review 1138 (1978).

[27] Those which caused the injured party to miss two or more games.

[28] Yeager, "The Savage State of Sports," Physician and Sportsmedicine 94 (1977).

survey of NFL team trainers revealed that injuries increased to an estimated record 1,638. That is 12 injuries for every 10 players.[29] In 1975, there was an increase in the injury rate to the point where one veteran NFL coach said that the 1975 season was the "worst I've seen since I began coaching in the NFL."[30]

At all levels, there are roughly 318,000 annual football injuries treated in hospital emergency rooms. About 30,000 are head and neck injuries, including fractured cervical vertebrae, subdural hematomas, spinal cord injuries, and severe concussions.[31] No part of the body seems immune from football injuries.[32]

---

[29] A. Hofeld, "Athletes--Their Rights and Correlative Duties," 19 Trial Lawyer's Guide 402 (1976).

[30] Id.

[31] H.M. Philo and G. Stine, "The Liability Path to Safer Helmets," 12 Trial 38 (1977).

[32] Trial Lawyer's Guide, supra, at 403. An anatomical breakdown of injuries suffered by NFL players and what percentage of total each represents, is as follows:

| | | |
|---|---|---|
| 1. | Head | 3.3% |
| 2. | Face/dental | 1.2% |
| 3. | Neck | 2.3% |
| 4. | Shoulders | 9.3% |
| 5. | Thorax | 5.2% |
| 6. | Arms/elbows | 3.3% |
| 7. | Wrist | 1.1% |
| 8. | Hands/fingers | 4.1% |
| 9. | Lower back | 3.5% |
| 10. | Abdominal | 0.9% |
| 11. | Hips | 4.0% |
| 12. | Groin | 3.6% |
| 13. | Thighs | 15.1% |
| 14. | Knees | 23.7% |
| 15. | Lower legs | 5.2% |
| 16. | Ankles | 9.4% |
| 17. | Feet/toes | 3.5% |

1. Acceptance of violence and physical intimidation as a "legitimate part of the game." Violence and intimidation in excess of that permitted by the rules of the sport are becoming integral parts of strategy.[43]

In hockey, players fight because "it has become a condition of the job."[44] Max McNab, General Manager and former coach of the Washington Capitals, indicated: "Intimidation is a factor. Physical courage is our primary requirement."[45] In fact, this "courage" that NHL management seeks may translate into the need for legitimate "fighters." Sports attorney Bob Woolf explains:

> The premium the NHL puts on this aspect of the game was reestablished every time I talked with a team on behalf of a draft choice. Invariably, the interview would get around to how well my client could fight. Sometimes, the hockey general manager sounds more like a boxing promoter trying to size up some kid coming out of the amateurs...To my endless amazement, the clubs, if they got the impression the boy wasn't tough, frequently offered to enroll him in boxing classes.[46]

In fact, there is an established "fighters etiquette" in the NHL which requires the combatants to drop their gloves and sticks and fight; the "player-spectators" are required to "pair off" by weight and position and "hold" each other until the fighters are through.[47] Pressure and duress

---

43 M. Partin, "Tort Liability for Players in Contact Sports," 45 University of Missouri-Kansas City Law Review 129 (1976).

44 B. Woolf, Behind Closed Doors 144 (1976).

45 Interview at Capital Centre, Landover, Md. (February 3, 1979).

46 Behind Closed Doors, supra, at 146.

47 A recent account of a January 20, 1979 brawl-filled Washington-Detroit NHL game had Detroit goaltender Vachon describing his role: "Normally, a goalie takes a goalie on this kind of thing. I was closest to Bernie [Wolfe; Washington goalie], so I had to go pick him up. "Detroit Victim of Capital Punishment, Postgame Penalties," Boston Globe, 32 (January 21, 1979).

on players to stand their ground to fight has been openly admitted by former NHL President Clarence Campbell.[48] More significantly, there appears to be an emerging trend to deliberately commence fighting at certain points in a game to reap strategic advantage. McMurtry explains: "What is recent and disturbing, however, is the emergence of a trend towards controlled and deliberate use of physical intimidation making full use of the present rules and the reluctance of the hockey establishment[49] to eradicate fighting as part of the game."[50] Boston Bruin star Brad Park, commenting on the "extracurricular" techniques of the Philadelphia Flyers[51], has stated: "Until this series I always considered a hockey fight to be something that happened after a flare-up. As to this team we find that fights are started deliberately."[52]

As a result of these pressures, it is not surprising to learn that most hockey players feel that fighting is "just part of the game." A series of interviews of 60 NHL players done for the Canadian Journal of Applied Sport Sciences indicates that most players use the word "violence" for only the most injurious acts, usually involving the stick. Fist-fights are not big deals because "no one ever gets hurt."[53] I sought confirmation of this and

---

48 McMurtry, supra, at 24.

49 See factor ten in this chapter. Text surrounding notes 155-170, infra.

50 McMurtry, supra, at 26.

51 The Flyers have been said to have a quote from Theodore Roosevelt tacked to the dressing room bulletin board: "The unforgivable crime is soft hitting. Do not hit at all if it can be avoided, but never hit softly." Criminal Law Quarterly, supra, at 434.

52 Toronto Globe and Mail 51 (May 6, 1974).

53 M. Smith, "Social Determinants of Violence in Hockey: A Review," prepared for Canadian Journal of Applied Sport Sciences 15 (December, 1978).

other theories through the use of surveys sent to all 425 active NHL players.[54] It was decided that while many players would disregard the survey because of apathy, ignorance, or fear of reprisal, enough "interested" players would respond to allow some conclusions to be drawn. A guarantee of confidentiality was made in hopes of mitigating the fear factor.[55] A letter was distributed to each team's Player Representative[56] suggesting that the Players' Association (NHLPA) sanctioned the survey in hopes of mitigating the apathy factor.[57] Judging by the quality of some of the responses, the ignorance factor was overestimated.[58] It was hoped that upon receipt of a packet of 25 surveys, the Player Representative would distribute them to all players, and that the players would respond individually. Some of the more instructive comments were as follows:

> There are so few court lawsuits "because most acts are not serious enough or are usually accepted as part of the game;"
> "It's accepted as part of the game; after the game mostly all is forgotten;"
> "99% of the players accept whatever they get;"[59]
> "It seems as though what happens on the ice is legal, always has been and always will be. If you have been physically abused--tough luck!"

---

54 I co-authored the survey with another third year student who was interested in exploring the First Amendment and its relationship to sports prohibition against public criticism of league management and officials.

55 A copy of the survey appears as Appendix B.

56 Each team designates one player to be its representative regarding matters involving the National Hockey League Player's Association (hereinafter NHLPA).

57 A copy of this letter appears as Appendix C.

58 See text surrounding note 266, <u>infra</u>.

59 It may be argued that the other eleven factors suppress the remaining one per cent.

Since they view their violent behavior as generally acceptable, hockey players seem to perceive no need for criminal law intervention. Dr. Michael Smith, who has been described as "probably one of the leading sports behaviorists who has contributed more to the study of hockey violence than any other academic,"[60] concluded that:

> Hockey players approve of violence, it seems, to the extent its use brings respect (expressive violence) and works as a game tactic (instrumental violence)...Analytically separate, these two uses merge empirically, each reinforcing the other. And though instrumental violence becomes increasingly salient as players learn the occupational culture, expressive violence remains important. Even when counterproductive in terms of winning, players --grown men--cling to rituals of fighting left behind by most males in the schoolyard. 61

In football, aggressiveness is the main quality desired in a prospective player; and sudden physical confrontations are not unusual.[62] John Ralston, the 1973-1976 Denver Broncos coach, recently indicated[63] that "the pre-game psychological preparation should be designed to generate an emotion equivalent to that which would be experienced by a father whose family had been endangered by another driver who had attempted to force the family car off the edge of a mountain road. The precise pitch of motivation for the players at the beginning of the game should be the feeling of that father when, after overtaking and stopping the offending vehicle, he is about to open the door to take revenge upon the person of the other driver."

---

60 Letter from William R. McMurtry (January 16, 1979). Appearing as Appendix D.

61 Smith, <u>supra</u>, at 17.

62 Georgia Law Review, <u>supra</u>, at 388.

63 In testimony before the Federal District Court of Colorado in <u>Hackbart v. Cincinnati Bengals, Inc.</u>, 435 F.Supp. 352, 358 (D. Colo. 1977). Discussed in greater detail in Chapter IV.

Coach Paul Brown[64] testified as to the "controlled rage" built up in pro football players.[65] The players refer to their actions as "intimidation;" not "violence." News stories preceeding Super Bowl XIII developed a consistent theme: "The Steelers and Cowboys are ready to club each other into submission on Sunday of they deem it necessary to win."[66] Said Dallas safety Cliff Harris: "If Swann comes into my territory he can expect to be jolted. That's part of the game. I don't mean anything dirty or illegal will happen, but sometimes it's clean shots that hurt the most."[67] Dave Klein describes the "intimidation" strategy further: "Intimidation usually works best when accompanied by a shattering blow to the opponent's body or a threat of such an act. You remember the pain, or you fear it, while the words and their implied threat may sometimes not even be heard."[68] Former football All-Pro linebacker Nick Buoniconti indicated that "most players assume that all of this is just part of the game."[69] Yet, players direct crippling, legalized violence toward the opposition; particularly the stars

---

[64] Then coach of the Cincinnati Bengals.

[65] Hackbart, supra, at 355-356.

[66] S. Marantz, "Intimidation Talk Getting Louder," Boston Globe 37 (January 18, 1979). It is important to note that newspaper reports are used in this paper merely to provide a general understanding, not for any critical information. I share Chief Assistant Prosecuting Attorney Carnovale's perception when evaluating news accounts of his office's decision not to prosecute a hockey incident (described in full detail in text surrounding notes 836-837 infra): "I would caution you against taking [the media releases] at their full fact value." (Letter of December 6, 1978).

[67] Id.

[68] D. Klein, The Pro Football Mystique 87-88 (1978).

[69] Mr. Buoniconti is now a practicing attorney in Miami. Interview on January 3, 1979.

in their lineup.[70]

In basketball, there is a pervasive sense of physical intimidation without overt violence. As a result, Jeff Cohen, Assistant General Manager of the Boston Celtics, noted that "there may have been only one or two litigable NBA violence cases in 36 years."[71]

Baseball, as has been previously mentioned, "is not particularly the type of sport which gives rise to violent activity."[72] Those acts which are exceptionally severe,[73] however, are "considered part of the game," according to Ray Greeby, Director of Player Relations.[74] Perhaps overstating the case, one commentator concludes: "Caught between club ethics, practical necessity and what they know inside to be wrong, players look away, certain that their frontier law--swift and sure justice--can tolerate headhunting well short of open warfare."[75]

---

[70] Criminal Law Quarterly, supra, at 437. A professional player is quoted as saying, "Why don't they stop arguing about the fine points of clean or dirty play and admit we're out there to murder each other?" Bob St. Clair of the San Francisco '49ers in "The Violent Life of the Greek Goliath," by Al Stump, True Magazine 69 (November, 1963).

[71] Interview at Boston Garden (February 9, 1979).

[72] Carnovale letter, supra. Peter Rose, Associate Counsel for the Major League Baseball Players Association, noted that, "Baseball, fortunately, has not experienced the acts of violence between or among players which have from time to time occurred in the other major sports." (Letter. December 7, 1978).

[73] The interviewee specifically referred to bat swinging (Roseboro), high-spike sliding (Munson) and the "beanball" (see text surrounding notes 37-39, infra).

[74] Telephone interview, New York City (November 10, 1978).

[75] Kram, supra, at 38.

2. Each league implicitly developes its own "criminal common law" distinguishing what is acceptable ("legal") from what is unacceptable ("criminal"). As each sport shapes its own category of intolerable "during the game" conduct, there is a tendency among players to (a) characterize the condoned conduct as "legal" and (b) "allow the league to self-police"[76] the conduct it does not condone.

In hockey, the September 21, 1969 Ted Green-Wayne Maki fight illustrates this "mentality." Green, then a Boston Bruin, "came off the boards and cuffed [Maki] with the back of his glove."[77] Maki retaliated with his stick, "coming straight overhead like a logger splitting a stump."[78] Milt Schmidt, the Bruin coach at the time, said it was "the worst thing he ever saw in a hockey game. He fell like a cut log."[79] Green sustained a serious concussion and massive hemhorraging. After two brain operations, he regained only partial sensation and "has never recovered 100 percent."[80] Two charges were brought; one against each participant. While the Maki stick swinging incident was condemned both in and out of hockey,[81] the judge on the Green case indicated that players think nothing of "ordinary fights and blows struck

---

[76] Confidential player survey (received February 21, 1979).

[77] Testimony at the NHL Disciplinary Hearing, as recounted by B. Woolf, *supra*, at 148.

[78] *Id.*

[79] R. Fitzgerald, "You Hear Green's Name, You Recall That Night," *Boston Globe* 19 (January 24, 1979). Photographs of Maki's "retaliation" appear as Appendix E.

[80] *Id.*

[81] Though Maki was acquitted on self-defense grounds. (See §IV).

by hockey players' gloves."[82] This distinction is pervasive. General Manager McNab has stated that "normal fighting is tolerable, stick swinging is repugnant."[83] In fact, "players are so afraid of an errant stick jeopardizing their careers that the NHLPA--the players' union--will not come to the stick swinger's rescue in any way."[84] Stick fights are abhorrent, "even to most hockey goons."[85]

In football, though the league and its players tolerate the occasional during the game fight, exceptionally severe clip, or late hit, the line is transgressed by a "blatant cheap shot well after the play is over,"[86] or a malicious forearm or stomach punch. Nick Buoniconti seemed to summarize player sentiment when he suggested that "players don't like the idea of a cheap shot artist threatening to shorten their careers."[87] In fact, one former football star has advocated "throwing cheap shot artists out of the league for life."[88]

3. <u>The league and players accept the fact that some less talented players frequently must use violence to compensate for inferior ability.</u>

---

82 <u>Regina v. Green</u>, 16 P.L.R.3d 137, 140 (1970).

83 See note 45, <u>infra</u>.

84 Telephone interview with Brian O'Neill, Executive Vice-President of the National Hockey League. Montreal, Canada (January 11, 1979).

85 J. Lapointe, <u>Detroit Free Press</u> (November 21, 1978).

86 Analogous to the <u>Hackbart</u> case facts, described in Chapter IV.

87 See note 69, <u>infra</u>.

88 The player had one specific person in mind. I have decided not to reveal his name.

As such, the "sports establishment" appears to condone the actions of certain "enforcers" even though these actions may go beyond those which would be tolerated from more skilled players.

In hockey, certain player types are required, among them tough, combative "grinders" who can win the physical battles for the puck and who can fight if necessary, which it inevitably is. Also needed is at least one "policeman," "enforcer," "hit man," "cement head," or "designated figher." Professional coaches, fans, and players "accept this as a fact of hockey life."[89] As for those whose role is to start fights, the professionals talk about two main types. Both, according to Smith, are supposed to (1) protect weaker teammates, (2) lift their team by clubbing an opponent, and (3) intimidate opposing players, star; especially.[90] But they go about their tasks differently. The "cement head" or "goon" does not adhere to the "rules" of fighting and is thus feared and disliked for his unpredictability and potential to injure. The "honest" policeman can be divided into two subtypes. "Both stick basically to the rules of fighting; both are respected, even admired. The first looks for fights--anyone, anytime--never avoiding a potentially faster gun. The second fights infrequently, but his menacing reputation acts as a deterrent on those who might think of challenging him, or one of his teammates."[91]

The hockey "establishment" does not deny this thesis. General Manager

---

89 Smith, supra, at 13.

90 Id., at 17.

91 M. Smith, "Towards an Explanation of Hockey Violence: A Reference--Other Approach," prepared for Canadian Journal of Sociology 4 (1979).

McNab admits that "there are a certain number of policemen."[92] Former NHL President Campbell participated in the following dialogue:

> McMurtry: Now it troubles me because I see this more and more in games where, when the play is stopped, quite often a player with less physical ability as a hockey player attempts to assert his physical superiority as a fighter or strongman.
> Campbell: I think there are efforts made by players to sucker other players off the ice of greater skill, yes. I agree with that.[93]

Enforcers, it seems, are cultivated from the youngest age. Smith suggests that "almost from the start, big kids who can handle heavy going are selected over smaller, less aggressive, though sometimes more skilled performers. By thirteen or fourteen, a boy's willingness and ability to hit are highly important in determining his upward mobility."[94] Smith concludes: "The adolescent bully is certainly not a recent phenomenon, but his sponsorship by adults on the scale evident in youth hockey may be somewhat unique."[95] Boston Bruins "enforcer" John Wensink and former Philadelphia Flyers "policeman" Dave Schultz seem to be products of this early "training." As for Wensink, "he was channeled to follow one road in hockey, the back road, the role of the enforcer...He was asked to punch other people in the chops whenever the occasion arose."[96] As for Schultz, he has been quoted as saying:

---

92 Now General Manager of the Washington Capitals, McNab coached the team for a brief period of time after an illustrious 14 year career in the NHL. See note 45, _infra._

93 McMurtry, _supra_, at 22-23.

94 Smith, _supra_, at 11.

95 _Id._

96 L. Montville, "Weinsink Still Drives the Pump Truck, But He's Added Frills," _Boston Globe_ 27 (December 14, 1978).

"I'm more valuable in the penalty box than I am sitting on the bench...I'm not gonna stop fighting even if I could. It's one of my assets and if it helps win games I'm going to keep fighting."[97]

Since most players tolerate the "enforcer's" actions as "legal," the mentality seems to perpetuate. Smith's 60 NHL interviews revealed responses similar to this one:

> I've got nothing against Schultz because he's trying to make a living and it's not his fault that he's there in Philadelphia. That's the type of player they wanted there and he's that type of guy so they put him in there and he's going to do the job. [98]

Occasionally, players will rebel at this type of activity. Though a few might go so far as to "sue a hit man,"[99] most retaliation will occur "on the ice," as Wayne Maki did to then Bruins enforcer, Ted Green.[100] In short, the criminal law may be ineffective in controlling such conduct that is not perceived by its participants as criminal. McNab explains in this context: "Keep the courts out. In this way, a player with lesser ability can hold his own by being rougher."[101]

In football, this mentality appears to be less significant. However, there is some indication that "enforcer-types" are tolerated. Following a 1976 incident similar to the one in Hackbart[102] involving George Atkinson of

---

97 McMurtry, supra, at iii.

98 Smith, supra, at 15.

99 Two players responding to my confidential survey suggested that they would sue.

100 Green was the undisputed enforcer at that time. Said Green: "I was a softie, but the way I learned hockey was to be an aggressor. That was the only way to get the respect of the other team." Fitzgerald, supra, at 19.

101 See note 45, infra. The prosecutorial rebuttal to this argument will be presented in Chapter III.

102 Discussed in Chapter IV.

the Oakland Raiders and Lynn Swann of the Pittsburgh Steelers, Coach Chuck Noll of the Steelers spoke publicly of a "criminal element" in the NFL and stated that Atkinson should be "kicked out of the league." Atkinson responded by filing a slander suit against Noll which was decided against Atkinson in a jury trial. During the proceedings, Noll implied that one of his players was part of the "criminal element" and was sued by that player as well. The suit was subsequently dismissed.[103]

4. The league and its players use the "catharsis argument" to justify any excessively violent conduct and, hence, do not perceive it as criminal. The argument is described by Smith: "That the speed and body contact--the very nature of the game causes an accumulation of aggressive impulses (usually described as "frustration") which must be released, if not one way, then another, and that prohibiting fist fighting thus would result in more vicious and dangerous illegal use of the stick."[104] This argument is usually coupled with the co rollary that "no one ever gets hurt in a fight because the technique is awful and the footing horrendous."[105] Of course, the argument has little merit.[106] However, the salient point is that the "hockey

---

[103] Georgia Law Review, supra, at 381.

[104] Smith, supra, at 1.

[105] McNab interview, supra.

[106] First, if violence were inherent in hockey, Smith argues that it would be more evenly distributed throughout the sport. Second, researchers have demonstrated that aggression does not automatically follow from frustration. Third, Smith argues that the real determinant of hockey violence is not innate aggressive tendencies, but "(1) the social organization of the hockey 'system'; (2) the ways in which the communications media portray the professional game; and (3) the attitudes of players' reference others, especially parents, coaches, and teammates." Fourth, fighting can cause severe harm. (See the Blonich-Paiement case study following Chapter IV). Fifth, there is nothing in the casebooks or statutes that condone a clear violation of law on the premise that a larger violation will be prevented.

establishment" believes in the argument strongly enough to shape its conduct accordingly. McNab suggests that most of hockey management supports this theory. Smith argues that "the majority of professional and amateur players appear to believe this."[107] Most survey responses resemble the following:

> I don't see any violence in two players dropping their gloves and letting a little steam escape. I think it's a lot better than spearing somebody. I think it's an escape valve because you know yourself pressure builds up and there's no way to release it and if fighting is not allowed then another violent act will occur.

This "justification" is taught as early as the "enforcer mentality" seems to be. Coaches do not approve of penalties per se, argues Smith, but they will accept a certain number as a consequence of "spirited, aggressive play and ubiquitous frustration. Then there is the 'good penalty.' 'You should have tripped him,' said a house league coach to a wide-eyed boy, eight."[108]

5. Sports violence is taught and accepted by its participants as non-criminal at a very early age.[109] This paper has already briefly explored some of the specific messages that are learned at a young age. This argument, however, suggests that the entire mentality of hockey and football revolves around the notion that each young "gifted athlete" is trained to believe that there is nothing "illegal" about fighting (or even more mali-

---

107 Smith, *supra*, at 1.

108 *Id.*, at 12.

109 This is the central theme of McMurtry's conclusion after his exhaustive investigation, labelled as "a guiding force on continuing efforts to reform hockey through criminal court intervention." [L. Halowell and R. Meshbesher, "Sports Violence and the Criminal Law," 12 *Trial* 27 (1977).] This was also the main thrust of the defense employed by Meshbesher in the *State v. David Forbes* hockey assault case (described in Chapter IV) which resulted in a hung jury.

cious conduct) if it is done during the course of a game.

In hockey, Canadian boys typically enter organizational hockey around age seven. The ablest are quickly funnelled into highly competitive "select" leagues and begin a training at the end of which, around sixteen, those who have remained emerge, as Vaz puts it, a "tough fighting unit prepared for violence whose primary objective is to win hockey games."[110] By Midget age (fifteen) Smith states that, "coaches are looking for players who can mete out, and withstand, illegal physical coercion."[111] McMurtry indicated in a telephone conversation that young leagues must produce "quality hockey players" rather than "good sports" because the Junior A Leagues have "become a mini-business, cultivating 14 year old professionals." These, "feeding grounds for the pros" survive mainly on the $40,000 they receive for each "professional player" they produce.[112] McMurtry's published conclusion seems obvious from what has been mentioned above:

> There is...substantial increase in violence in amateur hockey, and more alarming, the use of violence as a tactical instrument to assert superiority over an opponent...Violent games which were once unheard of at the pee wee (12) and minor bantam (13) level are now not uncommon.[113]

Given the prevalence of the preachings of violence at a young age, the fact that it is so universally accepted should not be so surprising, especially since "a youth's conduct should be expected to reflect his relative lack of

---

110 E. Vaz, "The Culture of Young Hockey Players: Some Initial Observations." In A. Yiannakis, T. McIntyre, M.J. Melnick, and D.P. Hart (eds.), Sport Sociology: Contemporary Themes 212 (1976).

111 Smith, *supra*, at 3.

112 Telephone interview, Toronto, Canada (January 12, 1979).

113 McMurtry, *supra*, at 17-18.

maturity and judgment."[114] Smith's study of the number of players who agree with statements regarding the utility of violence (Appendix F) is quite revealing.[115]

Some have argued that a youngster learns that violent hockey acts are "legal" by watching, and thus emulating, professional hockey.[116] In a sample survey of 604 Toronto junior players 56 percent suggested that they had learned "how to hit a player illegally" from watching pro hockey, and 60 percent had actually used some of these tactics "at least once or twice."[117] (Detailed descriptions of what they had learned appear as Appendix G.) McMurtry concludes that "it is not surprising that virtually every boy playing hockey is profoundly influenced by examples portrayed in the NHL."[118]

It may be instructive to learn that this "early violence education" is an exclusively North American phenomenon. General Manager McNab indicated that after a recent suspension of a Washington Capital star defenseman,

---

[114] S. Langerman and N. Fidel, "Responsibility is Also Part of the Game," 12 Trial 23 (1977).

[115] As one example, Smith found that 88 percent of the 15 year olds he interviewed agreed with this statement: "If you want to get personal recognition in hockey, it helps to play rough. People in hockey look for this." 84 percent agreed with the following: "To be successful, most hockey teams need at least one or two tough guys who are always ready to fight."

[116] The blame, of course, must not rest solely with the hockey establishment. Smith places much of the responsibility upon some parents who, as Smith suggests, "see fisticuffs as character building." Smith spends many pages giving examples of some parental comments, and concludes: "Fathers' approval of fighting has been statistically related to the number of fights their sons are in over a season's play...The more violence approval, the more violence." Smith, supra, at 8-10.

[117] J. Eastwood, "The Effects of Viewing a Film of Professional Hockey on Aggression," 6 Medicine and Science in Sports 158-163 (1974).

[118] McMurtry, supra, at 20.

a Swedish player was the only one who thought the penalty was not severe enough. "No one else thought he did anything bad enough to be suspended."[119]

In football, much the same situation appears to exist, though the causes may be somewhat different. One commentator notes that: "Intentional injuries will continue as long as high school players feel that they must demonstrate ability to play "a hard nosed game" in an effort to obtain a football scholarship to college; the same holds true for college players who, in desiring to make a career in athletics, emulate the professionals in hopes of being drafted.[120] Legendary coach Vince Lombardi indicated: "Pro football, like the college game, is a violent, dangerous game. To play it other than violently would be imbecile."[121]

6. Media portrayal of the most violent parts of the sport in a relatively attractive manner reinforces the belief that such action is not criminal. The proportion of media hockey violence that could be said to have a pro violence slant is not known, but unquestionably the media conveys the idea that fighting and the like is acceptable, even desirable behavior. Smith notes a recent "tribute" to Gordie Howe appearing in McLean's Magazine:[122]

> It is not as if he plays some Caspar Milquetoast game, shying from the corners, relying on speed and finesse...He never was one to skate from a fight. After he was nearly killed from a check into the

---

[119] See note 45, supra.

[120] "Contact Sports Injury Cases," 7 Am Jur Trials 237 (1964).

[121] V. Lombardi and T. Cohane, "Why Pros Play Better Football," 25 Look 107 (October 24, 1961).

[122] Smith, supra, at 5.

> boards by Ted Kennedy of Toronto Maple Leafs--a skull operation saved his life--he returned as one who knows it is better to give than to receive, that retribution is best administered quickly and decisively. With Lou Fontinato of New York Rangers he participated in what many regard as the greatest hockey fight in the history of the NHL. Fontinato was the terror of the league then, intimidating everyone, pulverizing even the mighty Rocket Richard, but Howe destroyed him in that fight. He broke his nose, splattered Fontinato's blood over his face and jersey, and Fontinato never was as terrifying again. 123

It appears that the hockey media exploits violence to pander to the unsophisticated American hockey fan, who will most easily understand and appreciate the brutality of the sport. Former hockey great Brian Conacher notes in his book, Hockey in Canada the Way It Is, that "the growing incidence of brawling in the game, I believe, is not unconnected with the 'image' of the game that is now being presented to the violence-oriented American hockey fan. The large numbers of people that are being exposed to the game now are often not aware of the skills and finesse that gives the game its real appeal. But brawling is something they do understand, so as far as the games, television acceptance, and crowd appeal is concerned, it probably doesn't hurt to have a few good brawls. If there is a little blood so much the better for people with color sets."

Football coverage seems no different. Shiela Brooks, NFLPA Staff Counsel, suggests that the public "is keenly aware of the more violent aspects of the game" because of increased media concentration upon it, not an increase in violence per se.[124]

---

[123] It is ironic to note that one of the reasons McNab gives for the decreasing interest in hockey is the "severe media criticism of hockey violence without a real understanding of what the game is really about." (See note 45, supra.)

[124] Telephone interview (see note 8, supra). From the perspective of Canadian hockey violence, McMurtry appears to approve of the football media's

7. Peer pressures by teammates and opponents encourage conformity to the generally accepted standard of violent behavior. In modern hockey, players are forced to fight when challenged or risk being branded as cowards by both their peers and spectators.[125] McMurtry indicates that "it is extremely difficult for the player who is being provoked and being pushed to turn his back and appear to be running. The pressure of his own team-mates and from the many millions of fans make it an impossibility for him to do that."[126]

That hockey players are thus forced to enter into fights has been grudgingly admitted by the President of the National Hockey League. The following exchange occurred between McMurtry and NHL President Clarence Campbell when Campbell testified before McMurtry's commission:

> McMurtry: To have the sanction there is being embarrassed and ridiculed and to be discussed among your peers and your coach and many million fans, that is not one of the most difficult decisions in the world for a person to turn his back and not fight.
> Campbell: I didn't say it wasn't difficult. I said it is an alternative.
> McMurtry: Then if you agree it is a very difficult alternative, it is apparently what you call the free alternative.
> Campbell: All right.
> McMurtry: There is incredible pressure and duress on that player not to turn his back--is that not true?
> Campbell: I don't think it is as great as you say, but it's real.
> McMurtry: There is real pressure and duress on that player to stand his ground and to fight.
> Campbell: I think so, yes, yes.[127]

---

coverage: "It is worth noting that the coverage in professional football seems to emphasize far more the finesse of the game, and this in a game that has more than its share of violence." McMurtry, supra, at 43.

125 R. Binder, "The Consent Defense, Sports, Violence, and the Criminal Law," 13 American Criminal Law Review 245 (1975).

126 McMurtry, supra, at 23.

127 American Criminal Law Review, supra, at 245.

The NHL players were asked by Smith how they and their teammates react to someone who refuses to fight when challanged. About half were unequivocal: "I'd rather see a guy fight and lose than turn his cheek and not fight at all, and I think a lot of the players are like that. You pretty well realize that you have to fight, otherwise the guys look down on you." The nonfighter threatens group cohesiveness. "You get a couple of guys trying to beat you up, you know he's not going to be there to help you out. That's a big thing. You don't look at these guys with much respect really."[128] In answer to my survey, some players made reference to "an overall 'macho' image" built into the league as the subtle pressure encouraging violent conduct.[129] In fact, it seems critical that a young player fight immediately upon entry into the league so as to "earn the respect" of his teammates and opponents. The <u>Boston Globe</u> provides an example:

> The Bruins have given rookie Al Secord a nickname. They call him "rockey," and after last night it probably will stick. Secord took Dave Hutchison's stock on the chin in the third period and both players dropped their gloves. Hutchison said, "come on" with his hands and Secord belted him with a left that buckled Hutchison's knees. "That's the best way to beat him," said Secord, "get in the first punch." [130]

Smith suggests that this phenomena begins to emerge around age twelve, when some leagues become violence prone. Youngsters "begin to evaluate one another's gameness. Reputations are being forged."[131] By fourteen, most boys are well versed in the informal norms that regulate the use of violence. Deviants, "chickens," suffer varying degress of contempt. The con-

---

128 Smith, <u>supra</u>, at 16.

129 Confidential survey (received February 22, 1979).

130 "Walton Returns," <u>Boston Globe</u> (December 6, 1978).

131 Smith, <u>supra</u>, at 14.

formity pressure seems to increase as players get older and continue through the professional ranks. First, as players get older and increasingly socialized into the occupational culture, attitudes toward violence tend to come into line. Second, as the less proviolent become older, they quit hockey at increasingly faster rates than the more proviolent. As a result, Smith and Russell argue that "socialization and selection processes operate jointly to produce relative homogeneity in the way performers feel about violence."[132] Smith's follow-up study of Canadian junior hockey players[133] indicated that by age 21, 78 percent of the performers saw their teammates as highly approving of their fighting.

8. Pressures by coaches encourage conformity to the generally accepted standard of violent behavior. In hockey, most coaches do not seem to expect everybody to be a fighter, or even highly physically aggressive "if it is not their nature and if they compensate with other valuable skills."[134] Yet, there are minimum requirements for these coaches: "You must help your teammates in trouble; you cannot let opponents' attempts at intimidation effect your performance."[135] In other words, a player at least has to be willing to grapple with a man in a melee, to prevent ganging-up, and tough enough to withstand opponents' coercive tactics.[136] Most coaches probably

---

132 Id., at 14.

133 Conducted in a manner similar to Eastwood's. See text surrounding note 117, supra.

134 R.R. Faulkner, "Making Violence By Doing Work: Selves, Situations and the World of Professional Hockey," 1 Sociology of Work and Occupations 288 (August, 1974).

135 Id.

136 Smith, supra, at 16.

do not overtly instruct a player to deliberately harm another player. In fact, McNab adamently contended that he never told a player to "get someone" when he was a coachnor heard it when he was a player.[137] However, studies have demonstrated that a coach's emphasis on "playing rough and being aggressive" frequently translates into the players' approval of "taking out opposing players any way you can."[138]

Though most coaches do not overtly encourage severe violence, there appear to be certain exceptions. Fred Shero, current coach of the New York Rangers, after a successful championship tenure with the Philadelphia Flyers, is described as "sending his men onto the ice looking for a fight."[139] He has been quoted in Trial as stating: "Players die like flies in football, why is everybody up in arms over violence in hockey."[140] Don Cherry, coach of the Boston Bruins, seems to have a similar reputation. Commenting on "enforcer" John Wensink's newly found ability to skate and score goals, Cherry noted: "I just hope he doesn't forget what got him there. I

---

137 See note 45, infra.

138 E.W. Vaz and D. Thomas, "What Price Victory? An Analysis of Minor League Players Attitudes Toward Winning," 2 International Review of Sport Sociology 47 (1974).

139 Time 71 (January 6, 1975). The Philadelphia Flyers are admittedly an unusual team, but the tactics they have perfected have long been practiced with less expertise by others. The article above describes a game early in the season in which Orest Kindrachuk of the Flyers and Mike Christie of the California Golden Seals continued fighting in the penalty box after being sent off the ice for fighting. Other members of both clubs joined the fray, creating a 40 minute delay, and resulting in 170 penalty minutes for ten players, ejecting eight from the game. Afterwards, Flyer Coach Shero stated: "Some people say I should have been fined for not controlling my players...Hell, I would have fined them if they hadn't gone in to support Kindrachuk." In a later feature article in Bernie Parent, the Flyer goalie, the record-setting pace of the Flyers in total penalty minutes is discussed: "The reason for all the violence is Shero's strategy of victory through fear-power. Freely admitting that Philadelphia lacks the quality players of other leading teams, Shero tries to make up for it with position play and intimidation. Time 53 (February 24, 1975)

140 Flakne and Caplan, supra, at 33.

mean the goals are nice, but I'll tell you the truth. I was happy he got the hat trick the other night, but not as happy as I've been when he's won some big fights for us. I know I shouldn't say that, but that's the honest truth.[141] Cherry was also quoted in Trial: "I only wish I had one man I could have sent after Mikita to send him back to Czechoslovakia in a coffin."[142] As with many other "pressures," the "violence coaching" begins early. McMurtry explains why:

> The majority of coaches are involved in minor league hockey, notwithstanding their good intentions, have really no concept of coaching other than the image portrayed by the professionals. Often it is easier for a coach to just stress the aggressive and violent side of hockey rather than the skills.[143]

Not surprisingly, Smith's study[144] revealed that 52 percent of the 21 year old players saw their coaches as highly approving of their fighting. Clark's research logically concludes: "The more coaches approve of fighting, the more players fight."[145]

9. Pressures by owners and general managers encourage conformity to the generally accepted standard of violent behavior. In hockey, since most General Managers grew up through the "hockey establishment," they would appear to preach the same violence dogma as others previously mentioned. Accordingly, I sent questionnaires to each of the 17 NHL General Managers asking them to comment on "formal and informal pressures which op-

---

141 Montville, Boston Globe, supra.

142 Flakne and Caplan, supra, at 33.

143 McMurtry, supra, at 32-33.

144 See notes 133 and 134, infra.

145 W.J. Clark, E. Vaz, V. Vetere, and T.A. Ward, "Illegal Aggression in Minor Hockey: A Causal Model," prepared for F. Landry and W. Orban (eds.),

erate to keep such cases out of the criminal courts."[146] Despite NHLPA Managing Officer Simpson's prediction that the General Managers would "be open,"[147] only two responded. One[148] formally directed my inquiry to the league office in Montreal. The other response, by Los Angeles Kings General Manager George Maguire, was, upon reflection, quite consistent with the mentality expressed above:[149]

> Not only do I not have time to answer your letter in the detail you request, I have no interest in exploring violence in professional sports with relationship to criminal law. I am not of the opinion that criminal violence exists in professional sports, and I feel that too many people try to make a mountain out of a mole hill when they have a tough time even finding the mole.

In football, the owners seem to encourage violence for the same reason that some lower level coaches do: they "are basically incompetent"[150] at the football business. However, Klein notes that " the owners are victimized by their own gigantic egos."[151] As a result, Klein argues that some owners will "meddle" in the internal affairs of running a football team, regardless of their competence. Hence, an owner will compensate for his lack of football knowledge by advocating the virtues of aggressiveness, rough play, and, possibly, criminality. Though Ed Garvey, NFLPA Executive

---

<u>Ice Hockey: Research, Development and New Concepts</u> (1979).

146 The questionnaire appears as Appendix H.

147 Telephone interview, NHLPA, Montreal, Canada (January 11, 1979).

148 Montreal Canadian General Manager Irving Grundman.

149 The letter appears as Appendix I.

150 Klein, Pro Football Mystique, <u>supra</u>, at 184.

151 <u>Id.</u>, at 178.

Director, maintains that owner pressure "is not even a factor,"[152] sportswriter Will McDonough[153] argues that owners condone potentially criminal contact as "just part of the game" because, "in their minds, violence is largely responsible for the success of football."[154]

10. Pressures created by the rule structure itself encourages conformity to the generally accepted standard of violent behavior. One implication of factors one through nine is that the hockey and football establishment, through a combination of covert and overt pressures and norms has substituted its own standard of "criminal conduct" in place of that which governs the society at large. Naturally, the league rules which purport to control this conduct become increasingly important. However, rather than control violent behavior, the NHL rules appear to encourage it.[155] Once a hockey rule proscribes a certain level of conduct, it is implicitly assumed that all conduct short of that level is tolerated, if not encouraged.[156] For example, NHL Rules 42 and 54 deal with "Abuse of Officials and Other Misconduct," and "Fisticuffs," respectively. There is nothing in either rule which prohibits fighting absolutely. These rules merely define two or five minute penalties for starting a fight[157]; intervening in an already existing

---

[152] Personal interview at NFLPA Office, Washington, D.C. (November 23, 1978).

[153] Telephone interview, Boston Globe (November 11, 1978).

[154] See factor 12, this section.

[155] The specific hockey, football, basketball, and baseball "anti-violence" rules will be discussed in greater depth in §II.

[156] The surveys that indicate that penalties, fines, and suspensions have no effect (see Chapter II) become more significant from this perspective.

[157] Rule 54(a).

fight;[158] fighting off the playing surface;[159] and taking too long to clear the ice after a fight.[160] The "note"[161] to Rule 54(b) does require a referee to "employ every means provided by these Rules to stop 'brawling',"[162] but this involves a level of violence far above a "normal fight."

McMurtry indicates that "the present rule structure in hockey is such that according to many players and coaches a [player] must fight whether he wants to or not. Because of the fact that very little attempt is made to prevent provocation, and only nominal penalties are assessed for fighting, a player has no reason or justification for turning his back and refusing to fight. In fact, if a player refuses to fight and an opponent for no particular reason deliberately punches him, and even renders him senseless, the 'appropriate' penalty at the present time is a two minute minor."[163] There is strong evidence from the social scientists that tolerating a rule structure such as that which exists in hockey reinforces and rewards violence outside the rules and leads to even more violence during the game.[164] Yet, the NHL has failed to consider this problem in any meaningful way. For example, though a rule currently in force allows a referee to assess a "misconduct penalty" on one whose "course of conduct [is]...designed to in-

---

158 Rule 54(d)

159 Rule 54(c)

160 Rule 42(e)

161 Seemingly similar to a Restatements' "commentary."

162 1978-1979 Official Rule Book of the National Hockey League 56 (1978) (hereinafter Rule Book).

163 McMurtry, *supra*, at 26.

164 *Id.*, at 29.

cite an opponent into incurring a penalty,[165] NHL President Campbell admits that this rule has had "relatively little use."[166] Further, the NHL has never "experimented with an attempt to give a match penalty for fighting."[167] Finally, when the media exerted some pressure on the NHL to amend its fighting rule structure,[168] rather than sanctioning fighting more severely, the league created a rule whereby a team is assessed a penalty if any player delays in proceeding directly to the penalty box.[169] McMurtry's conclusion is quite appropriate in this context: "The sick situtation in professional hockey is further aggravated by the structure of their rules. In particular, it is perhaps the only sport which tolerates fighting as 'part of the game'."[170]

11. Even if exceptionally violent conduct were considered "criminal" by the sports establishment (despite one through ten), the intense competition encourages such conduct, notwithstanding its "criminal" quality. In hockey, since winning is viewed "as the sole criterion for success,"[171] the

---

165 Rule 42(g). Since there are "penalties" for all of hockey's criminal-like acts, this presumably could be the vehicle for strict enforcement of an anti-violence policy.

166 Campbell dialogue with McMurtry, *supra*, at 25.

167 *Id.*, at 26.

168 Not because of an inherent dislike of hockey violence, but because the "TV networks did not like the inordinate delays caused by the interminable fighting which once consumed over three and one-half hours of prime time." *Id.*, at 29.

169 Rule 42(e).

170 McMurtry, *supra*, at 22.

171 *Id.*, at 21.

means used to achieve that end become less scrutinized. This "winning only" mentality appears to begin early. Thomas Tutko, sports psychologist, observes:

> The pre-occupation with, 'winning only,' and being Number 1 is a sick pre-occupation for sports. It is very painful to think of all the youngsters who love sports but who are being eliminated at every stage, just because they're too slow or too weak. [172]

As players reach the "big leagues," the competition for positions grows more keen because the number of teams progressively diminishes. Goode notes that "the structure of the system compels aspirants to conform increasingly to prevailing occupational standards, which include the necessity of employing at least a minimal amount of what might be called 'force threat'."[173]

In football, intense competition against teammates (for roster positions) and opponents (for victory) leads to the mentality that the law of survival is the only law that governs. In testimony before the Hackbart court,[174] coaches Ralston and Brown admitted that it was normal behavior in the NFL for players "to disregard the safety of opposing players."[175] Dwight White, defensive end for the Pittsburgh Steelers, attributed the violence to intense competition and to the law of survival. "You either hit or be hit... Yes, it is brutal." When confronted with the statistics showing the high rate of injuries to players in the league, Mr. White responded: "Just put it down as [an] occupational hazard. I am very uninterested in how many people got

---

[172] T. Tatko, "In Sports Winning Really Isn't Everying," 11 People 49.

[173] W.J. Goode, "Force and Violence in the Family," in S.K. Steinmetz and M.A. Straus (eds.), Violence in the Family (1975).

[174] See note 63, infra.

[175] Hackbart, supra, at 355-56.

hurt; how many people didn't get hurt....It's really a law of survival; [if] you play the game you assume certain liabilities...you might get hurt or might get maimed or your neck broken....All that is part of the game."[176] The Hackbart court noted that "professional football players are conditioned to 'play with pain'[177] and...are expected to perform even though they are hurt."[178]

12. Even if exceptionally violent conduct were considered "criminal" by the sports establishment (despite one through ten), the belief that violence enhances the marketability of the game encourages such conduct, notwithstanding its "criminal" quality. The NHL appears reluctant to stop violence for monetary reasons. Canadian Attorney-General Roy McMurtry[179] has stated: "The truth of the matter is that they're just afraid to do it because they are convinced that a number of people go to the games because they like to see the brawling."[180]

---

[176] Criminal Law Quarterly, supra, at 438.

[177] This factor is quite relevant in determining why so few sports victims use the courts for redress. (See Chapter I, §B.)

[178] Hackbart, supra, at 355. "'Suck it up!' 'Play with pain!' 'It's a hitter's game!' They are the litanies of the cult. They must be accepted if you wish to survive in a game that has clearly become vicious." Criminal Law Quarterly, supra, at 438. In fact, in the Hackbart case itself, defensive back Hackbart was severely injured. Although experiencing pain, he continued to play in several games and did not receive medical attention until after he was put on waivers by the Denver Broncos.

[179] Brother of William R. McMurtry, author of the oft-cited Investigation and Inquiry into Violence in Amateur Hockey.

[180] Criminal Law Quarterly, supra, at 432.

Jack Mehlenbacher, a former NHL referee, laid the blame on the owners, asserting "[t]he big wheels of the NHL figure they have to have blood to fill the arenas. I refereed for five years and that was all they were interested in."[181] The President of the NHL, Clarence Campbell, admitted as much during the McMurtry hearings: "It is the businss of conducting the sport in a manner that will induce or be conducive to the support of it at the box office...Show business, we are in the entertainment business and that can never be ignored. We must put on a spectacle that will attract people...."[182] This appears to be the "outsiders" view as well. Football Players' Association Executive Director Ed Garvey commented that: "Hockey owners go crazy when criminal charges are brought because they believe that violence sells tickets."[183]

This policy may be dictated by the nature of the audience. The National Hockey League sells hockey to a wide audience in the United States and Canada. This audience understands a hockey brawl far more easily than the skill and finesse demanded of European players who are applauded by a more sophisticated audience.[184] McMurtry notes that every American media characterization of the game involves "brutal top heavy Neanderthal types who were shown demonstrating every conceivable type of foul with great gusto and relish."[185] McMurtry's emotional conclusion to his argument suggests

---

181 W. Kuhlmann, "Violence in Professional Sports," Wisconsin Law Review 776 (1975).

182 McMurtry, *supra*, at 21.

183 Personal interview, see note 152, *infra*.

184 Criminal Law Quarterly, *supra*, at 428.

185 McMurtry, *supra*, at 22.

the reason that this "criminal" conduct is condoned and encouraged:

> When the evidence strongly indicates that there is a conscious effort to sell the violence in hockey to enrich a small group of show-business entrepreneurs at the expense of a great sport (not to mention the corruption of an entire generation's concept of sport), then one's concern grows to outrage. [186]

In football, the mentality appears to be similar, and for the same reasons. Football, as Klein notes, is played for the financial benefit of athletes, coaches, team owners, and the television networks.[187] One commentator concludes, as expected, that "brutality is profitable: the NFL's mystique of raw, explosive fury has filled stadiums and swelled TV audiences to 100 million a week."[188]

In short, the twelve factors above seem to be significant pressures which encourage conformity to "generally accepted" "during the game" violence. Faced with such realities, the Criminal Law Quarterly forcefully concludes:

> There is no socially useful element to an unprovoked, premeditated assault, on or off the playing field. Football, baseball, ahd hockey are socially useful activities whose value is threatened by league rules and policies which encourage criminal assault. [189]

---

186 McMurtry, *supra*, at 30.

187 Klein, Pro Football Mystique, *supra*, at 2.

188 Criminal Law Quarterly, *supra*, at 437.

189 *Id.*, at 453.

B. Pressures Which Operate to Suppress Those Who Wish to Challange the "Generally Accepted" Norms and Practices Through the Courts.

Even if a certain minority of participants view exceptionally violent sports conduct as "criminal and unnecessary," they will most probably not rely on the courts as an instrument for effecting change for six reasons.

1. There appears to be a "conventional understanding" that all disputes are best resolved "within the family." General Manager McNab seems to be speaking for the NHL when he argues: "The league has policed itself pretty well; we need no outside interference."[190] The sports establishment appears to "feel more comfortable with disputes beginning and ending with the league."[191] Most owners suggest that the league's internal disciplinary proceedings provide an adequate means of controlling players' behavior on the ice. For example, Walter Bush, the owner of the team for which Boucha played when he was injured by Forbes, told the press at the time of the verdict in that case, "I still believe any action between professional and amateur athletes on their fields of play should be handled by their respective leagues."[192] The pervasive justification is that the league, most notably Brian O'Neill,[193] "knows the sport better than any court does."[194] The official NHL policy is that though the league "prefers"

---

190 Personal interview. See note 45, infra.

191 Personal interview with Pierce Gardner, Public Relations Director, Washington Capitals. Interview at Capital Centre, Landover, Md. (February 3, 1979).

192 Minneapolis Tribune §1A (July 19, 1975).

193 NHL Executive Vice-President in charge of assessing fines and suspensions. (See Chapter II.)

194 Telephone interview with NHLPA Office Manager Simpson, Montreal, Canada (January 11, 1979).

to handle a case internally, and will be "upset" when it reaches the indictment stage, it will not "inhibit the legal proceedings or comment adversely." In fact, an occasional symbolic prosecution might be productive to "let players know they're not immune from the courts."[195] Though the league has been cooperative in numerous investigations,[196] the Dickinson Law Review concludes that this is not the exclusive practice: "It is significant to note here that even when courts have intended to protect all the players in a sport, the leagues will react as they see fit, regardless of the spirit of the decision. For example, leagues persist in barring undergraduates even though the practice has been declared illegal."[197]

The players,[198] seem to have adopted a similar attitude. Most players feel that they are "subject to league rules, and not local rules, once they sign their contracts."[199] Klein notes that players "suddenly freeze" when a media representative asks them to question the internal league structure.[200] One player responded to my survey question concerning "why there are so few lawsuits" thusly: "There is no such thing as a lawsuit; discipline is handled by league officials, and that's that!"[201] Another survey

---

195 Telephone interview with Executive Vice-President O'Neill, Montreal, Canada (January 11, 1979).

196 See County Prosecutor Carnovale's perceptions of the NHL involvement in the Biement-Blonich stick swinging incident. (Case study after Chapter IV)

197 Comment, "Contracted Rights and Duties of the Professional Athlete--Playing the Game in a Bidding War," 177 Dickinson Law Review 399 (1973).

198 Probably because of the cumulative pressures mentioned in this section.

199 Interview with P. Gardner. See note 191, infra.

200 Klein, Pro Football Mystique, supra, at 142-43.

201 Confidential survey (received February 15, 1979).

notes that "most players may think it's taboo to bring the courts into it."[202] The generally accepted, pervasive attitude appears to require dispute resolution "within the family."

The preference for "in the family resolution" is apparently based on fears based upon what are perceived as past court "failures." Professional hockey, baseball, football, and basketball each have been subjected to lawsuits which have succeeded in drastically altering the framework of the sport or in dramatically shifting the bargaining power within the sport so that drastic revision followed from negotiation. With changes in every facet of the sports, most attention was and is given to the economic changes which shifted a large portion of the fruits of the enterprise from the owners to the players.[203] Brody concludes that:

> Almost immediately after the litigative success (some would say because of it), hockey plunged into a period of contraction or retrenchment. In such times, there must perforce be restraint in the exercise of the judicially won freedom. 204

League officials worry that if judicial emphasis shifts to violence, "the game will become more tame, less competitive, and less appealing."[205] The biggest fear is that "the minute the courts have the power to litigate the game, a Pandora's Box will be opened."[206] Though possibly overstating the case, the diminutive Fred Shero demonstrated this mentality in commenting

---

202 Confidential survey (received February 12, 1979).

203 Brody, Trial, <u>supra</u>, at 35-36.

204 <u>Id.</u>, at 36.

205 Personal interview with McNab. (See note 45, <u>infra</u>.)

206 Personal interview with Gardner. (See note 191, <u>infra</u>.) This will be explored in greater detail from the prosecutorial perspective. (See Chapter III.)

upon the prosecution of David Forbes: "If they put him [Forbes] in jail, and I don't think they will, it will destroy all sports. Professional sports can police their own games. The only way the police should be involved is if we attack the fans. We're big enough and smart enough to handle our own problems."[207]

2. Pressures from teammates and opponents encourage conformity with the "conventional understanding" of internal dispute resolution. The same peer pressure that induces passive players to hit appears to induce those same players not to overtly complain when they become the victims. One survey summed it up best: "It [court dispute resolution] probably goes against the unwritten rule of survival of the fittest. If you can't survive on the ice, don't go running to the courts for protection."[208] Seven surveys and three sports attorneys that I interviewed all referred to the "macho code" as being the single most influential reason for the lack of victim complaints.[209] Hockey players who are victims of exceptionally violent conduct will, according to one source, "settle it their own way."[210] The "natural hesitancy on the part of an injured player...

---

[207] Washington Post D7 (February 10, 1975).

[208] Confidential survey (received February 15, 1979).

[209] Including personal interview with Ken Fishkin, attorney in Bob Woolf's office, Boston (November 15, 1978).

[210] Personal interview with Gardner (see note 191, infra). Presumably, he is referring to incidents such as Wayne Maki's brutal "retaliation" against "enforcer" Ted Green. (See text surrounding notes 77-82, infra.) Colorado Rockies player Wilf Paiment was banned from further participation against the Detroit Red Wings this year after Red Wing Dennis Polonich threatened "blood revenge" following the stick swinging incident on October 25, 1978. (See case study following Chapter IV.)

to sue an opponent"[211] with whom he has an ongoing playing relationship also appears to be a significant deterrent factor.

Most players surveyed indicated that court relief is rarely, if ever, considered. One adament player replied, "No one thinks of suing anyone; it's just not done."[212] Another player suggested that every player is implicitly immune except possibly for the overzealous "hit man."[213] General Manager McNab noted that "reacting in a legal way" "never entered his mind in all his [14] years in the NHL."[214] As for the players of "this generation," McNab explained that "while he can't answer for everybody, most players will complain after they get hit, but will usually stop after the game is over."

Interestingly, however, many players responded that, if a player really wanted to sue, he "could sue without most players saying or doing anything unusuall [sic]."[215] "By and large," says one Washington Capital official, "there is no conspiracy to prevent people from acting; you won't be ostracized."[216] This is also the view of Ed Garvey, NFLPA Executive Director, regarding the mentality in football.[217] The apparent reason for this

---

211 Chicago-Kent Law Review, <u>supra</u>, at 97.

212 Confidential survey (received February 22, 1979).

213 Confidential survey (received February 15, 1979).

214 Personal interview. (See note 45, <u>infra</u>.)

215 Confidential survey (received February 17, 1979).

216 Personal interview with Pierce Gardner. (See note 191, <u>infra</u>.)

217 Personal interview. (See note 152, <u>infra</u>.) However, the recent case of Mike Barber in this season's AFC Championship Game may leave room for doubt. Barber was hurt in the second quarter on an incomplete pass over the middle. Barber began slowing up, after the ball sailed over him when Wagner chopped Barber at the knees. After being helped off the field,

is that "the vast majority" of players who are not directly involved just do not care."[218] In hockey, McNab notes that "players will not get involved until the harm becomes individualized."[219] In football, Buoniconti notes that "most players are complacent; only the most intense ones will care one way or the other, for various reasons."[220]

In short, even if the peer pressures are not as significant as one might think, "victims" appear to perceive these pressures as being strong enough to deter any attempts at court resolution.

3. <u>Pressures from coaches, management, and the "sports establishment" encourage conformity with the "conventional understanding" of internal dispute resolution.</u> The "winning is everything" dogma[221] is apparently coupled with a "conservative, paternalistic mentality" that disdains any at-

---

Barber pointed a finger at Wagner and yelled angrily at him. Barber said, continuing the sentence with a string of expletives, "I'm going to get him. I'll get him back," Barber repeated, "and when I do, he won't play a game again." <u>Miami Herald</u> 3D (January 8, 1979). The next day (January 8, 1979), Barber talked of going to court, saying "He's not a dumb player. He saw the ball was over my head and incomplete. I had started to slow down, he just went ahead and took the shot. It could have been a career-ending blow." Within a week, NFL players "expressed shock" at Barber's press statements and intentions. (<u>Boston Globe</u> 37, January 18, 1979) No court action has been taken, though it presumably is still possible.

[218] Telephone interview with Will McDonough. (See note 153, <u>infra</u>.)

[219] Personal interview. (See note 45, <u>infra</u>.)

[220] Personal interview. (See note 69, <u>infra</u>.) The reasons for this "complacency" are detailed in the remaining factors in this sub-section.

[221] See text surrounding notes 171-78, <u>infra</u>.

tempts to challenge the structure. The "quasi-militaristic, do it for the team"[222] attitude encourages, if not requires, conformity. Klein cynically notes:

> The general locker-room mentality is not overly elevated, which is not to say that every football player in the NFL reads only the sports statistics and comic books. But the thinkers don't last long. The intellectuals draw more than their share of suspicious glances. The questioners are quickly drummed out.[223]

This fear of change seems to be shared by coaches and management alike, stereotypically labelled as "Neanderthal cretons" by McMurtry.[224] Most coaches and managers, concerned about the security of their jobs as well,[225] will rebel against anyone who challenges the "conventional understanding."

The players must understand and accept the perceptions of the coach or manager, for he holds the key to the athlete's success or failure. The competition is intense. There are often more than 120 players who report to summer football training camp with only 47 roster spots to compete for. This is especially true for the fringe veterans...the reserves who will never become starters...are just as paranoid as the free-agent and low-draft rookies. They know their status on the team, and they study each rookie who enters camp. "Sometimes, looking back on it now, the most exciting times of camp came on each cut-down day," said Charley Harper, a nondescript of-

---

[222] Telephone interview with Will McDonough. (See note 153, infra.)

[223] Klein, Pro Football Mystique, supra, at 65.

[224] Telephone interview. (See note 112, infra.)

[225] Bob Woolf notes that, "As a type, coaches and managers are driven men, consumed by their jobs, restless, insecure and wound tight. They are also more than a little paranoid. The job encourages that condition, whatever their qualities going in." Behind Closed Doors, supra, at 151.

fensive lineman who stayed several years with the Giants. "Each week that passed and didn't claim me was a moral victory. I was a nervous wreck then."[226] There is a great deal of pressure even for the "successful player." The average span of a player's career in the NFL is just short of five years (4.7). "For those who hit right on the average, there isn't much time to earn money. And suddenly, at the age of twenty-seven (or thirty, or thirty-five, or forty), the athlete is washed-up, over the hill, out of work."[227]

This pressure is exacerbated by the fact that most players could not readily find employment elsewhere, especially at a pay level commensurate to the one existing in pro football. Players who make the pros may often have disregarded their education or technical skills in concentrating on their football skills.[228]

The result of these job pressures is that most players fear that the

---

[226] Klein, Pro Football Mystique, supra, at 209.

[227] Id., at 60. Klein concludes: "Suddenly, the All-America is out-of-work. The all-pro needs a job. He can go from earning six-figure incomes to almost nothing. There's no security and no longevity and no guarantee. It can be over tomorrow [and beginning yesterday they can limp a lot]. And doctors don't get traded, either, and have to live apart from their families [and maintain two residences] in a city they would never pick in the first place. We have to make it all in a very concentrated period of time. It's not greed, it's practicality. No one wants you to make a speech or appear in a commercial after you stop being a star." Id., at 61.

[228] Connecticut Law Review, supra, at 371. Klein describes the NFL players situation: "Most NFL players have been to college. Several have even graduated. A few actually majored in subjects that required a great deal of intelligence and concentration. But most, given their qualitative education, would not have an easy time finding well-paying work. If lawyers and accountants are having difficulty in the current job market, not to mention all the poor souls who majored in elementary education or, God forbid, liberal arts, a physical education major with a minor in deodorant application might have some problems earning in excess of $10,000 annually. Pro Football Mystique, supra, at 58. The NHL players situation is much worse since, being drafted as teenagers, few go to college at all.

surrounding court involvement "will hurt their chances of getting ahead."[229] The fear of being condemned "as a clubhouse lawyer" appears to be significant,[230] especially since "the underground is such that everyone knows what everyone else is doing."[231] One NHL player responding to the survey replied that "the fear of being labelled" is "the <u>only</u> reason that players don't go to court."[232] Buoniconti suggested that "players naievely expect that they can't exist if they alienate coaches and management."[233] Social scientist Mertens explained this mentality from a behaviorist perspective: "conformity works within the system to achieve cultural goals by institutionalized means. This congruence is suggestive of generally conservative behavior with limited risk taking."[234] On a practical level, this suggests that a victim will not "risk" taking his claim to the court system for redress. The <u>Georgetown Law Journal</u>, in its definitive work on player discipline, concurs in this conclusion:

> It is also probable that disciplinary abuses will often remain unlitigated as a result of an athlete's reluctance to appeal to the courts for fear of being informally excluded from his sport or "black-listed" as a troublemaker or clubhouse lawyer.[235]

---

[229] Telephone interview with Shiela Brooks, NFLPA Staff Counsel. Washington, D.C. (November 11, 1978).

[230] Though some, such as Jeff Cohen, Assistant General Manager of the Boston Celtics, deny that it is a dispositive factor. Personal interview. Boston Garden. (February 9, 1979)

[231] Personal interview with Pierce Gardner. (See note 191, <u>infra</u>.)

[232] Confidential survey (received February 15, 1979).

[233] Personal interview. (See note 69, <u>infra</u>.)

[234] Mertens, "Congruence Theory," in <u>Crime and Justice American Style</u> (1971).

[235] Comment, "Discipline in Professional Sports: The Need for Player Protection," 60 <u>Georgetown Law Journal</u> 793 (1972).

4. <u>Pressures from the threat of trades, demotions, blacklisting, termination, and pension, compensation, and grievance manipulation encourage conformity with the "conventional understanding" of internal dispute resolution.</u> The risk avoidance mentality prevalent in factor three is further encouraged by the myriad of mechanisms available to management for dealing with "deviant" players.

First, the threat of a trade can be an effective weapon against recalcitrant players. For example, the NHL Standard Player's Contract specifically refers to the assignment of a player's contract being pursuant to disciplinary action: "The Club shall pay the actual moving expenses incurred by a player during the playing season when such move is directed by the Club <u>and is not part of disciplinary action</u>."[236] Should a player refuse to report to his assigned team because he deems the form of discipline unfair, then he is in breach of his contract and faces suspension and loss of salary: "If the Player fails to report to such other Club he may be suspended by such other Club and no salary shall be payable to him during the period of such suspension."[236] The <u>Manitoba Law Journal</u> describes the effect of such a threat:

> In discussing assignment of contracts as a form of discipline with several professional hockey and football players, it was learned that this form of sanction is very real and is particularly feared by players because of disruptions in family life caused through moving. One particularly telling incident of discipline through trade was related to the author by a professional hockey player and involved a player that the club management regarded as a "troublemaker" and a "loudmouth" because of his alleged irreverent attitude to the coach and general manager.[237]

---

236 Clause II of the Standard NHL Players Contract (March, 1972). Both the National Football League Standard Contract and the Canadian Football League Standard Player Contract (Clause 14) have similar clauses.

237 K. Alylvia, "Professional Contracts and the Player's Association," 5 <u>Manitoba Law Journal</u> 369-370 (1973).

> Management had decided to assign the player's contract to one of its farm teams as a disciplinary action but the player was not informed of the assignment until he was seated on a chartered bus with his teammates waiting to go to what he thought was his next game with the team. To add insult to injury that particular player's suitcase was at the rear of the bus' baggage compartment and he was forced to retrieve it himself by moving all other baggage aside. The point the player interviewed wished to make was that the team purposefully set out to humiliate the player in front of his teammates as an added measure of punishment, as if the contract assignment were not sufficient. Obviously, management had known well in advance of the trade, but chose this very inopportune time to inform the player of it. [237]

Nearly all professional team athletes have standard assignment clauses[238] in their contracts. Thus, this seems to be an extremely potent threat, especially to the "marginal" player.

Second, a threat of demotion to the "minor leagues" would appear significant to the "marginal" player. Each assignment clause is usually broadly written so as to include assignment to clubs in the minor leagues (as in the NHL Clause 11 set out in note 238). Coaches, it seems, might not be afraid to employ such a threat. In the words of Don Cherry, head coach of the Boston Bruins, the professional hockey player who disdains violence "would be sent back to the minors."[239]

Third, a team may "terminate" a player's contract at any time if he does not show "sufficient skill." The usual Standard Player Contract clause

---

[237] K. Alylvia, "Professional Sports Contracts and the Player's Association," 5 Manitoba Law Journal 369-370 (1973).

[238] NHL Standard Player Contract, Clause 11: "It is mutually agreed that the Club shall have the right to sell, assign, exchange, and transfer this contract, and to loan the Player's services to any professional hockey club, and the Player agrees to accept and be bound by such sale, exchange, assignment, transfer, or loan, and will faithfully perform and carry out this contract with the same purpose and effect as if it had been entered into by the Player and such other Club."

[239] Flakne and Caplan, Trial, supra, at 35.

is one which allows a head coach to terminate a contract if the player's performance does not conform to the requirements of the team or measure up to the capacity of the other players on the team. Of course, this is vague enough such that management may "cut" a player for any reason under the guise of his "not conforming to the requirements of the team."[240] It is conceivable that a victim could perceive that his team would rather terminate his playing contract than have him bring criminal charges against an especially violent player.

Fourth, since a player is negotiating a new contract on the average of every 1.9 years, there appears to be a perception that pursuing a criminal claim will hurt later contract negotiations. When asked this question specifically on the survey, a number of players mentioned that this was a "significant pressure."

Fifth, some players fear that taking a claim to court will result in an informal "blacklisting" of that player around the league. Blacklisting can arise from a tacit agreement among club owners not to deal with a certain player. This usually occurs when a player does something that team owners feels is prejudicial to their interests. Many owners adamently deny that such a blacklist exists. However, there is evidence to the contrary.

---

240

The Standard NFL Player Contract, Provision Six, reads as follows: "If in the opinion of the Head Coach the Player...fails at any time during the football seasons included in the term of this contract to demonstrate sufficient skill and capacity to play professional football of the caliber required by the League and by the Club, or if in the opinion of the Head Coach the Player's work or conduct in the performance of this contract is unsatisfactory as compared with the work and conduct of other members of the Club's squad of players, the Club shall have the right to terminate this contract...."

The NHL Standard Contract allows "termination...at any time...if the player materially breaches his contract" (Clause 7B), operationally defined as, among other things, "being unfit to play hockey" (Clause 5). The new 1977 contract includes a clause which permits the Club "to terminate a player's contract for one third of his National Hockey League salary." (Letter from

Bernie Parrish, a former defensive star with the Cleveland Browns of the NFL, suggests that he was blacklisted because of his activities in the NFLPA. Another former football player stated that blacklisting is used against a player who "...refuses to accept rigid authority" or who has "...different values either morally or otherwise than a coach." In short, the blacklist can be used against any player whom the team management (including the coach) feels is a "troublemaker" or whom the club feels is becoming too political or a "clubhouse lawyer."[241] A Canadian Football League incident provides an appropriate example. In 1973, two Winnipeg Blue Bomber football players were released from the team because of narcotics charges. The players, Mack Herron and Jim Thorpe, could both be classed as "star" players, with the term being especially appropriate for Herron who had been an All-Canadian running back in 1972. Despite the obvious talents of these players, no other CFL team picked them up when placed on waivers by Winnipeg. Earl Lunsford, General Manager of the Bombers, emphatically denied that the other

---

NHLPA Executive Director Eagleson to all NHLPA Members. September 19, 1977).

The Canadian Football League clause is similar to the NFL's (Clause 10). The Standard CFL Player Contract is included as Appendix J.

The National Basketball Association clause allows termination if, "in the sole opinion of Club's management [the Player does not] exhibit sufficient skill or competitive ability to qualify to continue as a member of the Club's team" [Clause 20(b)(2)].

241 B. Parrish, <u>They Call it a Game</u> 172 (1974). Another example is the baseball lockerroom assault of then Texas Ranger Manager Frank Lucchesi by one of his ballplayers, Lenny Randle. The <u>Boston Globe</u> describes the aftermath: "The attack—which one eyewitness says privately was so violent that Randle is fortunate not to have gotten two years—was completely wrong, whether Lucchesi had, in fact, called him a 'punk' or not. But the whole incident had marked Randle. He was suspended, fined and held up in baseball's stocks. A year later, last spring training, teammate Tom Grieve, who played with him in Texas and New York, told me he thought Randle was on the brink of a nervous breakdown." P. Gammons, "Neither Lucchesi Nor Randle Can Celebrate," <u>Boston Globe</u> 44 (December 15, 1978).

CFL teams had discussed Herron and Thorpe with the result that no team would pick them up. To quote Lunsford: "I've been in the League six years and no player or players was ever discussed in this kind of situation. There has never been what you'd call a blackball, never an arrangement at any table."[242] Even if management denies the existence of such a "conspiracy," player perception of such a threat is the key deterrent in this context.

Sixth, since compensation for an injured player's lost earning capacity is mainly a matter of team discretion, victims may fear that seeking a criminal complaint could result in an unfavorable injury compensation ruling. Each standard player contract contains a "fitness clause," whereby a team will only pay the remainder of an injured player's contract if, "on the sole judgment of the Club's physician [the player] is unfit to play skilled hockey for the balance of the season or any part thereof."[243] Similar clauses appear in the NFL arrangement,[244] as well as the Canadian Football League Standard Player Contract.[245] Additionally, if an injured player's contract is terminated the next year because of the previous year's injury, the player is theoretically entitled to additional compensation. Again, however, such a decision is within the sole discretion of team officials.[246] There

---

[242] Manitoba Law Journal, supra, at 371.

[243] NHL Standard Players Contract, Clause 5. This contract appears as Appendix K.

[244] Codified in Article IX, §1 of Collective Bargaining Agreement.

[245] Clause 21.

[246] Each league purports to have an ostensible neutral grievance procedure for precisely these matters. The NHL allows the matter to be submitted to arbitration (Collective Bargaining Agreement, Article 17.01). The NFL allows a claim to be presented to a neutral physician within twenty days (NFL Collective Bargaining Agreement, Article IV, §4). The Canadian Football League has an identical arrangement (Standard Players' Contract, Clause 21). However, Shiela Brooks, NFLPA Staff Counsel, maintains that "99 percent of the players go uncompensated." (Telephone interview, November 11, 1978).

are additional injury compensation mechanisms which a player may take advantage of at the team's discretion. In the NFL, for example, though a player must complete four years to be "vested" for pension plan purposes, an injured and incapacitated player may be deemed "eligible" earlier. Further, a team may voluntarily apply its state's Workman's Compensation laws to an injured athlete.[247]

It is not suggested that teams deliberately conspire to use any of these six mechanisms to destroy an injured player financially.[248] The point is merely that players perceive the consequences of these mechanisms as severe enough such that the risk of alienating the establishment by proceeding through the court system becomes overwhelming. Clearly, many players are afraid. McMurtry encountered such fear during his hockey investigaiton:

> Some individuals specifically requested that their interviews not be publicized in view of the fact that they had some specific criticism of the hockey establishment...They were concerned as to whether or not this might have an adverse effect on their careers as they are active either as players or officials in professional hockey.[249]

Sheila Brooks of the NFLPA warned that the chances of NFL players "giving any kind of controversial information is quite unlikely."[250] Though representatives in each sport adamently deny that there is a "conspiracy of si-

---

[247] NFL Collective Bargaining Agreement, Article XXXIII.

[248] Though given that owners are perceived by some as treating players only "as chattels, disposing of them when they no longer produce," this may not be entirely impossible.

[249] McMurtry, <u>supra</u>, at 13. The case study following Chapter IV will reveal that one of the main roadblocks in the Detroit investigation was victim Polonich's fear of signing the complaint.

[250] Telephone interview (November 11, 1978).

lence per se,"[251] the fear which operates to restrict controversial action is readily apparent.

5. <u>The fact that the league has been extremely generous to most of the players encourages conformity with the "conventional understanding" of internal dispute resolution.</u> With the tremendous salaries and ancillary protections accorded by the league, most players seem to feel that the sport has been too kind to them to "drag it through the courts." In football, the average salary for NFL players last season was $62,585, a 13.2 percent increase over 1977's $55,288 average.[252] In addition, the minimum salary will be increased to $26,000 in 1980,[253] an $8,000 increase since 1974.[254] This is complemented by a Retirement Plan,[255] a life insurance plan,[256] a major medical plan,[257] and dental coverage.[258] Hence, according to Buoniconti, most players are "happy and love the game."[259] Even those injured by it would appear to prefer internal dispute resolution, if they believe the pervasive mentality that court interference would "destroy what they've got." Even the liberals, according to Klein, realize that their paychecks "are too good to risk."[260] In hockey, the same benefits spawn the same mentality.

---

[251] Pierce Gardner, Washington Capitals, NHL. (See note 191, <u>infra</u>.) Ed Garvey, NFLPA Executive Director. (See note 152, <u>infra</u>.)

[252] <u>Miami Herald</u> 5C (January 30, 1979).

[253] NFL Collective Bargaining Agreement, Article XXII, §2.

[254] Klein, Pro Football Mystique, <u>supra</u>, at 71.

[255] NFL Collective Bargaining Agreement, Article XXII.

[256] <u>Id.</u>, Article XXX, §1.

[257] <u>Id.</u>, Article XXX, §2.

[258] <u>Id.</u>, Article XXX, §3.

[259] Personal interview. (See note 69, <u>infra</u>.)

[260] Klein, Pro Football Mystique, <u>supra</u>, at 224.

One responding player noted:

> I think everybody feels that when you accept your pay check (which all are very good) you know and everybody knows that--that locks you into the 'fraternity' and you accept the expected. [261]

6. Even if an injured player desired to seek a court remedy (despite the cumulative pressures), the intricacies and inconvenience of litigation encourage conformity with the "conventional understanding" of internal dispute resolution. This is, of course, a significant problem for any crime victim contemplating a civil or criminal remedy. It is more pronounced in this context because the athlete-victim has a more familiar and convenient mechanism for dispute resolution should he decide to take advantage of it. Rather than seeking criminal punishment against the perpetrator,[262] or seeking a civil settlement, most of the athletes playing professional football handle their injury grievances through a union arbitration procedure. Aimed at stopping "the tendency to cut a player who is injured," the procedure calls for a physician to determine if the player was injured at the time of his release, and an arbitrator to determine compensation if he judges that the injury was the cause of the player's release.

In the past few years, the number of grievances have averaged from 30 to 35 per year, with the arbitrator deciding in favor of the athlete and the team equally as often.[263] If a player is merely seeking compensation, this

---

[261] Confidential survey (received February 15, 1979).

[262] Certainly inappropriate if compensation is desired.

[263] L. Schmidt, "In Football, It's Arbitration," 14 Trial 38(1978). This mechanism merely covers intra-team disputes. The Hackbart court noted that, "no provision covers disputes between players of different teams." Supra, at 354.

procedure is the desirable alternative. Furthermore, the NFLPA provides support services geared toward directing complaints exclusively through this mechanism. For example, the Association provides no help in criminal cases, either in defense or counselling the victim upon what is required for a successful prosecution. Also, the Players Association makes it a policy not to represent athletes in civil matters because of the staff that would be needed to pursue torts in the various states and jurisdictions covered by the NFL. The Players Association takes part in civil suits of its athletes only by assisting in the determination of damages, providing expert testimony, and, more recently, acting as an information clearinghouse.[264]

Therefore, the injured player who wishes to proceed through the court system "must do everything himself."[265] Some claim that most athletes lack the intelligence to begin the process.[266] The more salient reason for inaction is that a professional athlete "pampered and coddled from his earliest days of stardom, will take the easy way out whenever possible;" hence, the grievance procedure route. Nick Buoniconti was a former NFLPA President and, as such, was on the 1970 negotiating committee which originally drafted the Article IX grievance procedure. He noted that "there was never any intention to use the procedure as an incentive to foreclose criminal action."[267] Nevertheless, for some injured athletes, it appears to have had precisely

---

264 Id.

265 Personal interview with Buoniconti. (See note 69, infra.)

266 Klein cynically notes: "Almost every player in the NFL went to college. Lots of them even have degrees. I have a feeling they all majored in Showering After the Game, and the ones who don't have degrees flunked the course." Pro Football Mystique, supra, at 52.

267 Personal interview. (See note 69, infra.)

that effect. When asked whether the "provision in the league rules" that provides the grievance procedure is "a reason for so few lawsuits," 33 percent of the responding players suggested that it was.

In conclusion, the two sets of pressures described in this chapter encourage conformity to the generally accepted standard of behavior and operate to suppress those who wish to challenge the "generally accepted" norms and practices through the courts. There seems to be some concern within the sports establishment about rampant violence, but not nearly enough. Each sport has demonstrated some isolated interest in "cleaning up the game." In football, concern led to issuance of a formal written statement in 1978 by the Commissioner of the NFL to the teams that violence on the playing field would not be tolerated and that multi-game suspensions might be employed as enforcement. Additionally, in a letter to the coaches of the players involved in the Atkinson incident, the Commissioner of the NFL condemned an action such as the one in the instant case: "In sixteen years in this office I do not recall a more flagrant foul than your clubbing the back of Swann's head totally away from the play....Our sport obviously involves intense physical contact, but it requires of all players discipline and control and remaining within the rules. Every player deserves protection from the kind of unnecessary roughness that could end his career."[268]

---

[268] Georgia Law Review, supra, at 390. More recently, the NFL Competition Committee proposed rules during the 1979 Annual Meeting deemed to be "the most positive step ever toward eliminating unnecessary violence." Will McDonough describes the proposals:

> Eliminate the use of the top of the football helmet in tackling and blocking. Surveys have shown the helmet to be the most deadly weapon in use in the game...

In hockey, some players are worried enough about the situation to take affirmative action, as did superstar Bobby Hull in his "one-man work stoppage" in 1977. The League itself appears to have made token gestures to "clean up the game."[269] There is _some_ evidence that past criminal prosecutions have indeed been a force in decisions by the NHL Players' Association to prompt the NHL leadership to establish new rules and penalties aimed at reducing fighting and violence in hockey.[270]

---

> Prevent blocking below the waist on all kickoffs and punt returns, where many serious injuries occur...
> Make every hit--block or tackle--that an official deems was made with the intent to injure a major penalty. This category would include a multitude of sins that pro football has allowed under the guise of 'hard nosed football' over the years. Gone would be the abuse of passers currently allowed. No more would defensive linemen or any pass rusher be allowed to spear him in the back from the blind side, or just whop him headfirst into the ground like linebacker Jim Youngblood of the Rams did to Vikings quarterback Tommy Kramer, putting Kramer in the hospital last season.

W. McDonough, "NFL May Blow Whistle on All that Roughness," _Boston Globe_ 24 (March 13, 1979). Informatively, _only_ the "kickoff blocking" rule was completely approved by full league management.

[269] A humorous example of the NHL's effort is the new set of officials illustrated signals appearing in the 1978 Rule Book. Each penalty is illustrated by a cartoon-like referee demonstrating the appropriate signal. For the non-violent penalties (holding, hooking, interference, and the like), the cartoon referee is presented as a neutral charicature. For the more violent penalties, however, the referee is presented with an extremely disapproving facial expression. Given the current hockey establishment, it will take much more than a disdainful cartoon illustration of a referee to remove the violence from the game.

[270] Halowell and Meshbesher, Trial, _supra_, at 29. The _Boston Globe_ describes NHL management response to an especially violent game between Philadelphia and Los Angeles on March 11, 1979:

> NHL vice president Brian O'Neill caught the Philadelphia Flyers at Philadelphia International Airport Tuesday and gave them a lecture on their record-setting brawl with the Los Angeles Kings. Five players were ejected and 10 records were broken during the 12-minute battle Sunday night at the Spectrum. Referee Wally Harris assessed a total of 372 penalty minutes in the first period, 310 for the 12-minute fight, and a total of 380 minutes for the game.

Clearly, much more needs to be done. The players, however, "keenly aware"[271] of all existing pressures, are neither desirous nor capable of using the courts as a mechanism to remove the violence from hockey and football. Charlie Krueger, one of the "toughest" players in NFL history, remarked, "Nothing will be done until someone dies."[272] One concerned NHL player quite appropriately summarized the pressures described in this chapter:

> There are many, many unwritten rules concerning violence in the league and management's stand on the issue. But when it boils right down to it, it's like any other job, you will be used, pampered, adored as long as you're useful--rules you break are ignored or overcome somehow. But, as soon as your usefulness is no longer needed--anything you do is breaking rules--the sooner they can get rid of you the better!! 273

---

Philadelphia's Bob Kelly and Mel Bridgman were each given one-game suspensions. O'Neill said his visit was intended "to curb the brawling and donnybrooks. There is no place in the game for brawls and after talking to the players I think they feel the same way."

271 Telephone interview with Shiela Brooks, NFLPA. (See note 124, *infra*.)

272 Krueger's comments were addressed to a different set of problems, but they are entirely appropriate in the context. R. Epstein, "The Case Against Artificial Turf," 14 *Trial* 42 (1978).

273 Confidential survey (received February 15, 1979).

II) INTERNAL LEAGUE DISCIPLINARY MECHANISMS WHICH PURPORT TO DEAL WITH "DURING THE GAME" CRIMINAL LAW VIOLATIONS.

One of the most significant factors mentioned by athletes[274] and prosecutors[275] alike when asked about the rarity of court intervention is the deference paid to internal fine and suspension mechanisms. The situation represents the criminal law's deference to the lawmaking capacity of "a virtual private government."[276] This system of private criminal law grew in response to management fears that their games were becoming "contaminated" by off the field legal disputes. The Nebraska Law Review explains:

> The public impression of sports as the great American pastime, exemplar of fair play and builder of character, is being shaken. The athletes' performance is suffering, and owners are forced to make unpopular trades and dismissals. Indeed, the fundamental notion of sports as a game is eroding away. Realizing this problem the sports industry has undertaken an extensive search for a system to resolve these disputes in an orderly and expeditious manner. 277

These procedures have become the usual method for league dispute resolution. In the early 1970's, over 500 disputes were decided through this system every three years. Many more were settled before a decision was rendered.[278]

---

274 Chapter I.

275 Chapter III.

276 John P. Marris uses this term to describe the entire sports industry. J.P. Morris, "In the Wake of the Flood," 38 Law and Contemporary Problems 85-86 (1973).

277 J.B. Gessford, "Arbitration of Professional Athletes' Contracts: An Effective System of Dispute Resolution in Professional Sports," 60 Nebraska Law Review 363 (1972).

278 Id.

The trend is increasing as each sport becomes more violent.[279] Given the critical position of these procedures in the scheme of sports violence regulation, this paper explores these internal mechanisms in the following manner: (A) General understanding of the power and discretion inherent in each league's procedures; (B) Specific sanctions available in each league's procedures; (C) Player perceptions of the stigma attached to (and deterrent value of) each league's sanctions; (D) Procedural protections against arbitrary judgment: the grievance procedures; (E) Legal rationales which may be employed to improve the grievance procedures.

## A. General Understanding of the Power and Discretion Inherent in Each League's Procedures.

In general, the Commissioner's powers in each league "are immense."[280] "It is a system of private criminal law," notes the Alberta Law Review, "practised without procedural safeguard at the fiat of the owners."[281]

---

[279] See "Scope of the Sports Violence Problem," preceeding Chapter I. Note that these are almost exclusively private mechanisms, as courts will not use the league rules and regulations themselves as a basis of enforcement. Courts initially refused to enforce baseball regulations binding a player to his team. See Metropolitan Exhibition Co. v. Ewing, 42 F. 198, 203-04 (C.C.S.D. N.Y. 1890) (reserve clause too indefinite to be specifically enforced); American League Baseball Club v. Chase, 86 Misc. 441, 465-66, 149 N.Y.S. 6, 19-20 (Sup. Ct. 1914) (reserve clause found unconscionable). But see Philadelphia Ball Club v. Lajoie, 202 Pa. 210, 217, 51 A. 973, 974 (1902) (player of unique ability enjoined from playing for another team). It is notable that in the "Black Sox" scandal organized baseball bypassed legal sanctions and relied on its own disciplinary measures to protect its vital interests. For a detailed account of these events, see E. Asinof, Eight Men Out (1963). Baseball is used here as an example of dissatisfaction with legal remedies since it was the first sport to encounter these problems. Few other sports have even attempted to use the courts to protect their interests. Georgetown Law Journal, supra, at 772.

[280] B.E. Lee, "A Survey of Professional Team Sport Player-Control Mechanisms Under Antitrust and Labor Law Principals: Peace at Last," 11 Valparaiso Law Review 409 (1977).

[281] D.I. Shapiro, "The Professional Athlete, Liberty or Peonage?," Alberta Law Review 218 (1975).

"After viewing the cases and the methods by which leagues and owners 'chattelize' its players, one cannot help but conclude that indeed the professional athlete is a glaring example of a contemporary slave."[282]

The vast power of league and club discipline is usually said to have its legal basis in the consent of the player. The standard contract is the vehicle through which this consent is secured.[283] Though the player ostensibly consents through his signature, he has little choice if he wishes to play football, for Article XII of the NFL Collective Bargaining Agreement requires the use of the Standard "NFL Player Contract form" for "all subsequent signings." In addition, all such information is contained in the

---

[282] Id., at 234.

[283] The Standard Player's Contract, National Football League, §4 (1975) states: The Player agrees at all times to comply with and be bound by the Constitution and By-Laws, Rules and Regulations of the League, of the Club and the decisions of the Commissioner of the League (hereinafter called "Commissioner"), which shall be final, conclusive and unappealable. The enumerated Constitution, By-Laws, Rules and Regulations are intended to include the present Constitution, By-Laws, Rules and Regulations as well as all amendments thereto, all of which are by reference incorporated herein. If the Player fails to comply with said Constitution, By-Laws, Rules and Regulations, the Club shall have the right to terminate this contract as provided in Paragraph 6 hereof or to take such other action as may be specified in said Constitution, By-Laws, Rules and Regulations, subject, however, to the right to a hearing by the Commissioner. All matters in dispute between the Player and the Club shall be referred to the Commissioner and his decision shall be accepted as final, complete, conclusive, binding and unappealable, by the Player and by the Club. The Player, if involved or affected in any manner whatsoever by a decision of the Commissioner, whether the decision results from a dispute between the Player and the Club or otherwise, hereby releases and discharges the Commissioner, the League, each Club in the League, each Director, Officer, Stockholder, Owner or Partner of any Club in the League, each employee, agent, official or representative of the League or of any Club in the League, jointly and severally, individually and in their official capacities, of and from any and all claims, demands, damages, suits, actions and causes of action whatsoever, in law or in equity, arising out of or in connection with any decision of the Commissioner, except to the extent of awards made by the Commissioner to the Player. The Player hereby acknowledges that he has read the present said Constitution, By-Laws, Rules and Regulations, and that he understands their meaning.

"playbook" distributed to each player upon joining the Club.[284]

Apparently, the "sentencing judge"[285] is empowered to do almost anything. All leagues have contractual constitutional clauses similar to that of the NBA, which follows:

> The Player agrees...(d) to be neatly and fully attired in public and always conduct himself on and off the court according to the highest standards of honesty, morality, fair play and sportsmanship; and (e) not to do anything which is detrimental to the best interests of the Club or the Association. 286

The important thing to note about such contractual provisions is their nebulous character. In most cases there are no clear guidelines as to what conduct would be considered as unacceptable. Rather, the clauses may be expressed in terms of what is "moral," a value judgment which could conceivably vary with the situation and the individual. With such provisions affecting the personal liberties of the individual, the athlete "may be open to arbitrary and unreasonable actions by team coaches and executives."[287] Commissioners frequently issue public statements ascribing theoretical limits to these nebulous clauses in an attempt to eliminate the inevitable criticism of rampant discretion. For example, during the testimony of Baseball Commis-

---

284 Klein, Pro Football Mystique, supra, at 105.

285 Almost always the Commissioner of the league. (In the NHL, the Executive Vice-President.)

286 NBA Uniform Player Contract, Clause 5. The following contain similar clauses: American Basketbal Ass'n Uniform Player Contract §3a(5); NFL Const. art. V., §8.13(D) at 33; Professional Golfers' Ass;n of America Const. art. IV, §1, in PGA Rules 22; World Boxing Ass'n Const. art.II(A), in World Boxing Ass'n Constitution, By-Laws, Championship Regulations, Safety Code 6 (1970); Standard Canadian Football League Standard Players Contract Clause 8; Major League Baseball Rules, Rule 15; NHL By-Laws §17(3).

287 Comment, "Contract Matters and Disciplinary Procedures in Professional Sport," 39 Saskatchewan Law Review 225 (1974-75).

sioner Ford Frick, it was pointed out that under Rule 15, the Commissioner has the authority to deny the use of stadium facilities, without notice or hearing, to any player who, in his judgment, is not acting in the best interests of baseball. Frick admitted this, but he insisted that the rule would be applied only to cases where a player was found guilty of throwing a game or of a crime involving moral turpitude.[288] Each league justifies its "best interests" clause on the basis of the inability to anticipate all violations and prohibit them with more narrow drafting. Former NFL Commissioner Bert Bell testified that: "Because there are situations of doubtful ethics which cannot be spelled out ahead of time, the commissioner is also empowered to punish for 'conduct detrimental to professional football.'"[289] Regardless of the justifications and public limitations for such ambiguous clauses, the fact that they exist allows for the potential of discretionary abuse. The Georgetown Law Journal's seminal article on disciplinary procedures maintained that "the rights of professional athletes may be circumscribed severely by artibrary enforcement of rules forbidding conduct detrimental to the best interests of a sport."[290] The Gonzaga Law Review notes in conclusion that:

> One finds, in the United States, a general willingness to permit the athlete to sacrifice his personal freedom in order that the public may take its sporting pleasure. In this sense the American public is parasitic upon its professional athlete. It could be argued that the relationship between the athlete and the public actually is a symbiotic rather than a parasitic one. It is submitted, how-

---

288 Georgetown Law Journal, supra, at 774.

289 Hearings on Organized Professional Team Sports Before the Subcommittee on Antitrust and Monopoly of the Senate Comm. on the Judiciary, 85th Cong, 2d Sess. 423 (1958)(testimony of Bert Bell).

290 Georgetown Law Journal, supra, at 776.

ever, that the constitutional and quasi-constitutional questions raised in a consideration of the status of the professional athlete in America are not answered simply by concluding that the relationship is a symbiotic one. 291

B. Specific Sanctions Available in Each League's Procedures.

In addition to the broad "best interests of the game" clause that each league possesses, there are a number of "sentences" available to each league for a variety of specific offenses.

In hockey, the NHL Rule Book contains a range of specific penalties to control the "excessively violent player." A minor penalty[292] is available for "causing violent impact with the boards,"[293] carring the stick "excessively high,"[294] "unnecessary roughness,"[295] and "unsportsmanlike conduct," including hair pulling and biting.[296] A major penalty[297] is available for "butt-ending" an opponent with a stick,[298] or "attemting to spear", or "actually spearing" an opponent with a stick.[299] A misconduct penalty[300] is

---

291 M. Schneiderman, "Professional Sport: Involuntary Servitude and the Popular Will," Gonzaga Law Review 64 (1971).

292 "The player is ruled off the ice for two minutes." Rule 27(a).

293 Rule 45(a).

294 Rule 58(a).

295 Rule 84.

296 Rule 42(n).

297 Player ruled off the ice for five minutes; an automatic $50.00 fine for a "foul causing injury to the face of head of an opponent by means of a stick." (Rule 28a); automatic game suspension plus $100.00 fine for "three major penalties in the same game" (Rule 28c).

298 Rule 48(b).

299 Rule 78(a).

300 Player ruled off the ice for ten minutes; an automatic $50.00 fine (Rule 29 a, b).

available for the same violations as above, but committed in an exceptionally violent manner. A game misconduct,[301] and a gross misconduct[302] are even more serious penalties for the same actions. A match penalty,[303] is available for "deliberate attempts to injure,"[304] and actual "deliberate injury of opponents."[305] There is also power for the Commissioner to make "at his discretion...any subsequent investigations...and assess any additional fines and suspensions...whether or not such offense has been"[306] previously penalized. Though this rule was "a response by President Campbell to give the league more discretion," it has been used only once, supplementing "normal discipline of a severe high sticking incident."[307] There are also special "fisticuff" rules,[308] employing a mixture of all available sanctions depending upon the severity of the incident. For an understanding of how these penalties are meted out, examine the NHL's response to the largest hockey fight of the 1979 season (in New York between the

---

301 The player is removed for the rest of the game; automatic $100.00 fine; and the case "shall be reported to the President who shall have full power to impose such further penalties by way of suspension or fine on the penalized player or any other player involved in the altercation" (Rule 29c). After three game misconducts, a player is automatically suspended for one game and his team fined $1000.00 (Rule 29f).

302 The player is suspended for "the balance of the game"; automatic $100.00 fine; and "the case shall be referred to the President of the League for further disciplinary action" (Rule 29e).

303 The player is "removed immediately"; automatic $200.00 fine; and "the case shall be investigated promptly by the President who shall have full powers" as in Rule 29c (Rule 30a,b).

304 Rule 44(a).

305 Rule 49(a).

306 Rule 34A.

307 Telephone interview with Executive Vice President O'Neill, Montreal, Canada (January 11, 1979).

308 Rules 54 and 66.

Philadelphia Flyers and the New York Islanders), as described by the _New York Times_:

> There were fewer than 13 minutes to play in the game when the altercation broke out. The Islanders were leading, 5-1, and they were coasting home.
>
> The Flyers sent out Hoyda, a right wing, who has not scored a goal this season. He got onto the ice while the Flyers were beginning to clear the puck from their end. Hoyda passed Denis Potvin of the Islanders at the Philadelphia blue line and gave him a high stick in what appeared to be a challenge. Putvin shrugged off the gesture and Hoyda then crossed the ice and the center line to cross-check Bossy from his blind side.
>
> At this point Gillies, who was near the play, dropped his gloves to fight Hoyda. Gillies is 6 feet 3 inches tall and weighs 220 pounds to Hoyda's 6-1 and 200 pounds, and the Islander was getting the better of the fight. As other players milled around the pair, Nystrom left the bench to join the altercation and in a moment both benches had emptied.
>
> There were numerous pairs of fights and wrestling matches, and players changed partners from time to time. A fight would subside in one place and another would break out elsewhere, as in a brush fire.
>
> Wicks and his two linesmen were helpless to stop the fray and they followed standard operating procedure which was to let the combatants tire themselves. It was 37 minutes before order was restored. Wicks imposed 166 minutes in penalties. For the game there was a total of 180 penalty minutes...
>
> Nystrom, a right wing, and seven other players, four from Islanders and three from the Flyers, drew game-misconduct penalties.
>
> Officials of the league also were studying what action, if any, they would take to supplement the automatic penalties that were imposed. The donnybrook, which occurred in the third period, led to 166 minutes in penalties and fines that will run into thousands of dollars...
>
> The National Hockey League also informed the Islanders that the club had been fined $1,000 under Rule 66B because it was their player who had left the bench.
>
> Brian O'Neill, executive vice president of the league, said he would study a videotape of the episode before deciding whether to supplement the automatic fines with league fines in money or suspensions.
>
> "There are a lot of automatics in cases like this, substantial ones that usually are adequate to cover the situation," O'Neill said in a telephone interview from

> Boston, where he was to attend an exhibition match between the Boston Bruins and the Wings of the Soviet. "I am not saying we cannot take additional action, but we do try not to inject league action unnecessarily."
> For each game misconduct there was an individual fine of $100. Fines of $100 apiece also were assessed on the 26 players from both teams, who left the benches.
> "These misconducts accumulate in the course of a season," O'Neill said. "When a player gets three game misconducts, he is automatically suspended for one game. If he gets four, he is suspended for two games.
> "We have these severe penalties to discourage this kind of thing, and they have been an adequate deterrent. If it becomes a persistent problem, then we take a hard look at the clubs involved." [309]

"Judge" O'Neill noted that he "uses his procedures judiciously."[310] Most discretionary suspensions have involved gross misconduct or match penalties. O'Neill said he has used this power twelve times since 1976; with eight suspensions for stick swinging, and four for "kicking the skate in an attempt to injure the opponent."[311] The World Hockey Association system works along similar lines.[312]

In football, the rules are much less elaborate. The NFL relies on three on the field penalty rules to control excessive violence: "unsportsmanlike conduct," "roughing the passer," and "unnecessary roughness." Furthermore, the referee, in his discretion, may suspend the player for the duration of the game. The fine and suspension powers are quite similar to those in hockey. Commissioner Rozelle views the film and notifies the guilty party of the fine or suspension,[313] using either the specific league rule or the

---

309 J.S. Radosta, "After the Brawl, Nystrom Sits One Out," New York Times (January 10, 1979).

310 See note 307, infra.

311 Personal Interview (see note 307, infra).

312 Alberta Law Review, supra, at 227.

313 Through a letter to the NFLPA office. (Personal interview with Sheila Brooks. See note 124, infra.)

broad "best interest" clause.[314]

In basketball, the "best interest" clause contained in the NBA Constitution,[315] incorporated by reference into the Uniform Player Contract,[316] allows the Commissioner to impose a fine of $500.00 "or...order for a time the suspension of any such person," or both. The NBA procedures are less detailed and more arbitrary than most, prompting specific criticism from the Georgetown Law Journal:

> The charter grants to the NBA president virtually unchecked power to determine cases of suspected misconduct, and to impose fines or suspensions therefor. In effect, NBA athletes must rely either upon their president's good judgment or upon public outcry as their protection against arbitrary or unreasonable disciplinary actions. The protection accorded by public empathy, however, is often minimal, for the details of such disciplinary actions are generally not made public.[317]

In baseball, until about 1962, beanball wars were common in the major leagues. Introduction of "...a rule requiring a warning to offensive players, followed by automatic ejection from the game, has aided considerably towards solving the problem."[318]

---

314 Canadian Football League procedures are similar.

315 NBA Constitution, §35(d).

316 Clause 5. See text surrounding note 286, infra.

317 Supra, at 774. National Basketball Ass'n Uniform Players Contract, Clause 21. Formerly even legal representatives were excluded from meetings between the Commissioner and the players because, as the then Commissioner Podoloff testified, the operation of the NBA is closely knit and he did not want interference from any "flannelmouths." Id., at 775.

318 Criminal Law Quarterly, supra, at 441.

C. Player Perceptions of the Stigma Attached to (and the Deterrent Value of) each League's Sanctions.

Given the widespread problem of sports violence, it seems that the only justification for deference by the criminal law in this area is that the internal sanctions are an adequate deterrent to such repugnant behavior. Too often, however, this is not the case.

1. Value of fines and short suspensions. Leagues frequently use their broad fining power. For example, in the five-year period prior to 1976 NFL Commissioner Rozelle collected $53,000 in fines from players and approximately $245,000 from NFL clubs.[319] The leagues regard fines and suspensions as part of a singular disciplinary system. The league's ultimate purposes in imposing punishment are basically the same in each case, and the choice of one sanction rather than the other may merely reflect differences in the seriousness of the offense, the mental state of the offender, or the quality of the factual proof.[320] In most cases, these fines and short suspensions have no deterrent value whatsoever. First, the penalties are usually too lenient given the nature of the offense and the high income of the average professional athlete. For example, in October, 1977, the NFL engaged in "the first suspension by the Commissioner for on the field behavior in almost 10 years--and the first for violence against another player for a "flagrant personal foul." The incident involved a "deliberate forearm blow" to the head of a player after the player had caught the ball and was in the clutches of a tackler and resulted in the suspension of one game and a loss

[319] Brief for the Appellants NFL & Alvin Ray Rozelle at 46, Mackey v. National Football League, 543 F.2d 606 (8th Cir. 1976).

[320] J. Weistart, "Player Discipline in Professional Sports: The Antitrust Issues," 18 William and Mary Law Review 736 (1977).

to the player of approximately $2000. The response of the suspended player was, "It don't faze me at all."[321] Gary Flakne, prosecutor in the Forbes hockey stick swinging case, miffed at the three-game suspension given Wayne Maki in 1969, and the ten-game suspension given Forbes in 1975, noted:

> Obviously, the same act, had it occurred outside the arena, would yield certain criminal prosecution. Since it receives only a token penalty inside the arena, there is no real compelling force to curtail that type of conduct. So the psychological conditioning drilled into the body contact athlete flourishes. [322]

With the large salaries that most players earn, "no one is going to care too much about a $200 fine."[323] Many of the players surveyed responded to my open ended question on "the fairness of the procedures" in a manner similar to the following response:

> The league's procedures have been pretty fair, although some of these fines and suspensions could have been more severe. [324]

Second, even if the fines were severe enough, some players claim that the team pays the player's fine. One player notes: "A fine is ignored usually. The team should pick it up and they usually do because they expect you to do what you get fined for."[325] This process may be illegal since most con-

---

[321] Georgia Law Review, supra, at 390-91.

[322] Flakne and Caplan, Trial, supra, at 35.

[323] Personal interview with Ed Garvey, NFLPA Executive Director (see note 152, infra.).

[324] Confidential survey (received February 22, 1979).

[325] Confidential survey (received February 15, 1979).

tracts require the player to pay the fine.[326] Third, many of the rule violations require that the team be fined directly for a player's action.[327] If, as has been suggested, a team actually encourages such conduct, the league's rationale of fining the team as an inducement to police its own players seems to have been miscalculated.

In short, there may be some cases where a fine is an effective deterrent. (For example, a "marginal" player being forced to pay a several hundred dollar fine.) For the most part, however, the situation is, as Flakne describes it: "The token fine or penalty has been ineffectual in eliminating violence in sports."[328]

2. Value of longer suspensions. If it is true that "professional discipline often operates only in the most extreme cases,"[329] then it might be expected that longer suspensions may be more effective in deterring severe sports violence. A suspended player is not paid for the duration of his suspension;[330] his suspension time is deducted from his salary on a pro rata basis.[331] Furthermore, a suspended player may not play for any other

---

326 NHL Contract, Clause 18: "The Club and the Player further agree that all fines imposed upon the Player under the Playing Rules or under the provisions of the League By-Laws, shall be deducted from the salary of the Player and be remitted by the Club to the NHL Players Emergency Fund." The same type of clause governs football (Canadian Football League Standard Players Contract, Clause 9. See Appendix J.) In basketball, the NBA Uniform Players Contract, Clause 15, requires the player to promise to pay the fine directly, with the Club deducting it from his salary only if he fails to so pay.

327 For example, NHL Rule 66(b) calls for a fine up to $5000.00 against the Club if a player leaves the bench to join a fight. In basketball, the NBA Constitution, §35(d) gives the Commissioner power to fine the Club $1000.00 if a player violates the "best interest" clause.

328 Flakne and Caplan, Trial, supra, at 33.

329 Hallowell and Meshbesher, Trial, supra, at 32.

330 Personal interview with Washington General Manager McNab (see note 45, infra.)

331 NHL Standard Player's Contract, Clause 15 (see Appendix K). (But see text surrounding note 325, infra.)

club during the period of his suspension.[332] In addition, many have accused the sports establishment of entering into an implicit "blacklisting" agreement not to employ the suspended player after his suspension is terminated.[333] In fact, one court specifically found that the "blacklisting" practice has been utilized.[334] Even if a player is not "blacklisted," some players have responded that an athlete is "treated differently by teammates, other players, coaches, and management" after returning from a lengthy suspension.[335] Though there are no statistics available, it is prob-

332 See, e.g., Major League Rule 13(a), in Blue Book 544; NFL Const. art.XVII, §17.12, at 60-61; ABA By-Laws, art. XV, §4, at 36.

333 See text surrounding notes 241-42, *infra* for the "blacklist" argument in the context of a "clubhouse lawyer" bringing a case to court.

334 The district court in *Mackey* concluded that a player who does not want to deal with the club that has drafted him or is not willing to accept that club's terms, "is effectively boycotted or blacklisted" by other clubs. *Mackey v. National Football League*, 543 F.2d 606 (8th Cir. 1976). Other examples involve former third baseman Clete Boyer, apparently blacklisted from baseball after publicizing a dispute he had with the general manager of his team. When football players tried to organize a union the owners blacklisted the organizer, Bernie Parrish. Valparaiso Law Review, *supra*, at 411. When NFL stars Paul Hornung and Alex Karras were suspended for gambling activities in 1963, the rival AFL stated that it would not attempt to recruit the players even though there was no agreement between the two leagues. *N.Y. Times* 41 (April 18, 1963). The *Manitoba Law Journal* describes the harm of such a "blacklisting":

> The effects of blacklisting can be devastating to a player's career. Once a player is placed on a team's blacklist, no other team will deal with him, as all other clubs in the league have been advised that the player is on the blacklist. Theoretically free to negotiate with any team since he has been cut from his former club's roster, the blacklisted player will find it impossible to get any other team in the league to sign him, or even give him a tryout. *Supra* at 371.

335 Seven respondents, however, claimed that players "are not treated any differently" after returning from a suspension. Given the mentality described in Chapter I, one wonders what "treated differently" actually means in this context. While in "normal society," a conviction creates a disadvantageous stigma in terms of future employment, in "hockey society," such an "internal conviction" may bring with it a certain amount of "respect".

ably the case that (given the attendant consequences) a lengthy suspension would have deterrent value. Unfortunately, however, severe punishments are rarely assessed.[336]

D. <u>Procedural Protections Against Arbitrary Judgment: The Grievance Procedures.</u>

The arbitrary powers discussed in Part A have been somewhat tempered by "procedural reforms [which] have been enacted as a result of mounting pressures from players associations."[337] Most of the reforms have been aimed at providing (1) a set of procedures to govern the fine and suspension determination and (2) a process by which these decisions may be reviewed.

In hockey, the penalty structure has a built in system of automatic fines and suspensions for certain offenses.[338] If an offense satisfies one of those criteria, the dispute is submitted to the president for final decision.[339] At that time, the Club must suspend the player from further action until the league's action is completed.[340] From the time of the notification of hearing and forward, "no publicity by any party" is allowed.[341]

---

[336] See, for example, Flakne's discussion of the "token" NHL Maki and Forbes suspensions for relatively serious offenses. (See text surrounding note 322, <u>infra</u>.) Further, although professional football has suspended players for disciplinary reasons for periods of time, it has never suspended a player for life, nor have its suspensions been challenged in court. K. Burr, "Player Control Mechanisms in Professional Team Sports," 34 <u>University of Pittsburgh Law Review</u> 649 (1973).

[337] Georgetown Law Journal, <u>supra</u>, at 775.

[338] See text surrounding notes 292-308, <u>infra</u>.

[339] NHL Collective Bargaining Agreement, §4.01(c).

[340] <u>Id.</u>, §15.01.

[341] Id., §4.05.

The hearing theoretically may be conducted at any site; but most are held in Toronto because of access to video equipment.[342] The player "presents his case" in the presence of the referee, his coach, his General Manager, and NHL Executive Vice President O'Neill (the "judge" for these purposes).[343] There "are no rules of evidence or trial procedure," because, as O'Neill suggests, "the purpose is not a legal inquiry, but rather a factual invesitgation."[344] There is "an opportunity for interchange," though the viewing of the game film is almost always dispositive.[345] Once a decision is reached, O'Neill sends a copy of the decision and officials' report to the NHLPA.[346] There is theoretically a right of appeal to the NHL Board of Governors.[347] However, since the "sentences are not stayed during appeal," O'Neill suggests that there is no incentive to do so.[348] Accordingly, "outside of a couple of threats to go forward, there have been no appeals."[349]

In football, the procedure is exclusively set out in Article VIII, §1, of the Collective Bargaining Agreement:

> All disputes involving a fine or suspension imposed upon a player by the Commissioner for conduct on the playing

---

342 Personal interview with Brian O'Neill, NHL Executive Vice-President (see note 307, _infra_).

343 Personal interview with General Manager McNab (see note 45, _infra_).

344 O'Neill, _supra_. Given the reasons behind the rules of evidence, this statement appears to make little sense.

345 _Id._ These hearings are apparently so informal, however, that O'Neill _frequently_ "conducts them on the telephone after reviewing the game film" himself.

346 For a copy of such a decision and report, see Appendices S and T, introduced in the Paiement-Polonich case study following Chapter IV.

347 NHL By-Laws, §17.

348 O'Neill neglected to mention another disincentive: The Board of Governors, being part of the "hockey establishment," could not be expected to overrule the initial decision.

349 O'Neill, _supra_.

> field, or involving action taken against a player by the Commissioner for conduct detrimental to the integrity of, or public confidence in, the game of professional football, will be processed exclusively as follows: The Commissioner will promptly send written notice of his action to the player, with a copy to the NFLPA. Within 20 days following written notification of the Commissioner's action, the player affected thereby or the NFLPA, with the approval of the player involved, may appeal in writing to the Commissioner. The Commissioner will designate a time and place for hearing, which will be commenced within 10 days following his receipt of the notice of appeal. As soon as practicable following the conclusion of such hearing, the Commissioner will render a written decision, which decision will constitute full, final and complete disposition of the dispute, and will be binding upon the player(s) and club(s) involved...

Additionally, the Agreement requires that "a player may be accompanied by counsel of his choice."[350] A representative of the NFLPA may also participate,[351] "and almost always does."[352] However, "each party will bear the cost of its own witnesses, counsel, and the like."[353] There is a pretense of formality. For example, the American Arbitration Association evidentiary rules are employed.[354] However, the process really merely involves "Rozelle looking at the film, sending out a letter with a fine sanction on it, and the player's routinely paying it."[355] Since there is no transcript recorded, nor a formal written disposition completed,[356] a meaningful review of the Commissioner's decision seems presently impossible.

---

350 NFL Collective Bargaining Agreement, Article VIII, §3.

351 Id.

352 Personal interview with Shiela Brooks, NFLPA Staff Counsel (see note 124, infra.)

353 "Unless the Commissioner determines otherwise." Article VIII, §4.

354 Brooks, supra.

355 Id.

356 Id.

In basketball, there is little concern with procedural formality. The NBA Constitution, §35(d), indicates that fines and suspensions will be assessed if "in the opinion of the Commissioner," the player has acted in a detrimental manner. Section 35(i) allows an appeal to the Board of Governors, "who shall determine such appeals in accordance with such rules and regulations as may be adopted by the Board in its absolute and sole discretion."

Baseball, on the other hand, has adopted a rigorous set of procedures. The major leagues have full blown Rules of Procedure,[357] providing for, among other things, written notice, a requirement to conduct the hearing "in general like judicial proceedings,"[358] following of "the established rules of evidence,"[359] summons and perjury clauses, allowance for depositions, and the opportunity for "a stenographic report" of the proceeding.[360]

In analyzing whether each set of procedures is both appropriate and adequate, it is important to explore the criteria upon which such a decision should be made. There appear to be three. First, the <u>reliability/consequences interrelationship</u>. Weistart explains:

> In resolving this question, there are two considerations which will deserve particular weight: the concern for the reliability of the decision and the significance of the consequences to the individual. There is a high degree of interrelationship between these factors; the more severe the consequences of a decision, the greater the need for a care-

---

[357] Rather than reproduce them here, they appear as Appendix L.

[358] Rule 3.

[359] Rule 4.

[360] Rule 8.

> fully structured proceeding. When the accused is threatened with a suspension or expulsion which seriously restricts his opportunity to earn a living, a high degree of deference to his interests will be required. [361]

Second, the public perception of reliability and/or formality. Thibaut, Walker, LaTour, and Holden report in their 1974 Stanford Law Review article "Procedural Justice as Fairness" that people strongly prefer adversarial procedures to procedures which provide them with less participation in the adjudicative process. For example, it may be more important to the "dignity" of the NHL player to have his suspension delivered in person rather than over the telephone or by letter (as is common practice), even if the decisional outcome would be identical. Third, available recources. The Supreme Court recognized the trade off inherent in such a determination in a "welfare hearing" decision, Matthews v. Eldridge:[362]

> At some point the benefit of an additional safeguard to the individual affected...and to society in terms of increased assurance that the action is just, may be outweighed by the cost.

In football, for example, NFL Counsel Jay Moyer notes the advantages of informality in his sports dispute resolution procedures. "This in-house system saves attorney fees, expedites settlements, keeps unseemly charges private, and assures that decisions will be made by a person familiar with football and its history."[363] In hockey, McMurtry notes that the league[364] "does not have the resources, financial or otherwise to launch or consider a comprehensive investigation..."[365]

---

[361] William and Mary Law Review, supra, at 714.

[362] 424 U.S. 319 (1976), at 348.

[363] J. Craig, "The Legal Question Could Become a Sticky One," Boston Globe (December 20, 1978).

[364] The Ontario Hockey Association.

[365] McMurtry, supra, at 18-19.

Using these three criteria as a framework, five specific types of procedural alternatives will be evaluated in an attempt to determine if any of them should be employed to supplement current league procedures.[366]

1. Right to counsel. There is no definitive answer. Weistart explains: "If the enforcing agency--the league--conducts its affairs through professional counsel and if the participant has no particular sophistication on the matter of how to present his defense, it would seem that the fairness of the proceeding could be insured only if there were a balance in the relative professionalism of the two sides."[367] But if the disciplinary proceeding is handled by non-legally trained personnel and otherwise has the attributes of impartiality, a court should accept that some individuals can adequately represent themselves, particularly if the factual issues are not overly complex. The primary concern should be whether the disciplined ath-

---

[366] Of course, there are many more types of procedural alternatives. The five explored in this paper are probably the most appropriate in the sports league context, given the desire for informality and the lack of resources. Judge Friendly, in his very useful article, "Some Kind of Hearing," 123 U.Pa.L.Rev. 1267 (1975), lists many of the ingredients of judicial due process:

(1) An unbiased tribunal;
(2) Notice of the proposed action and the grounds asserted for it;
(3) Opportunity to present reasons why the proposed action should not be taken;
(4) The right to present evidence, including the right to call witnesses;
(5) The right to know opposing evidence;
(6) The right to cross-examine adverse witnesses;
(7) Decision based exclusively on the evidence presented;
(8) Right to counsel;
(9) Requirement that the tribunal prepare a record of the evidence presented;
(10) Requirement that the tribunal prepare written findings of fact and reasons for its decision.

[367] William and Mary Law Review, supra, at 714.

lete was seriously disadvantaged by the denial of counsel, and that would seem to be a matter upon which no a priori judgment could be made. As mentioned earlier, the NHL and NFL[368] provide that counsel may be present, though at a cost to the appealing player. Both leagues report, however, that an "outside attorney" is rarely, if ever, present."[369]

2. Rules of Evidence and Standard of Proof. On a general level, the private group should not be expected to conform to the strict standards imposed in the criminal area. The tribunals used in the sports area generally do not have the sophistication of a court of law; and to expect them to operate with the same care and precision as found in criminal proceedings would require a fundamental restructuring which is not warranted in light of the nature of the decision involved. A primary antitrust concern is for the reliability of the decisions which are made. This can be insured even if some hearsay evidence is presented, the traditional notions of privileged testimony are ignored, and the decision is made on the preponderance of the evidence. If the opportunities for bias are removed and if there is an orderly presentation of evidence bearing on a particular issue, there would seem to be no inherent reason why the tribunal's decision should be suspect. But, of course, this does not mean that a reviewing court should be unconcerned about the quality of proof. If the tribunal ignores opportunities to hear relevant testimony, admits considerable prejudicial evidence, or fails to pursue important issues, the resulting decision is not likely to be one which generates confidence and may properly be rejected.[370] While baseball

---

[368] See text surrounding note 350, infra.

[369] O'Neill, supra.

[370] William and Mary Law Review, supra, at 715.

employs strict rules of evidence, and the NFL uses those of the American Arbitration Association, the NHL and NBA Rules contain no provisions for any evidentiary rules or standards.

3. Independence of the Decisionmaker. This is perhaps the most significant procedural infirmity. Each league vests initial decisionmaking power in the hands of its highest executive.[371] There are a number of problems with this procedure. First, disciplinary decisions are often made by a commissioner or similar official who is not totally removed from the internal politics of the league's venture. The league commissioner typically is selected by the club owners and is viewed as dependent upon them. The owners usually determine and pay the commissioner's salary; they have authority to modify the documents defining his powers, and they retain the right to fire him. Under these circumstances, it is alleged the commissioner is not likely to render decisions contrary to the owners' basic interests.

---

371

| SPORT | FINAL DECISION BY COMMISSIONER |
|---|---|
| (1) National & American Baseball Leagues | Fines and suspensions for conduct on the field, or conduct which involves the integrity of the game. |
| (2) National Football League | All non-injury grievances. |
| (3) National Basketball Association | Fines and suspensions for conduct on the court or for conduct that involves the integrity of the game. |
| (4) Hockey | |
| a. National Hockey League | General grievances. |
| b. World Hockey Association | General grievances. |

Gessford, Nebraska Law Review, supra, at 363. Additionally, individual sports such as golf and tennis have also found it advantageous to organize associations of those involved in the sports and to place disciplinary powers in executive committees. See Professional Golfers' Ass'n of America Const. art. IV, §3 & art. VIII, §2, in Constitution, By-Laws and Regulations of the Professional Golfers' Ass'n of America 5, 22-24, 31-32 (1970); The Constitution: United States Law Tennis Ass'n art. IV, §2 & art. VI, §2(b). Finally, boxing

The William and Mary Law Review tactfully condludes that while it is inappropriate to conclude generally that league-appointed commissioners are inherently biased, there may be cases in which the commissioner does not act with the appropriate objectivity.[372] Congressman Emanuel Celler was less diplomatic in testimony before the 1958 Hearings on Organized Professional Team Sports:[373] "It should be borne in mind that the office of the commissioner cannot be relied upon to protect the public, the players, or the sport. The commissioner is paid by, and his office is controlled by, the club owners."

Second, it is argued that the commissioner himself is so involved in matters that come before him for arbitration that it is unrealistic to expect that he can treat them impartially. For example, in addition to his role as arbitrator, the commissioner often is given power to promulgate rules governing such subjects as player conduct and personnel procedures. The Constitution and By-Laws for the National Football League provides that: "The Commissioner shall interpret and from time to time establish policy and procedure in respect to the provisions of the Constitution and By-Laws and any enforcement thereof."[374] He may be required to arbitrate a case in which the meaning of the rule or his authority to promulgate is called into question. As a result, the players contend that the commissioner cannot be expected to remain objective when his own actions are under review.[375]

---

and wrestling, due to past histories of corruption, are regulated by state-appointed commissions where such sports are legal. See, e.g., D.C. Code Ann. §§2-1210 to1226 (1967); N.Y. Unconsol. Laws, §§8901-31, 8933 (McKinney 1961); Tex. Pen. Code Ann. art. 614-1 to -17 (1952).

[372] William and Mary Law Review, supra, at 715-716.

[373] Georgetown Law Journal, supra, at 797.

[374] §8.5.

[375] William and Mary Law Review, supra, at 715-716.

Third, there may be a temptation by sports authorities to use players caught in rule infractions as scapegoats. For example, if it develops that there are widespread rumors of gambling in a particular sport, there may be a tendency to "throw the book" at the first player to be caught.[376] One NHL player responded that players are treated differently after their return from a suspension because "they are watched more closely by league officials."[377]

Fourth, the current procedure maintains the "appearance of impropriety," even if the Commissioner is, in reality, completely fair. When interviewed, Ed Garvey of the NFLPA suggested that though "Rozelle himself is quite fair, it's the set up that we're worried about."[378] Regardless of the intent of the individual Commissioner, the fact that he has both "investigative and judicial power"[379] produces a less credible appearance. Weistart notes that the system is therefore perceived of as less rational:

> Unless some legal control is introduced, there is a risk that the disciplinary power may be used to achieve improper economic goals or to require conformity with a standard of morality which reflects more the idiosyncrasies of a commissioner or a group of owners than the needs of the sport.[380]

At least one court[381] has adopted this "illegal per se" type of analysis. In Blalock v. Ladies Professional Golf Association[382], Jane Blalock was accused

---

376 Id.

377 Confidential survey (received February 13, 1979).

378 Personal interview (see note 152, infra).

379 C.H. Lowell, "Collective Bargaining and the Professional Team Sport Industry," Law and Contemporary Problems 18 (1974).

380 William and Mary Law Review, supra, at 720.

381 The legal arguments will be explored more fully in Part E of this chapter.

382 359 F.Supp. 1260 (N.D.Ga. 1973).

of cheating in an LPGA sponsored tournament and upon being found guilty was suspended from tournament play for a year. She sued, alleging that the suspension constituted a group boycott. The court accepted the plaintiff's characterization and found the defendant's action to be per se illegal. The court was primarily concerned about the structure of the disciplinary organ in the LPGA. The committee which imposed the suspension was composed of golfers who competed with Blalock on the LPGA circuit. Moreover, in the court's view, the group was given "completely unfettered, subjective" discretion in determining the appropriateness of exclusion as the sanction for the alleged offense. Although the court did not dwell on the question of how this discretion might be affected by bias, it clearly was concerned about the fact that the decision was made by players who stood to gain if Blalock were removed as a competitor.[383] It should be noted that the court did not find that any of the players on the discipline committee was actually biased. Rather, the central objection was that the disciplinary process had not been structured to guard against this possibility.[384] Although Blalock dealt with a sport involving individualized competition, the dicta in the case suggests its applicability to the league sports context. This is especially true since each league's Commissioner is essentially given the "completely unfettered, subjective discretion"[385] that the Blalock court disdains.

4. Independent Review of Decisionmaker's "Sentence." The four harms of a coopted Commissioner could be largely alleviated if there were some mechanism for an objective appellate review. Unfortunately, there is no such pro-

---

383 William and Mary Law Review, supra, at 717-19.

384 Id.

385 See text surrounding notes 338-360, infra.

cedure. The NFL[386] and Canadian Football League[387] accord the Commissioner the power to render "full, final, and complete disposition."[388] The NHL and NBA[389] allow appeals to the respective Boards of Governors. These Boards are usually composed of former coaches or current owners or general managers, and, hence, are not independent. In these cases, therefore, there is no mechanism for independent review.

In short, as Nick Buoniconti notes, "the situation is anything but clean, with the Commissioner acting as judge, jury, and Supreme Court."[390] Though the current NFLPA staff dislikes the procedure also, their feeling is that, since this was a legitimate concession negotiated into the Collective Bargaining Agreement, "we must wait until the next contract is up for negotiation."[391] In the meantime, Garvey estimates that about half of the players fined "would say they'd like to appeal Rozelle's decision."[392] The _Valparaiso Law Review_ concludes: "It is obvious that the integrity of a sport must

---

386 NFL Collective Bargaining Agreement, Article VIII, §1.

387 CFL Standard Player Contract, Clause 17. (See Appendix J)

388 NHL By-Laws, §17.

389 NBA Constitution, §35(i)

390 Personal interview (see note 69, _infra._)

391 Personal interview with Shiela Brooks (see note 124, _infra_). Labor law cases appear to forclose a court remedy as long as there is a provision in the collective bargaining agreement to the effect that the arbitrator's decision "shall be final and binding on the parties." _United Steelworkers of America v. Enterprise Wheel and Car Corp._, 363 U.S. 593 (1960). As such, the Commissioner is the "arbitrator" for these purposes and each relevant Collective Bargaining Agreement does contain the appropriate "finality" provision.

392 Personal interview with Ed Garvey (see note 152, _infra._).

be maintained. A decision should be appealable to an independent arbitrator. This would give the player at least one review to insure the correctness of the commissioner's decision."[393]

5. <u>Approximate Guidelines to Insure Decisional Consistency.</u> If some general standards were created to guide a Commissioner's decision, not only would the majority of outcomes tend to become more consistent, but the isolated repugnant decision would be more easily cognizable. Impeccable accuracy is not necessarily the goal. In fact, studies suggest that there is little evidence that court decisions imposing procedural formalities have led to markedly more accurate decisions in the context of "mass justice" welfare bureaucracies.[394] However, given the vague and arbitrary rules with which a Commissioner has to work,[395] some parameters must be considered. In search of such guidelines, Weistart has developed a sliding scale which shall govern how much deference to allow a Commissioner's decision. Least deference, he argues, should be given to "off the field conduct of a non criminal nature." Weistart notes that: "A player may insist that he is hired primarily for his athletic prowess and that as long as he maintains his physical condition and performs to the best of his ability in practice and competition, he has fulfilled his contractual obligation. What he does off-the-field, it will be contended, is his own business."[396] More deference should be paid to

---

[393] <u>Supra</u>, at 411.

[394] Drawing on studies by Baum and others. Mashaw, "The Management Side of Due Process: Accuracy, Fairness and Timeliness in Adjudication of Social Welfare Claims," 59 <u>Cornell Law Review</u> 772 (1974).

[395] See, for example, the discussion of the "best interest" clauses in Part A of this Chapter.

[396] William and Mary Law Review, <u>supra</u>, at 730.

a decision involving "off the field conduct" which the society defines as criminal or serious.[397] Even more freedom should be given the Commissioners on matters involving "the integrity of on the field competition." Weistart suggests the following standard as the relevant guide: "For most rules related to the integrity of league competition, the relevant inquiry is whether the action is reasonable in light of the goals sought to be achieved, on the one hand, and the effect upon the players' competitive opportunities on the other."[398] Finally, Weistart suggests that the most deference should be accorded to decisions in the area most critical to this paper:

> Fighting among players, although it does not involve the type of dishonesty found in other rule infractions, is often a source of concern for league officials. There have been numerous instances in which fighting and other activity which threatens the safety of participants have resulted in players being suspended from competition, although the suspensions are usually for short periods of

---

[397] A case which illustrates the difficulty in defining the league's prerogatives in this area is that involving football player Lance Rentzel. Rentzel, a star performer as a wide receiver for the Dallas Cowboys, was suspended from the NFL following two convictions of indecent exposure and an arrest for drug possession. League Commissioner Rozelle suspended Rentzel under a rule that authorized such action when a player engages in "conduct detrimental to the welfare of the League or professional football...." NFLPA Executive Director Garvey publicly criticized the suspension and assisted in filing legal actions to enjoin the continuance of the punishment. The public debate raised the issues which are considered here. For example, the club owners argued for the need for discipline among players and expressed concern for the distraction that might be caused by the presence of a controversial figure on the field. Garvey, on the other hand, saw the suspension as an attempt by the Commissioner to legislate the moral standard to be followed by the players. Others viewed the matter as illustrating the difficulty of drawing a line between "life-style" and truly detrimental conduct. Id., at 733.

[398] Id., at 723.

> time. There should be little doubt that the league can take action to control such conduct. It has a legitimate concern not only for the physical well-being of its players but also for the problems which might result if a brawl developed to the point where fans joined in. Finally, major altercations among players disrupt the contests in which they occur and tend to attract attention away from the regular competition, a result which undermines the league's efforts to focus fan attention on the game itself. [399]

However, though Weistart advocates broad deference to a Commissioner's fine or suspension sentence for violent during the game conduct, he does not suggest that those decisions should be unreviewable. In fact, he concludes, "that the league may be justified in controlling such unauthorized combat does not mean that its action will not be reviewed. As with other types of misconduct, the punishment for fighting which is imposed must not be excessive. Moreover, the league should be prepared to show that it has pursued an even-handed enforcement policy."[400]

It is precisely this type of policy that the Players' Associations have been unanimously advocating. One commentator concludes that, "...when some form of disciplinary action is necessary to protect the best interests of a particular sport, such action will be undertaken in...an inconsistent manner."[401] McMurtry, perhaps overemphatic in his characterization, suggested that the NHL procedure is run by men "who have no moral or legal duty to anyone. Where due process is concerned, they never know what they're doing."[402]

---

[399] Id., at 728-29.

[400] Id., at 729-30.

[401] Georgetown Law Journal, supra, at 777.

[402] Telephone interview (see note 112, infra.). Contrast this with "insider" McNab's statement that he has "never seen an unfair result." (See note 45, infra.) The fact that there are differing perceptions, alone, should

Most players responding to the survey appear to accept the system as "fair." In reality, however, most players fall into two groups. One group really does not care about a set of procedures "that will never really effect them."[403] Garvey suggests that if this group is concerned with anything, it is with "the intra-Club disciplinary rules such as curfew, training, and the like."[404] For this group to be "excited," says Buoniconti, "something really unfair will have to happen to someone close to them."[405] The other group is less apathetic. However, as the Wisconsin Law Review notes, they will not do anything to change the system of light fines and penalties in a game [hockey] where everybody must be violent to survive:

> At present, players suspended or fined for serious misconduct have rather dutifully accepted their punishment. No doubt now they realize, after the Forbes indictment, how relatively mild their punishment has been. However, should the league sanctions become significantly more severe, such as a full year suspension without pay, the players will undoubtedly be more reluctant to accept the present informal system of hotel room arbitration without the assistance of counsel or other due process protections. The same problem has been discussed with respect to disciplinary proceedings for other forms of misconduct (e.g., betting suspensions).[406]

---

suggest some form of neutral review or meaningful guidelines. In football, there are also diverse opinions. Some commentators suggest that the NFL procedure is "administered arbitrarily" (Georgetown Law Review, supra). Others contend the opposite. Alan Page, former Minnesota Viking All-Pro Defensive Lineman, now with the Chicago Bears, stated: "They [the NFL] have taken certain rules, enforced them, and have done a very good job of stopping [players] from fighting." (Criminal Law Quarterly, supra, at 439.)

403 Personal interview with McNab (see note 45, infra.)

404 Personal interview (see note 152, infra.)

405 Personal interview (see note 69, infra.)

406 Wisconsin Law Review, supra, at 788-89.

E. Legal Rationales Which May Be Employed to Improve the Grievance Procedures. [407]

Part D recommends certain specific procedural reforms which would serve to improve the internal disciplinary mechanisms. Part E suggests two legal bases that could be used as vehicles to implement these reforms.

1. Argue that as a member of a private association, a player is entitled to certain minimum due process protections. First, the respective league must qualify as a "private association" for the purposes of this doctrine.[408] Second, the "association" must qualify as the type of association into whose internal affairs courts are willing to intervene. A number of recent decisions, however, indicate an increasing judicial willingness to review association actions where it is shown that an association serving a public purpose bars nonmembers from engaging a particular profession or occupation. The Georgetown Law Journal,[409] after summarizing these decisions, noted that judicial intervention in such disciplinary matters is

---

407 Though this inquiry is directed at both fines and suspensions, the relevant case law has mostly dealt with the restrictive act of suspending someone from his employment for a period of time. There is little authority, either generally or in the sports area, specifically considering the authority of private groups to use fines to achieve compliance with their rules. In the few instances in which fining systems in other industries have been reviewed, the focus has usually been on whether the group can properly impose discipline at all, and the issue of whether monetary penalties are entitled to greater, or lesser, deference typically has not been raised. See, e.g., Mechanical Contractors Bid Depository v. Christiansen, 352 F.2d 817 (10th Cir. 1965), cert. denied, 384 U.S. 918 (1966).

408 By their own description, the organizations governing team sports are associations. See, e.g., NFL Const. art. I, §1.1 at 9; ABA By-Laws, art. I, §1 & art. II, §6, at 2; National Hockey League Const., art. 1. As one court has stated: "Each of the leagues is an unincorporated association ...." American Football League v. National Football League, 205 F.Supp. 60, 62 (D. Md. 1962), aff'd, 323 F.2d 124 (4th Cir. 1963). Baseball is somewhat different in that there are two major leagues, the National and the American, each describing itself as an association and each voluntarily submitting itself to the authority of the Commissioner. Blue Book 601-06. Georgetown Law Journal, supra, at 788.

409 Supra, at 782.

founded upon three criteria: 1) membership is essential to an individual's livelihood;[410] 2) the association performs a quasi-public function;[411] and 3) judicial action will not seriously impair the proper goals of the organization.[412] Assuming these criteria are satisfied,[413] before a court can apply constitutional protections to a given case, it must find that the con-

---

410 In setting aside the disciplinary action imposed by a labor union on one of its members, one court noted that "by the judgment of expulsion for life...a man approaching middle age with a lifetime of experience in a chosen field...is for all practical purposes economically destroyed." Sanders v. International Ass'n of Bridge Workers, 330 F.Supp. 253, 258 (W.D. Ky. 1955). Other courts have intervened in the internal affairs of associations for the same reason. See James v. Marinship Corp. 25 Cal.2d 721, 155 P.2d 329 (1944); Carroll v. Electrical Workers Local 269, 133 N.J.Eq. 144, 31 A.2d 223 (Ch. 1943).

411 See Marjorie Webster Jr. College v. Middle States Ass'n, 302 F.Supp. 459, 469 (D.D.C. 1969) (college excluded from an accreditation society performing a public function); Falcone v. Middlesex County Medical Soc'y, 34 N.J. 582, 170 A.2d 791 (1961) (qualified physician excluded from medical society which served the public interest).

412 Falcone v. Middlesex County Medical Soc'y, 34 N.J. 582, 170 A.2d 790 797 (1961). See generally Hurwitz v. Directors Guild, 364 F.2d 67, 72 (2d Cir. 1966) (association's method of protecting its legitimate interests held improper); Deesen v. Professional Golfer's Ass'n, 358 F.2d 165, 172 (9th Cir. 1966) (an association's enforcement of reasonable rules to promote its objectives is not a violation of antitrust laws); Bernstein v. Alameda Contra Costa Medical Ass'n, 139 Cal.App.2d 241, 293 P.2d 862 (Dist. Ct. App. 1956) (association's by-laws not enforcible if against public policy).

413 Where courts refuse to extend the status of private associations to professional sports organizations, or where courts determine that a particular organization does not satisfy the criteria of association essential to judicial intervention, one could argue that "the public function" performed by sports leagues entitles a player to due process protections guaranteed by the Fourteenth Amendment. Early cases held similar private endeavors absolutely free of fourteenth amendment restrictions. This strict interpretation of the law has been modified recently by a line of cases finding state action wherever private organizations perform a public function. The Connecticut Law Review argues that this test has been satisfied: the most important factor in classifying spectator sports as a "public" function is that the facilities which sports teams use are most often paid for by the taxpayer. Of the twenty-eight stadiums that currently house professional football, only two are privately owned. Therefore, municipal and/or state governments already have the inherent authority to regulate various aspects of spectator sports through control of their own property. S. Nelson, "Bringing Sports Under Legal Control," 10 Connecticut Law Review 256 (1978). For a thorough discussion of this "public function" doctrine, see Georgetown Law Review, supra, at 790-92.

nection between the organization and the state is sufficient to support a conclusion that the organization's activities constitute "state action." The same "quasi-public function" arguments used above, as well as in the "public function test," may be used here.[414] Once these problems are overcome to the extent that it is clear that some procedures are required, the relief requested by an excluded athlete must be balanced against any harm resulting to the interests of the sport. In general, an athlete will be denied relief where the basis for his punishment was a rule fairly enforced[415] and reasonably related to the proper goals of the organization. From a Constitutional perspective, dicta from Mr. Justice Powell is relevant in this context.[416] He argues, in essence, that the procedures necessary to assure a fair trial rest upon a balance of three considerations: (a) the complexity of the offense charged; (b) the probable sanction imposed; and (c) the individual factors peculiar to each case and other matters which "a sensitive and diligent judge would recognize as crucial to fundamental fairness."[417] Professor LaFrance suggests a similar balancing in his "neo-special circumstances" approach,"[418] weighing the needs of the

---

414 See note 411 and 413, infra. In addition to state action problems, the NHL reformers are faced with the problem of applying the United States Constitution and common law to disciplinary proceedings which occur, for the most part, in Toronto.

415 As one court expressed this concept: "We hold that a private organization, particularly if tinged with public stature or purpose, may not expel or discipline a member adversely affecting substantial property, contract or other economic rights, except as a result of fair proceedings which may be provided for in organization by-laws, carried forward in an atmosphere of good faith and fair play." McCune v. Wilson, 237 So.2d 169, 173 (Fla. Sup.Ct. 1970).

416 Argersinger v. Hamlin, 92 S.Ct. 2006.

417 Id., at 2026.

418 A. LaFrance, "Criminal Defense Systems for the Poor," 50 Notre Dame Lawyer 44 (1974). Though Professor La France was dealing with attorney representation in criminal cases, the balancing analogy seems appropriate here.

organization (the league in this case) against the needs of the individual (player).[419] A derivative of this flexible balancing approach has been applied to quasi-governmental administrative agencies as well.[420] In the sports context, while this balancing process clearly permits those disciplinary actions necessary to the maintenance of competition, it must not be applied to allow arbitrary or heavy-handed disciplinary actions by sports organizations under broad "best-interest" clauses. There has been only one case dealing with the necessity of due process protections in league[421] sport fine and suspension proceedings. In <u>Molinas v. National Basketball Association</u>[422], the plaintiff, who admitted placing bets on his team to win, was suspended indefinitely by the commissioner. The court stated that Molinas had failed to show an unreasonable restraint of trade

---

[419] For both LaFrance's and Powell's tests to apply, the satisfaction of the "private association" criteria is not enough. The individual must "be deprived of an interest of sufficient consequence" (Argersinger, <u>supra</u>). In this context, the harm that attaches to a suspended player may be enough of a "sufficient consequence," given the text surrounding notes 329-334, <u>infra</u>.

[420] The Georgetown Law Journal, <u>supra</u>, at 787 notes that the concept of due process is not subject to fixed rules, but rather is related to the time, place, and circumstances of each case. <u>Joint Anti-Fascist Refugee Comm. v. McGrath</u>, 341 U.S. 123, 163-63 (1951). (Frankfurter, J., concurring). In an administrative case, the practices generally equated with due process include the right to a fair hearing upon adequate notice in which the parties are apprised of the charges against them, permitted representation by counsel, afforded the opportunity to present evidence on their behalf, and allowed to cross-examine witnesses. See <u>Greene v. McElroy</u>, 360 U.S. 474, 496-97, 506-08 (1959). See generally <u>Reilly v. Pinkus</u>, 338 U.S. 269, 275-76 (1949). In addition to these procedural safeguards, it also has been held that the due process clause affords certain substantive protections such as the prohibition of arbitrary rule enforcement.

[421] See text surrounding notes 382-385, <u>infra</u>, for the description of the <u>Blalock</u> case, applying such protections to "individual sports" (golf) and suggesting that the leap to league sport protection may be made through <u>Blalock</u> itself.

[422] 190 F.Supp. 241 (S.D.N.Y. 1961).

as defined by the antitrust laws. The court held that the league provision seemed "not only reasonable but necessary for the survival of the league." Unfortunately, the court failed to make any mention of the possible due process violation that may have occurred as the player had not been given a hearing prior to his suspension.[423] However, despite the favorable ruling in Molinas, the NBA settled with another complainant[424] in 1969 for over a million dollars. As a direct result, the NBA instituted procedures requiring that a player be given notice and an opportunity to be heard prior to any suspension or disciplinary action by the commissioner.

In summary, the private association/due process argument is by no means universally accepted. However, there is some case law which supports its extension to require impartial review of a Commissioner's decision, for example. The NFLPA maintains that the Collective Bargaining Agreement locks the organization into the current procedures "unless there is a total lack of good faith."[425] However, if such protections were found to be Constitutionally guaranteed, the Collective Bargaining Agreement would be ineffectual in "contracting away" those rights. Furthermore, even if the current Agreement were dispositive, these disciplinary powers are clearly within the concept of the terms and conditions of employment and would, therefore, be mandatory subjects of bargaining about which the owners must negotiate during the next bargaining period. Thus, the players could demand that they be given full procedural due process rights in all disciplinary matters and this would be a subject about which the owners would be required to bargain in good faith.

---

423 Valparaiso Law Review, supra, at 410.

424 Connie Hawkins, who had been restricted from NBA employment for five years.

425 Personal interview with Ed Garvey. See note 152, infra.

2. Argue that antitrust law protects the athlete against arbitrary disciplinary procedures in violation of the "rule of reason" standard. Professional athletes have traditionally sought judicial relief from arbitrary disciplinary actions through application of federal antitrust law. Under the Sherman Act, an athlete can recover damages if he can establish a clear causal connection between antitrust violations by a professional sports organization and legal injuries he has sustained.[426] The determination of what constitutes an actual violation of antitrust law in relation to organized sports has been based primarily upon a "rule of reason" standard.[427] Under this standard, courts are called upon to weigh the reasonable regulatory objectives of a professional sports organization against the anti-competitive effects of its rules.[428]

Under the rule of reason approach, courts are required to examine the agreement or practice in relation to the history and economics of the industry in which it is employed. If supported by clear economic necessity, and if its dominant purpose is not a restraint of trade, the practice is declared reasonable and not violative of the antitrust laws. After the rule of reason became the recognized standard by which antitrust violations would be measured, the Supreme Court declared on numerous occasions that in certain cases the detriment of an illegal activity by itself outweighed any possible rationale that could be advanced for its continuance. Henceforth, these particular activities were deemed illegal per se, thereby avoiding the necessity

---

[426] Tepler v. Frick, 204 F.2d 506, 507 (2d Cir. 1953); Molinas v. National Basketball Ass'n, 190 F.Supp. 241, 243 (S.D.N.Y. 1961).

[427] The Sherman Antitrust Act provides, in part: "Every contract, combination in the form of trust or otherwise, or conspiracy in restraint of trade or commerce among the several states...is declared to be illegal." 15 USC §1 (1970).

[428] Georgetown Law Journal, supra, at 779.

for prolonged economic investigation. Among those practices which have been held to be so pernicious as to be per se violations are group boycotts and concerted refusals to deal.[429]

In 1957, an action for treble damages reached the Supreme Court. The suit was brought by a player who had been blacklisted by the National Football League and its affiliate The Pacific Coast League, for playing in the rival All-America Conference. In Radovich v. National Football League,[430] the Supreme Court held the Sherman Act applicable to professional football because of the volume of interstate business involved.[431] By implication, Radovich ruled that all professional team sports except baseball[432] were subject to the antitrust laws. This has since been confirmed. Cases involving both basketball[433] and hockey[434] have held that the antitrust laws were applicable. Hence, the antitrust "rule of reason" standard appears to condemn "restrictive practices" in all major professional sports leagues except baseball.

---

429 Valparaiso Law Review, supra, at 384-85.

430 352 U.S. 445, reh. denied, 353 U.S. 931 (1957).

431 Id., at 452.

432 Baseball was specifically exempted from the antitrust laws by the seminal decision of Federal Baseball Club of Baltimore v. National League, 259 U.S. 200 (1922). In Flood v. Kuhn 407 U.S. 258 (1972), the Supreme Court held that the precedential value of Federal Baseball survived the holdings in Radovich and other sport antitrust cases. As such, the Court stated that any remedy would have to come from Congress. Id., at 285. Dissenting, Mr. Justice Douglas confessed that although he had previously supported the majority position, he now felt that the Court should correct its own "fundamental" error and should not depend on Congress to do so. Id., at 286. Mr. Justice Marshall urged the Court to overrule its previous mistake as a substantive federal right--free competition--was being denied. Id., at 292-93.

433 Haywood v. National Basketball Association, 401 U.S. 1204 (1971) (Douglas, J., as Cir. J.).

434 Nassau Sports v. Peters, 352 F.Supp. 840 (E.D.N.Y. 1972); Philadelphia World Hockey v. Philadelphia Hockey Club, 351 F.Supp. 462, 517 (E.D.Pa. 1972).

It may be appropriate to argue, therefore, that a disciplinary proceeding which has the potential of restricting a player's liberty through fine or inordinate suspension is "unreasonable" unless it conforms to certain requirements (such as independent review, for example). The "rule of reason" standard has been applied in a number of analogous areas to end unreasonable player restriction. The Valparaiso Law Review notes: "Antitrust laws...have had a large impact on other professional sports. Specifically, they have been fairly effective in attacking the use of the player-control mechanisms."[435] There are a number of examples. First, the basic draft systems used by two professional leagues were ruled illegal in Smith v. Pro Football (NFL)[436] and Robertson v. National Basketball Association[437] (NBA) as unreasonably restrictive on player movement. Second, the courts overturned as restrictive the NBA rule prohibiting a player from being eligible to play until four years after his high school class had been graduated.

---

[435] Supra, at 381.

[436] 420 F.Supp. 738 (D.D.C. 1976). The plaintiff, Jim "Yazoo" Smith, had been drafted and signed in 1968 by the Washington Redskins. In the last game of his rookie season Smith sustained a serious neck injury that ended his professional football career. Smith asserted that because of the draft he was unable to negotiate a contract reflecting the free market value of his talents and that it was impossible for him to negotiate a clause to guarantee against the loss of earnings in the event of injury. The court found the draft to be per se violative of the antitrust laws: "This outright, undisguised refusal to deal constitutes a group boycott in its classic and most pernicious form, a device which has long been condemned as a per se violation of the antitrust laws...There is no question but that the restrictions comprising the draft are 'naked restraints of trade' with no purpose except stifling of competition." In the alternative, the court also found that the draft was a violation of the antitrust laws when tested by the rule of reason. It found that the NFL draft was the most restrictive system possible, leaving no room for competition for the service of the draftees. Since less restrictive alternatives were possible, it was decided that the present provisions could not be protected by the rule of reason. Valparaiso University Law Review, supra, at 389.

[437] 389 F.Supp. 867 (S.D.N.Y. 1975). Though the court denied a motion for summary judgment based on "per se" reasoning, it left open the possibility of

This rule was designed to protect collegiate athletic programs which the NBA utilized to develop talent in lieu of an expensive minor league system. Ironically, even if a player did not attend college, he had to wait four years to play in the league. The NBA provisions, comprising what is commonly known as the four-year rule, were challenged successfully in 1971 by a player[438] so excluded in Denver Rockets v. All-Pro Management, Inc.[439] One of the major factors in the court's ruling that the rule was unreasonable was that there were no "procedural safeguards which assure that the restraint is not arbitrary and which furnish a base for judicial review."[440] Third, the "reserve system" and "option clauses" of the NFL (Kapp v. National Football League[441] and Mackey v. National Football League[442]) and NHL (Philadel-

---

a "rule of reason" violation. No decision was reached on this issue, however, as the case was settled in conjunction with approval of the NBA Collective Bargaining Agreement.

438 Connie Hawkins.

439 325 F.Supp. 1049 (C.D.Cal. 1971).

440 Id., at 1064-65.

441 390 F.Supp. 73 (N.D.Cal. 1974).

442 407 F.Supp. 1000 (D.Minn. 1975), aff'd 543 F.2d 606 (8th Cir. 1976). The District Court held the Rozelle Rule to be illegal in that it restrained the players, was overly broad, and afforded no procedural safeguards. The court rejected the justification for the reasonableness of the Rule presented by the defendants. The NFL argued that the Rule protected its investment in player development; the court reasoned that other businesses incur like expenses. The NFL also argued that player continuity was important to the success of a team and was aided by the Rule. The court found that all teams would be equally affected and that the quality of play in the NFL would not decrease. Furthermore, even if the quality of play would decrease, that would still not justify the anticompetitive nature of the Rule. Finally, the court found that the elimination of the Rule would not be immediately disruptive, nor would it cause irreparable damage to the NFL.

The Court of Appeals for the Eighth Circuit affirmed the district court's finding of antitrust violations. Valparaiso University Law Review, supra, at 407. This holding produced major alterations in the 1977 Collective Bargaining Agreement.

phia World Hockey Club v. Philadelphia Hockey Club[443]) were also found to be unreasonable under antitrust analysis. The Valparaiso University Law Review suggests that the key fault in such a scheme is the automatic restrictiveness inherent in the process, therefore analogous to an unreviewable fine and suspension proceeding:

> Both clauses allowed a team, at the expiration of the first contract, to unilaterally renew a player's agreement for one year, usually at a reduction in salary of ten percent. The reserve clause renewed the contract upon all the same terms and conditions contained in the contract. Since the reserve clause was in the original contract it was deemed to be in the renewed contract as well. Therefore, the team could indefinitely renew the contract of a player effectively binding him to that club for his entire playing career. 444

---

Under the new agreement, a player choosing to leave his club can play out his option year at 110% of his previous year's salary rather than at the earlier 90% rate. The player's former team is still to receive compensation from the team acquiring him. Now, however, if compensation cannot be agreed upon, it will be assessed not by the Commissioner but according to a predetermined schedule. If the free agent is offered a salary of $60,000 to $65,000, his former team will receive a third round draft choice as compensation. Compensation for a player offered $65,000 to $75,000 will be a second round draft choice. A player offered $75,000 to $125,000 will cost the acquiring team a first round draft choice. A player offered over $125,000 will require two successive first round selections as compensation from the new team. In all cases, the player's original club will have a right of first refusal. If it matches the other club's offer, the player must stay where he is.

443 351 F.Supp. 462 (E.D.Pa. 1972). The WHA brought suit to enjoin the further enforcement of the NHL reserve system. The WHA alleged that the reserve system and the monopoly enjoyed by the NHL were violations of Sections 1 and 2 of the Sherman Act. Reacting to the monopoly charge, NHL Commissioner Clarence Campbell made the ill-advised statement that the purpose of the affiliations with the other leagues was to insure that the NHL would always be "the only major professional hockey league operating from coast to coast in the United States or Canada." Nor surprisingly, the court granted the injunction.

444 Supra, at 392.

The unreasonableness of these three sets of restrictions seems compellingly analogous to the fine and suspension grievance procedures described earlier.[445] For three reasons, however, the courts have not adopted the analogy to scrutinize these procedures. First, in cases involving athletic skill, gambling,[446] or contractual control over an athlete's services, for example, courts have consistently found anticompetitive actions by sports organizations justified under the rule of reason. Second, once the fine and suspension proceeding is incorporated into a bona fide Collective Bargaining Agreement, it is apparently immune from antitrust attack under current case law.[447] Third, as was suggested earlier, since the

---

445

See text surrounding notes 337-400, infra.

446

Molinas v. National Basketball Association, supra. See text surrounding note 423, supra.

447

This is a product of the labor law exemption from the antitrust laws embodied in Sections 6 and 20 of the Clayton Act. Specifically, Section 6 of the Clayton Act, 15 U.S.C., §15 (1970) provides:

"The labor of a human being is not a commodity or article of commerce. Nothing contained in the antitrust laws shall be construed to forbid the existence and operation of labor, agricultural, or horticultural organization, instituted for the purposes of mutual help, and not having capital stock or conducted for profit, or to forbid or restrain individual members of such organizations from lawfully carrying out the legitimate objects thereof; nor shall such organizations, or the members thereof, be held or construed to be illegal combinations or conspiracies in restraint of trade, under the antitrust laws."

Section 20 of the Clayton Act, 29 U.S.C., §52 (1970), provides in pertinent part:

"No restraining order or injunction shall be granted by any court of the United States, or a judge or the judges thereof, in any case between an employer and employees, or between employees, or between persons employed and persons seeking employment."

The Mackey court (543 F.2d 606, at 616) listed three requirements to be satisfied before this exemption may apply to a league Collective Bargaining Agreement: the restraint must affect only the parties to a collective bargaining agreement, concern a mandatory subject of bargaining, and be a product of bona fide bargaining. In Mackey, the court found that the first two requirements were met and, because the new procedures appear to have been genuinely bargained-for in each agreement, the third requirement is also met. Kansas Law Review, supra, at 132. For example, NHLPA Executive Director Alan Eagleson's September 19, 1977 letter to all NHL players contains the statement

since the Commissioner is viewed as the "arbitrator" in each respective Collective Bargaining Agreement, labor law cases require extreme judicial deference to an "arbitrator's" decision.[448] Hence, court review of specific fine and suspension decisions appears to be foreclosed. Therefore, some commentators argue that the sole remedy now lies with the National Labor Relations Board.[449] In fact, Ed Garvey of the NFLPA suggests that it would be "against public labor policy" to challenge these procedures in court.[450]

This deference does not mean that the "rule of reason" can never be applied in the sports fine and discipline context, especially if it can be unequivocally demonstrated that non-objective decisionmaking and lack of independent review is de facto unreasonable. First, the NLRB itself has shown some willingness to review a Commissioner's decision. The Board has upheld a rule under which 106 players were fined for leaving the benches while fights were in progress in 3 pre-season games. However, the Board rejected the management position that it should defer to arbitration conducted by the NFL Commissioner of these non-injury grievances. The Board

---

that since all the negotiations were freely entered into, all players signing the Standard Player Contract will be "bound of those negotiations."

448 In Kansas City Royals v. Major League Baseball Players Association, ___F.2d___ (8th Cir. 1976), the court reiterated the judicial attitude on reviewing an arbitrator's award: "The Supreme Court articulated the legal principles applicable to the arbitration of labor disputes in the Steelworkers trilogy, and recently reaffirmed them in Gateway Coal Co. v. United Mine Workers of America...We do not sit as an appellate tribunal to review the merits of the arbitrator's decision. We hold that the arbitration panel had jurisdiction to hear and decide the Messersmith-McNally grievances, that the Panel's award drew its essence from the collective bargaining agreement and that the relief fashioned by the District Court was appropriate. Accordingly, the award of the arbitration panel must be sustained, and the District Court's judgment affirmed.

449 Valparaiso University Law Review, supra, at 374.

450 Personal interview. (See note 152, supra.)

stressed that the Commissioner was not a disinterested figure but had been actively involved in the investigation of the events in question, the formulation of the rule, and the levying of the fines.[451] In dicta, four years earlier, the Board left open the possibility of overturning the system altogether. It noted that: "[T]he system appears to have been designed almost entirely by employers and owners, and the final arbiter of internal disputes does not appear to be a neutral third party freely chosen by both sides, but rather an individual appointed solely by the member club owners themselves. We do not believe that such a system is likely either to prevent labor disputes from arising in the future, or, having once arisen, to resolve them in a manner susceptible or conducive to voluntary compliance by all parties involved. Moreover, it is patently contrary to the letter and spirit of the Act for the Board to defer its undoubted jurisdiction to decide unfair labor practices to a disputes settlement system established unilaterally by an employer or group of employers."[452] Second, the union (Player Association) may be liable for breach of the "duty of fair representation" if it is proved that it failed to negotiate a fine and suspension system that was consistent with the demands of procedural due process.[453] Third, despite the ostensibly well-settled case law, it appears that a court may well intervene to overturn a Commissioner's ruling or declare the entire process illegal if (a) the fine or suspension was severe enough and (b) the procedures were egregious enough.

---

451 National Football League Management Council and The Constituent Member Clubs of The National Football League and National Football League Players Association, Cases 18-CA-3380, 18-CA-3437; 203 NLRB 165 (1973).

452 American League of Professional Baseball Clubs, 180 NLRB 189 (1969).

453 Though there is no case law or arbitration decision to support this theory, NFLPA Executive Director Ed Garvey suggests that this is a possibility. (See note 152, infra.)

In Gardella v. Chandler[454] a baseball player under contract to the then New York Giants was blacklisted by major league baseball upon his return from playing with the outlaw Mexican League. The case was settled out of court for $60,000 after the judge suggested that he would "come down" on baseball's procedures. In Silver v. New York Stock Exchange,[455] the Supreme Court suggested that the "reasonableness" of internal procedures is critical regardless of whether they have been contractually negotiated or not. The Court required that procedural safeguards be present to ensure that the industry did not act arbitrarily or impose restraints that exceeded the scope of its need to self-regulate.[456] Thus, Silver requires an examination of the totality of the circumstances. Support for this

---

[454] 79 F.Supp. 260 (S.D.N.Y. 1968).

[455] 373 U.S. 341 (1963).

[456] Comment, "The Sherman Act and Professional Team Sports: The NFL Rozelle Rule Invalid Under the Rule of Reason," 9 Connecticut Law Review 341 (1977). In addition, dicta in Silver gives added emphasis to earlier parts of this chapter. The Court noted that the procedural aspects of private self-regulation were an appropriate matter for inquiry by the antitrust court. The concern for procedural safeguards is supported by a number of considerations. It is thought that the requirement of notice and a hearing will facilitate the administration of the antitrust laws. Such procedures serve to define more precisely the factual basis for the group's actions as well as the defenses and contentions of the accused. Thus, a court called upon to review the matter in an antitrust proceeding will be in a better position to determine whether a basis exists for the discipline and whether the action is justified in light of the group's purposes. In addition, the requirement that a group use reasonable and deliberate procedures tends to discourage arbitrary action and thus serves to foster compliance with the substantive antitrust rules. If the group is required to state and defend its reasons for imposing the discipline, it will constantly be reminded of the need to adopt defensible rules and to apply them only when the proper factual basis exists. A structured hearing will serve to expose weaknesses in the group's position and is likely to encourage adjustments--such as a reduction in the offense charged or the punishment imposed--

position is found in Mackey,[457] where the court notes that "restrictive rules in general impose severe hardships on a player;" and in Kapp, where the court calls certain NFL procedures "mere formalities."[458] Hence, though some maintain that the case law disallows any antitrust "rule of reason" inquiry into the fine and suspension procedures, three arguments advocate its expansion.[459]

In conclusion, each league, as a "private criminal lawmaking body," possesses tremendous power and discretion. This is true with both the general ("best interest" clauses) and specific rules which permit punishment. Though

---

which will bring its actions into antitrust compliance without the need for litigation. William and Mary Law Review, supra, at 711.

457 407 F.Supp. 1005.

458 390 F.Supp. 73.

459 This paper has focused on the two main arguments to be used to alter internal procedures: (1) private association/due process; and (2) antitrust/rule of reason. However, some commentators suggest that an argument grounded in "contract law" is available. The first approach is to argue that the club breaches its contract with the employee player if it fails to provide adequate procedures for suspension or termination. The Georgetown Law Journal, at 780-81, criticizes this argument:

"Since an employer's major obligation under such a contract is generally payment of a specified salary, the contract affords an athlete little protection from unreasonable restrictions on personal liberties. In fact, the employment contract may form the legal basis for finding an athlete subject to a myriad of rules and regulations which serve only to abridge his personal liberties. Most uniform player contracts provide that the employer can terminate the agreement on short notice if a player's services are unsatisfactory, and though an employer's dissatisfaction must be real and in good faith, the reasonableness of the grounds for termination are not subjected to close judicial scrutiny. Thus, although an athlete's contract can protect him from dismissal without cause, it is obvious that this protection, standing alone, is incapable of protecting the athlete from arbitrary or unreasonable regulations."

A second approach would be to argue that since league rules require that all player contracts must be in standard form required by the league, courts should treat athletic contracts as adhesion contracts. However, as Dickinson Law Review, supra, notes at 399, courts are extremely reluctant to terminate contracts based upon adhesion.

minor fines and suspensions have little deterrent value, the longer suspensions and "blacklistings" may have a profound effect on a player's career.

## III) FACTORS WHICH INFLUENCE A PROSECUTOR'S DECISION CONCERNING WHETHER OR NOT TO USE THE JUDICIAL SYSTEM TO DEAL WITH "DURING THE GAME" CRIMINAL LAW VIOLATIONS.

The basic theme of Chapter II is that the sports league cannot be relied upon exclusively to deter and enforce sanctions against "during the game" criminal law violations. Seemingly, a literal application of the assault and battery statutes to the more excessive incidents of sports violence would be successful in many cases.[460] This chapter explores this possibility from a prosecutorial perspective. Taking the flexibility inherent in prosecutorial discretion as a starting point, this chapter analyzes nine factors involved in the decision of whether or not to prosecute a sports violence case.

Much of the information was obtained through responses from surveys sent to thirty-four county prosecutors who, collectively, have jurisdiction over all professional hockey, football, basketball, and baseball teams in the United States. The survey asked ten specific questions concerning the factors influential in the decision to prosecute past sports cases in their offices, or hypothetical cases if none have actually been investigated. The final question solicited the prosecutors' "perceptions of the role of criminal prosecution on controlling exceptionally severe acts of sports violence." A copy of the survey indicating the final total of all responses appears as Appendix M. An example of the cover letter explaining the project appears as Appendix N. The overall interest and response rate was extraordinary. Twenty prosecutors responded. Offices in Wayne County (Detroit), Michigan and Ala-

---

460 The actual problems of proving such a case are the concern of Chapter IV.

meda County (Oakland), California were extremely helpful.[461] Only one office[462] declined to respond for confidentiality reasons. After all responses were received, the more "interesting" ones were followed up by telephone interviews.

The most consistent comment was that most offices would, "theoretically", prosecute any sports violence case that satisfied the elements of the appropriate assault and battery statute in that jurisdiction. Alexander Yankelove, Associate Deputy State's Attorney of Baltimore, responded that "the position of our office is that if any case appears on our docket for trial, we will prosecute."[463] John Van de Kamp, District Attorney for Los Angeles County, somewhat ambiguously noted: "Should any such case come to the attention of the district attorney we would, of course, investigate it if evidence of a violation of the penal code was indicated."[464] Similarly, Carol S. Vance, District Attorney of Harris County (Houston), Texas would prosecute a sports violence case "Like any other violence if it is a violation of law."[465] Three respondants maintained steadfast loyalty to the Model Penal Code preamble, suggesting that a violation merits prosecution, regardless of other

---

461 In fact, the Wayne County response, telephone interview, and subsequent material is the basis for the case study following Chapter IV.

462 Office of the District Attorney of Nassau County, New York. District Attorney Dillon wrote: "Since the subject matter of your thesis involves questions which may come before me in future cases, I would prefer to deal with the questions raised in a particular factual context and not as a subject of a hypothetical question." (December 12, 1978. See Appendix O.) Ironically, the largest fight of the 1979 hockey season occurred in his jurisdiction on January 9, 1979, merely 28 days after he dictated his response. (See text surrounding note 309, *infra*.)

463 Letter received December 18, 1978.

464 Letter received December 14, 1978.

465 Survey response to Question III. (Received December 28, 1978)

"intrinsic factors":

> Whatever views one holds about the penal law, no one will question its importance in society...This is the law on which men place their ultimate reliance for protection against all the deepest injuries that human conduct can inflict on individuals and institutions. By the same token, penal law governs the strongest force that we permit official agencies to bring to bear on individuals. Its promise as an instrument of safety is matched only by its power to destroy. If penal law is weak or ineffective, basic human interests are in jeopardy. If it is harsh or arbitrary in its impact, it works a gross injustice on those caught within its tails. The law that carries such responsibilities should surely be as rational and just as law can be. Nowhere in the entire legal field is more at stake for the community or for the individual. [466]

These responses are not atypical. A Toronto Star poll of prosecutors in 12 professional hockey cities revealed that 11 of 12 would prosecute sports violence cases.[467] Some commentators have noticed more than a mere "theoretical" trend toward judicial intervention. The Missouri-Kansas City Law Review maintains: "The old belief that sports should be free from unwarranted legal interference has been challenged by a newer belief which sees no valid reason for sports to enjoy any special legal immunity. More and more today, sports law problems are being resolved by judicial intervention of a sort rarely witnessed in earlier times."[468] The Criminal Law Quarterly agrees: "There is a clear trend that the criminal justice systems in Canada and the United States are becoming more and more willing to control illegal violence in sports."[469]

---

466 Wechsler, "The Challenge of a Model Penal Code," 65 Harvard Law Review 1097, 1098 (1952). Charles F. Hyder, Maricopa County (Phoenix), Arizona, Attorney suggested that this philosophy "is his most important consideration." Cover letter to survey response (received January 9, 1979).

467 Halowell and Meshbesher, Trial, supra, at 29.

468 University of Missouri at Kansas City Law Review, supra, at 119.

469 Supra, at 453.

However, not everyone is in agreement that such a trend exists. Hennepin County (Minneapolis), Minnesota District Attorney Gary Flakne stated that before his prosecution of David Forbes, "prosecutors had been reluctant to enforce criminal codes on any playing field."[470] The Wisconsin Law Review agrees: "Because the elements of an athlete's assault and battery seem to present no difficulty of proof,[471] and the most likely defenses would appear to be of no value in a sports setting, the athlete's tacit immunity must be largely attributed to nonlegal factors affecting the discretionary decision not to prosecute."[472]

Apparently, sports violence would be vigorously prosecuted in some jurisdictions, while completely ignored in others. Haphazard enforcement without a rational strategy is a significant problem here. Vorenberg notes in another context: "It seems clear that no valid purpose is served by the enormous breadth of prosecutorial discretion and that it represents power resulting from default rather than a conscious legislative judgment."[473] Of course, this paper does not advocate that the prosecutor present all charges which the evidence might support. As the ABA Standards on the Prosecution Function recognize, "the prosecutor may in some circumstances and for good cause consistent with the public interest decline to prosecute, notwithstanding that evidence may exist which would support a conviction."[474] However, this paper does maintain that some standards should be created to guide future sports violence prosecutions. Specific black letter standards will not

---

[470] Criminal Law Quarterly, supra, at 431.

[471] This, of course, is an area of much dispute. See Chapter IV.

[472] Supra, at 778.

[473] J. Vorenberg, "Narrowing the Discretion of Criminal Justice Officials," Duke Law Journal 651, 680 (1976).

[474] Standard 3.9, "Discretion in the Charging Decision."

be suggested. However, it is hoped that once the implicit criteria which guide a prosecutor's decision in the sports violence area are exposed, some effort at more specific guidelines can be made at a later date. Accordingly, this paper will suggest nine factors which are relevant in a decision to prosecute "during the game" sports violence.

A. The Perceived "Societal Value" to be Gained by Prosecuting a Sports Violence Case. Stigler suggests that the "significance of an offense to society"[475] is a critical factor in determining whether or not to prosecute. Apparently, some prosecutors perceive sports violence as not worthy of their attention. D. Lowell Johnson, Alameda County (Oakland), California District Attorney suggested that, "We have enough straight line criminal violence to keep us busy--without entering a new media game."[476] George A. Peach, St. Louis, Missouri Circuit Attorney, responded that: "Criminal prosecution has little or no role in controlling this kind of violence when it is confined to game time...I've got more important things to do."[477]

However, many commentators argue that these and other prosecutors have underestimated the problem for three reasons. First, it is argued that prosecutors have a duty to attempt to control sports violence because of the effect that it has on young children. Players are emulated by "young, aspiring athletes who look to the professionals for guidance and example."[478] As a

---

[475] G.J. Stigl er, "The Optimum Enforcement of Laws," Journal of Political Economy 528.

[476] Survey response to Question I(6)(7). (Received December 6, 1978)

[477] Survey response to Question III. (Received December 4, 1978)

[478] Comment, "Consent in Criminal Law: Violence in Sports," 75 Michigan Law Review 174 (1976). A recent UPI dispatch detailed the great concern of the Pittsburgh Steelers superstar receiver Lynn Swann after he received the fourth

result, some have expressed concern about the effects of such violence on these young athletes.[479] McMurtry notes that "the influence has been compounded with the advent of television. Professional sport by its very nature dominates the mass media in its quest for spectators. Now the images presented by TV dwarf the effect of home and school on the mind of most sports-conscious younsters."[480] Second, a similar "susceptibility argument" has been advanced to suggest that spectator violence is reinforced if sports violence is implicitly condoned by prosecutorial inaction. Violent outbursts by fans at games are not uncommon. Oakland District Attorney Jensen provided an example of what he termed "peripheral violence": "Last year an en-

---

brain concussion of his career in the opening game against the Oakland Raiders. Concerned that "nothing significant has been done to protect people" and by warnings from his own doctors that the concussions have reduced his tolerance to further surgery, Swann related a conversation with a young fan:

"There was a little boy I met the other day who told me he's almost got my record beat," Swann recalled.

"And I said, 'What record's that?'

"And he said, 'I've got three concussions!'

"I said, 'Well son, concussions are not something you want to get.'

"And he said, 'I know. My doctor said I can't ride my bike anymore. I can't play contact sports.'

"This is just a little child," Swann said."

Philo and Stine, Trial, supra, at 38.

[479] Georgia Law Review, supra, at 381.

[480] McMurtry, supra at 21. Several psychological experiments provide support for this hypothesis and the related hypothesis that viewing such rule-breakers being rewarded for their aggression may increase child aggression. In 1963, Bandura, Ross and Ross tested preschool children in a laboratory experiment. The children viewed an adult model attacking a Bobo-doll and being either rewarded or punished for that behavior. Those who had viewed the model being rewarded were more likely to express aggression in the same manner as the model; those who had viewed the model being punished were less likely to do so. Kaplan & Singer, "Television Violence and Viewer Aggression: A Reexamination of the Evidence," Journal of Social Issues, Fall 1976, 35, 43. In 1975, Hartnagel, Teevan, and McIntyre analyzed questionnaire data from adolescent television viewers. Those children who perceived violence on their favorite television show as an effective means to an end reported significantly more violence behavior than those who did not. Hartnagel, Teevan and McIntyre, "Television Violence & Violent Behavior," 54 Social Forces 341, 345 (1975). Capetta, Connecticut Law Review, supra at 381.

thusiastic Warrior fan attacked Bob Lanier[481] and was fortunate enough to be pulled away before total confrontation was achieved."[482] He was charged with and convicted of assault.[483] Klein notes:

> Fans are not always decent and understanding. Their money, they often feel, entitles them to manifest any type of behavior. There have been instances of fans physically assaulting players. Booth Lusteg was once beaten in Buffalo on a Sunday night after he missed a field goal that cost the Bills a victory.[484]

Further, one of the main catalysts behind McMurtry's massive investigation into amateur violence was the finding in the game in question[485] that the 750 fans "were orderly until the game became violent, and by the end of the second period large numbers of them were out of control."[486] Third, it is argued on a larger scale that if violence is condoned in one (albeit specialized) sector of society, it becomes more likely that violence will increase in other parts of society. Professor Michael Smith, after reviewing all relevant behavioral research, concluded for the McMurtry investigation that:

> ...If this violence is legitimized, research suggests at least two consequences that go beyond the game itself. First, the scope of what may be considered legitimate behavior in and out of sport, may be widened; acts once considered deviant become accepted as normal. Second, where there is a climate of approval of violence, conduct that may precipitate collective outbursts is likely to occur.[487]

---

[481] The humongous Detroit Piston center.

[482] Survey response to Question II. (Received December 6, 1978)

[483] It could be argued that DA Jensen was treating a symptom rather than the disease.

[484] Klein, Pro Football Mystique, _supra_, at 148.

[485] Hamilton-Bremelea OHA game of April 16, 1974.

[486] McMurtry, _supra_, at 17.

[487] _Id._, at 29-30.

One court has intimated as much, noting that inadequately regulated football could have "adverse effects on the population as a whole."[488]

If any or all of these arguments are even partially correct, the prosecutor would appear to have a right, even "an obligation" (as NFLPA Executive Director Garvey puts it),[489] to prosecute exceptionally severe violence which occurred in front of a large number of spectators or television viewers. One commentator concludes: "Quite apart from society's interest in the safety of participants, the effects of violence in sports on its audience

---

[488] Hackbart, *supra*. Georgia Law Review, *supra*, at 389. It is enlightening to note that there is a contrary position similar to the "catharsis/frustration" hypothesis adopted by the violent players. (See text surrounding notes 104-108, *infra*.). S. Fischler, *Slashing* (1975), quoting another psychologist, observed: "For professional people there are few outlets where we can expose the baser side of ourselves. A game like hockey is one of the few areas for the ventilation of primitive feelings....Every adult, no matter how mature or responsible, needs an opportunity to regress, to be something other than this mature, responsible adult, and that is what hockey does for some people." See also *Time* 51 (March 3, 1975) containing a letter from Dr. W. Walter Menninger of the Menninger Foundation and a former member of President Johnson's National Commission on the Causes and Prevention of Violence: "Despite the recent indignation over violence in professional hockey, it should not be surprising that the spectator following should be so rapid, particularly in the congested metropolitan areas where legitimate expressions of violence are so limited. Many of the 'silent majority' who feel so frustrated, angry and helpless today can readily identify with the beleaguered, assaulted hero of the 'war on ice.' They experience a vicarious satisfaction from the open aggression and mayhem on the ice, and indeed, it is powerfully exhilarating to let one's emotions 'all hang out.'...Until enough people decide it is not worth the price, we may expect little change in the trend toward increasing violence in hockey and other contact sports. See also the arguments advanced in Chapter IV to support the "social utility of sports" defense to assault and battery. However, Smith concludes that "the weight of scientific evidence, however, is against the catharsis hypothesis. Behaving aggressively, or watching others behave aggressively, tends to lead to more, not less, aggression." Smith, *supra*, at 2.

[489] Personal interview. (See note 152, *supra*.)

suggested by outbursts by spectators and emulation by children justifies public concern over sports activities."[490]

B. <u>Given Finite Resources, the Relative Importance of Prosecuting Sports Violence Cases as Compared With Other Types of Crime.</u> The ideal of "full and impartial enforcement of the laws" is largely tempered by available resources and enforcement strategies. This is especially salient since "resources are not infinite, nor are they spent with uniform prudence."[491] Hence, the relevant consideration in this context is Packer's fifth variable: whether controlling sports violence through the criminal process will "expose that process to severe qualitative or quantitative strains."[492]

An analysis of relevant factors suggests that "sports violence" should be higher on the priority list than it currently is.[493] Most criminologists consider assault and battery in general to be a high priority crime. It ranks very high on the President's Commission's scale of the "Economic Impact of Individual Crimes."[494] Sports-related assault and battery must be critical, as well, if one accepts that the "victim" is not only the assaulted player, but children, spectators, and the society at large.[495] Furthermore,

---

490 Personal interview. (See note 152, <u>supra</u>.)

491 H. Packer, <u>The Limits of the Criminal Sanction</u> 301.

492 <u>Id.</u>, at 296. Stigler notes, perhaps obviously, that "the extent of enforcement of the laws depends upon the amount of resources devoted to the task." Stigler, <u>supra</u>, at 527.

493 Remember Circuit Attorney Peach's comment: "I've got more important things to do." (See text surrounding note 477, <u>supra</u>.)

494 "Crime and its Impact--An Assessment," <u>President's Commission on Law Enforcement and the Administration of Justice</u> (1967), at 45.

495 See factor one. Text surrounding notes 475-490, <u>infra</u>.

the costs of investigation are comparatively small, as the victim and the assailant are "captured" on film and can be identified by thousands of fans. Though there are additional resource costs,[496] Greenwood's problem of apprehension and clearance[497] is not a concern in this context. If Packer's cost-effectiveness argument is credible, sports violence prosecution would seem to be a relatively efficient priority: (A) the act is widely disliked (Even if, assuming arguments, most hockey fans like "violence," most of society will condemn exceptionally severe stick swinging, for example); (B) enforcement will be relatively cheap (the efficiency of investigation, as noted above); (C) prosecution will pose few threats to civil liberties because private citizens will shoulder much of the burden of gathering evidence (fan and victim complaints). In a sense, the following factors explore these arguments further.

C. <u>Appropriateness of the Criminal Sanction in Controlling Violent "During the Game" Behavior.</u> This factor has three components.

First, it is argued that criminal penalties have little deterrent value in this context, given that most players do not perceive such action as criminal. Since the goal of enforcement is to achieve that degree of compliance with the rule of proscribed behavior that the society believes it can afford,[498] it would be inefficient to enforce a sanction that achieves a low

---

[496] The Paiement-Polonich case study (following Chapter IV) reveals these problems: (a) reluctance of victim and/or hockey "fraternity" to testify; (b) difficulty of locating season ticket holders who could accurately recount the incident; (c) low probability of success, as four previous prosecutions had failed. These and other problems are related in more detail in factors 3-9.

[497] Greenwood, et al. <u>The Criminal Investigation Process</u> 121 (1977).

[498] Stigler, <u>supra</u>, at 526.

degree of compliance. This appears to be especially relevant in the sports violence context. Additionally, the fact that the four major hockey assault cases have all ended in an acquittal or a hung jury reinforces the players' notion that such activity is not criminal. Sports attorney Bob Woolf indicated that within a year after the 1969 Green and Maki acquittals the players were "raising their sticks and using them again."[499] Further, "enforcer" David Forbes noted immediately after the July, 1975 Forbes hung jury: "I'm disillusioned with the whole system. I just don't see, no matter how wrong the act is, how anything that happens in an athletic contest can be criminal."[500] In fact, some argue that real deterrence can only be achieved through some punishment which will effect the competitiveness of the team, giving it the incentive to control its own players' behavior. This may only be accomplished internally The Wisconsin Law Review argues that: "There is the possibility that controls that affect team competitiveness, such as player suspensions, are the greatest deterrent to such conduct because the team itself will soon discourage fighting. If the courts chose to impose fines, for example, feeling incarceration was too drastic, the richer teams would be at a competitive advantage. Thus, internal control is arguably more effective because of the intervention and deterrence problems raised by legal control."[501]

Even though the deterrence value of sports violence prosecution is not overwhelming, this should not mean that such prosecution should be attemped

---

[499] Woolf, Behind Closed Doors, supra, at 150.

[500] Flakne and Caplan, Trial, supra, at 34.

[501] Wisconsin Law Review, supra, at 786.

infrequently or not at all. Symbolic intervention is required, at least to remind the players that they are not absolutely immune from the criminal law. If the major roadblock is the low probability of conviction (as it was on four surveys[502]), one prosecutor has suggested that plea bargaining will be especially effective given the sports' desire to "keep courts out of the process." Edwin L. Miller, San Diego County District Attorney, described a minor league hockey incident where a player "slammed his stick into the face of a fan, fracturing his jaw," and a college basketball incident where a player "punched an opponent, fracturing his jaw." Both cases were resolved by pleas before trial, with both defendants fined and placed on probation for three years, "the normal sentence in these charged acts." Of course, Miller notes that the problems of proof, dispositive in the four previous hockey acquittals, were not relevant "since neither case went to trial."[503] Seemingly, if plea bargaining sports violence cases is used as part of an overall rational strategy of symbolic enforcement (as it was in San Diego), it would increase the potential deterrent effect of the criminal sanction.

The second argument for the inappropriateness of the criminal sanction is "the widespread feeling that sports comprise a unique institution that

---

502 See factor 6.

503 Survey response to Question II(6)(3). (Received December 26, 1978) Most jurisdictions have assault statutes which allow for flexible reduction consistent with a plea. While assault and battery with a dangerous weapon and aggravated battery are usually felonies, simple battery is most times a misdemeanor.

cannot be legally ordered without grave damage to the institution itself."[504] It is agreed that the criminal sanction will reduce the competitiveness of the sport.[505] The court in Green emphasized this point in acquitting the defendant: "It is very difficult, in my opinion, for a player who is playing hockey with all the force, vigour, and strength at his command, who is engaged in the rough and tumble of the game, very often in a corner of the rink to stop and say, 'I must not do that. I must not follow this up because maybe it is an assault."[506] A similar argument was adopted by the appellee in Nabozny v. Barnhill:[507]

> As suggested by the very name it carries, a contact sport involves a good deal of physical contact and collision between participants. Often, in the heat of a contest, a participant's concentration will be on performance of his appointed tasks and not at all on exercising reasonable care so as not to injure an opponent. Imposition of liability on a participant in a contact sport for mere negligence, it was contended, would place unreasonable burdens and liabilities upon participants. Furthermore, the purpose of the contact sport--promotion of intense concentration and activity by participants--would be weakened or defeated. [508]

---

504 Schuett, Nebraska Law Review, supra, at 1137.

505 Of course, this argument, and the argument that criminal sanctions have no deterrent value, appear to be mutually exclusive. Nevertheless, anti-competitiveness argument was expressed by Pittsburgh Steeler Defensive Lineman Dwight White in an interview with Criminal Law Quarterly, supra, at 438. Mr. White was questioned at length on his views concerning the prosecution of football players for illegal actions on the gridiron. He stood vehemently opposed to intervention by the legal system into his profession. He believes that the rules, and not the courts, must control the sport. "If they ever started [prosecuting] in football, I think I would definitely want to get out." That he might be charged with violation of a criminal code for actions during a game never crossed his mind, and he expressed displeasure about discussing the subject.

506 Regina v. Green, 16 D.L.R.3d 137, 141 (Ont.Prov.Civ. 1970).

507 31 Ill.App.3d 212, 334 N.E.2d 258 (1975). Though a tort case, the arguments are equally applicable in the criminal contaxt. The case is described further in Chapter IV.

508 Brief for Appellee at 21-25.

The Michigan Law Review notes that, "an announcement that certain conduct will subsequently make a player subject to criminal prosecution might not only eliminate or reduce the frequency of the undesirable conduct, but will also eliminate some desirable conduct necessary to the continued vigor and popularity of the game. Players who know that certain conduct will subject them to prosecution are likely to avoid doing anything that remotely resembles the conduct."[509] It is also argued that occasional prosecution of athletes could "deter others from participating in such sports," with some NHL figures believing that this could lead to "the destruction of professional hockey."[510] At least one responding prosecutor emphasized this argument, suggesting that "the criminal law must not be suited as an extra umpire for that might seriously detract from the activeness of the game."[511] If any of the above is correct, sports violence prosecution may run counter to Packer's third criteria: "Suppressing it will [not] inhibit socially desirable conduct."[512]

Again, while these arguments seem persuasive, they should not compel a conclusion that sports violence should never be prosecuted. First, a victim

---

509 Supra, at 176. This argument was successfully made as early as 1921 in Gibeline v. Smith (Mo.App.), 81 S.W. 961, which denied any relief to plaintiff who was injured in a "friendly scuffle," holding: "To hold otherwise, would be to say that all untoward results from the play of men or boys in which they mutually engaged, would furnish a cause for an action by the injured party. Play, even though rough, or dangerous, if mutually engaged in, is not unlawful, otherwise, athletic games now, and always common to the people would not have had the sanction which ages have given them."

510 American Criminal Law Review, supra, at 244-45.

511 Cover letter of Charles F. Hyder, Maricopa County (Phoenix), Arizona Attorney. (Received January 9, 1979.)

512 Packer, supra, at 296. "There are two great national institutions which simply cannot tolerate either internal dissension or external influence--our Armed Forces and our sports programs." Slusher, "Sport: A Philosophical Perspective," 38 Law and Contemporary Problems 129 (1973).

should not be required to sacrifice the benefit to him of seeing his assailant punished, regardless of the consequences to the sport.[513] Second, those that hypothesize the downfall of sport are assuming full prosecution of every technical violation of the assault and battery laws. If a symbolic enforcement strategy were pursued, the harm would be marginal. Responding prosecutors seem to prefer symbolic enforcement in this context. Hennepin County Prosecutor Flakne explains:

> Obviously, with respect to any sport involving body contact, technical assaults amongst the participants are occurring throughout the entire contest. Therefore, those who oppose the entry of the criminal justice system into the sporting arena argue that by the criminal prosecution of every technical violation of the law, the prosecutor will quickly bring about the demise of sporting events. As a practical matter, however, the likelihood of prosecutions for technical violations of the law on the part of a sports participant is virtually non-existent. In the first place, it is unlikely that any jury would be willing to convict under those circumstances and, secondly, the prosecutor would not derive any support from the law.[514]

Multnomah County (Portland), Oregon District Attorney Harl Haas suggests that anything other than symbolic enforcement in this context might be a violation of ABA Standards. "The state," he explains, "should not become involved in setting unreasonable standards for any segment of society even when technical violations of law exist. The duty of the prosecutor is to seek justice [ABA Standard 1.1(c)]. In cases of sports violence, the standard should be set by way of prosecution if necessary that seek justice for all involved and also preserve the freedom of action inherently necessary

---

513 Dicta in Nabozny v. Bainhill, <u>supra</u>, though discussing tort principles, is applicable to this argument: "A participant should not be required to bear the cost of injuries inflicted upon him by conduct that goes beyond the limits of what can be expected in ths sport...A participant relies upon the assurance that other participants will exercise reasonable care to prevent injuries. When this assurance is not met and a participant who relied upon it is thus injured, liability should be imposed on the wrongdoer."

514 Flakne and Caplan, Trial, <u>supra</u>, at 35.

in each respective sport. (See ABA Standard 3.9)."[515] It is precisely this balance that this paper advocates.

The third argument for the inappropriateness of the criminal sanction is what has been referred to as "the community subgroup rationale."[516] It argues that the act becomes less criminal since everyone else in the subgroup performs similar acts. Therefore, it is unfair to ascribe and punish an individual member of the subgroup. This rationale recognizes that illegal activity carried on by members of a definable group are tolerated because the conduct is widespread in the group, or perhaps looked upon as less serious by the members of that group than by society as a whole.[517] Chapter I demonstrates this attitude in hockey, for example. For this reason, officials and courts have been reluctant to interfere with the savagery of the game.[518] When the system does intervene, however, the problem of drawing the line above which individual responsibility should be actionable is an inherent difficulty. Ronald I. Meshbesher, defense counsel in the Forbes case, elaborates: "Among the problems in linking the harmful act with the criminal definition is the failure to clearly meet the premise of legal individualism. This problem has two interrelated subparts: determination of responsibility, and punishment for the act. Sports violence trials have raised the question of whether the sport or the individual is on trial. Thus, the individual can be seen as a 'scapegoat' for the legal of violence in the sport and, by some

---

[515] Survey response to Question III. (Received December 13, 1978.)

[516] Wisconsin Law Review, supra, at 779.

[517] W. LaFave, Arrest: The Decision to Take a Suspect into Custody 110 (1965).

[518] Criminal Law Quarterly, supra, at 432.

standards, unjustly punished..."[519] Meshbesher concludes:

> That excessive violence in sports might be reduced is admirable, but that it may be achieved at the expense of individual justice is questionable. The verdict in the Maloney case demonstrates the ambivalence over these dual issues of reforming the sports organization and securing justice for the individual. After 9 1/2 hours of deliberation, the jury found Maloney not guilty, but, following an Ontario jury verdict feature, attached a rider to the result expressly asserting that the verdict did not signify condonement of the fighting involved but rather rather 'hope that similar occurrences do not happen in

---

519

Meshbesher draws support for his argument from an analogue to the Calley case. Trial, supra, at 28:

> The most dramatic illustration of public ambivalence and opposition to criminalizing conduct under these circumstances is shown in responses to the Lt. Calley trial in which a majority disapproved of the trial per se, irrespective of its outcome. A research effort under way several months after the trial found 58% disapproved of criminal sanctions being applied to an individual acting in a legitimate role and following what he believed to be at least implicit orders. Similarly, contemporary sports involve the explicit expectation that violent conduct is "part of the game."
>
> Aside from boxing, which has as its aim the disabling of the opponent, most contact sports include varying degrees and types of aggressive action as a means of winning the contest. Recent social science research on ice hockey concludes that assaultive behavior is legitimate and normatively organized in both amateur and professional settings. Mirroring these findings, defense testimony and argument in sports violence trials have emphasized the violent milieu of the sport as mitigating individual responsibility. One point brought out in hockey is that the player operating in a setting in which violence is customary and approved does not act with criminal intent but merely follows the established practices of the sport.
>
> But, as in the Calley, case, people do not assess responsibility similarly; the two sides in the Forbes case exemplify this. One conviction juror said: "any man is responsible for his own actions regardless...", whereas a non-conviction juror urged no responsibility: "just like if I had committed some crime because of my job then my employer should suffer or should answer [for] it--not me." Prosecutors reject these arguments indirectly, asserting that their indictments relate only to individuals and that

the future. [520]

Given the "individual responsibility" problems, it can be argued that the serious penalties attached to criminal assault indicate to those with prosecutorial discretion that the legislature did not intend to reach such conduct which, until the present, has been accepted as part of the game. The great disparity between hockey's internal, league-enforced penalty (a few games suspension) and the penalties found in the assault statutes (fines and imprisonment) further emphasizes this limitation of a literal application of the statute.[521] In analyzing the significance of these arguments, Alameda County District Attorney Jensen concluded that criminal prosecution is a "completely ineffective mechanism"[522] for controlling exceptionally severe acts of sports violence.

While this argument strongly condemns the appropriateness of the criminal sanction in this context, a strategy of symbolic enforcement of only the most egregious acts would maximize the deterrent value[523] with a minimum of harm to the sport and its participants.[524]

---

questions of sports organization and customs are irrelevant. In Hennepin County Attorney Falkne's words: "There seems to be a line...beyond which something other than goodnatured hard contact becomes assault."

[520] Id., at 29-32.

[521] Wisconsin Law Review, supra, at 780.

[522] Survey response to Question III. (Received December 6, 1978.)

[523] See reasons given in sub-argument one. (Text surrounding notes 502-503, infra.)

[524] See reasons given in sub-argument two. (Text surrounding notes 513-515, infra.)

D. The Degree of Public Awareness and Concern About the Nature and Severity of the Act of Sports Violence. Judging by the responses received, prosecutors seem to proceed through a two-step analysis in determining whether the public is concerned enough with this particular crime such that it should be prosecuted. The prosecutor first observes the degree of public awareness and concern. Then, if enough of the community appears interested, the prosecutor will decide if the act is severe enough to involve the criminal justice system.

1. Degree of Public Awareness and Concern. Packer's first criteria for the effectiveness of the criminal sanction is relevant in this context: "The conduct is prominent in most people's view of socially threatening behavior, and is not condoned by any significant segment of society."[525] More specifically, LeFave suggests that prosecution is more likely when the conduct is "glaringly obvious to the community."[526] In cases of sports violence during a game in front of thousands of fans, there is usually no problem of prosecutor or community awareness. The mass media is the most significant influence. Sports attorney Ken Fishkin suggested that publicity is the "most important variable in deciding whether a case will be prosecuted."[527] In "traditional" criminal cases, "fair trial" Constitutional imperatives have forced the media to be somewhat restrained in their coverage. (Referring to the suspect as the "alleged assailant," for example). However, because traditional "restraint" has not yet influenced sports media reporting, sports violence reports tend to be extremely explicit and inflammatory. For example,

---

525 Packer, supra, at 296.

526 Wisconsin Law Review, supra, at 781.

527 Telephone interview (November 15, 1978).

the photographs of the Green-Maki incident (Appendix E) were published in Boston newspapers the day after the game.[528] NFLPA Executive Director Ed Garvey argues that the fact that the NHL violence is more exploited by the media "explains why there are no NFL violence cases."[529] Forbes prosecutor Flakne noted the significance of media coverage on his decision to prosecute: "From the time of the incident, the activities surrounding the alleged aggravated assault and the action taken by the Hennepin County Grand Jury touched off a controversy which was the rage of private conversations, newspaper articles, and radio and television, for the next six months."[530]

Complaining fans are another significant factor in prosecutorial awareness and action. The Forbes case is a primary example. Apparently the facts of the case came to the attention of Hennepin County Attorney Gary Flakne and the foreman of the grand jury at virtually the same time. As Flakne was pondering action, he was contacted by the grand jury foreman who asked if the grand jury might consider the case. Although the standard procedure in the county calls for the prosecutor to bring an information in assault cases, sensitive (usually political) cases are referred to the grand jury. Thus Flakne let the grand jury make the prosecutorial decision to avoid any inference of personal bias. Flakne also told the press that his decision to investigate the Forbes case with an eye toward filing criminal charges was activated by

---

528 For inflammatory editorials concerning the Paiement-Polonich stick swinging incident and subsequent investigation, see the case study following Chapter IV.

529 Of a criminal nature. Hackbart, described later, was an NFL violence case based on tort law. (Personal interview, see note 152, infra.)

530 Flakne and Caplan, Trial, supra, at 34. One example was provided by Alameda County (Oakland) District Attorney Jensen where he claims to have decided not to prosecute Jack Tatum's "contact" that paralyzed New England Patriot Darryl Stingley because "the consensus from the media was that Tatum [was] not at fault." (Survey answer to Question I. Received December 6, 1978.)

the telephone calls of irate citizens.[531] Some have expressed concern at this method of "investigation." First, this reflects more of a random, haphazard approach than a uniform, rational procedure. "Extraneous factors may play a role in the filing of sports assault charges because the impetus to investigate in this area is more likely to be triggered by spectator complaints than prosecutorial concern."[532] Second, it allows for a broad prosecutorial discretion capable of being influenced by such extraneous factors as whether the victim was a member of the home or visiting team.[533] Both of these criticisms suggest violation of Packer's fourth criteria for the effectiveness of the criminal sanction: "It may be dealt with through evenhanded and nondiscriminatory enforcement."[534]

Sports violence incidents "come to the prosecution's attention" through a variety of means. The twenty responding prosecutors (see Appendix M) suggested that most cases "came to their attention" through the media (five); "victim complaints" were the next highest means (three); then "attending fans" (two); and one indicated that the "grand jury" brought the case to his attention. On the other hand, if the community and the prosecutor are not "aware" of any sports violence incidents, such cases will, of course, not be

---

531 Minneapolis Tribune D4 (January 16, 1975).

532 American Criminal Law Review, supra, at 244.

533 In his summation to the jury, Forbes' attorney made this point using as an example the failure to file criminal assault charges against a member of the home team who struck an opponent across the head with a hockey stick and was penalized by the referee for deliberate intent to injure . This incident occurred in the same game as the incident for which Forbes was indicted. Id. The Paiement-Polonich case study demonstrates the influence of the home town Detroit Red Wing fans.

534 Packer, supra, at 296.

prosecuted. "Mere inattention"[535] is a significant factor. Of the twenty responding prosecutors, all but two have a hockey or football team in their jurisdictions. As has been previously noted, these teams play games in which "technical assaults amongst the participants are occurring throughout the entire contest."[536] Yet, twelve of the twenty attorneys perceived no "exceptionally severe acts of sports violence" which had come to their attention within the last five years.[537]

2. Assuming There is Enough Community Concern, Then the Prosecutor Will Analyze the Nature and Severity of the Act of Sports Violence. This characteristic does not refer so much to the number of spectators who are present at events, but rather to the nature of the assault.[538] The severity of the assault is a key in any prosecution, even for "traditional" assault and battery. What is interesting is that many prosecutors treat this as the single dispositive factor. Maricopa County (Phoenix) Attorney Hyder notes that, "Prosecution must only be warranted in those cases of sport violence where assault is so intentioned, so gross, and so disregarding of human welfare as to shock the conscious of society."[539] Allegheny County (Pittsburgh) District Attorney Robert E. Colville suggested that he would prosecute "only the excessively bad case...and/or cases that arise as a result of sports, but

---

535 Wisconsin Law Review, supra, at 780, suggests this is one of four reasons for prosecutorial inaction.

536 Flakne. See note 514, infra.

537 A typical response is one similar to that of Harris County (Houston) District Attorney Vance, whose cover letter appears as Appendix P. Her office has jurisdiction over the Oilers (football), Rockets (basketball), and Aeros (hockey; now defunct).

538 Wisconsin Law Review, supra, at 781.

539 Cover letter of Charles F. Hyder. (See note 511, infra.)

off the field."[540] Multnomah County (Portland), Oregon District Attorney Haas, based upon experience gained from prosecuting a "high school football practice player fight," suggested that:

> Our probability of a successful prosecution rested on the extreme deviation from the violence standard deemed to be the risk inherent in the sport. Such extreme and apparently calculated deviations from the violence inherent in the sport are prime candidates for review by the state in the interest of justice and an eye toward the pure preservation of sport.[541]

At the extreme, Alameda County District Attorney Jensen goes so far as to suggest that "the first non-hockey [football] prosecution will involve a death."[542]

In short, once the public is aware of an incident, prosecutorial deference will vary commensurate with the perception of the seriousness of the conduct and severity of the injury. Kuhlmann[543] proposes a continuum similar to the deference scale proposed by Weistart to govern court intervention into internal disciplinary proceedings.[544] The less severe conduct[545], he

---

540 Survey response to Question III. (Received December 11, 1978.)

541 Survey response to Question I(6)(7). (Received December 13, 1978.)

542 Survey response to Question III. (Received December 6, 1978.)

543 Wisconsin Law Review, supra, at 782-83.

544 See text surrounding notes 396-400, infra.

545 The first of these is conduct which is prohibited by the rules of the game but occurs relatively frequently, and the penalty for which never extends beyond the immediate contest in which it occurs. Examples of this are two-minute roughing penalties in hockey; or, for more serious fights, a ten minute or even a game misconduct. The distinguishing characteristic of such activities is that they are controlled entirely by the referees, officials, or umpires as part of the game-to-game routine of the sport. It may be argued that as to this type of conduct, normal legal sanctions are incapable of effectively intervening and thus the localized control of the referee will always be necessary.

The second category of conduct is more serious, giving rise to league-imposed penalties that extend beyond the contest in which the misconduct oc-

Because of the confidential nature of certain portions of this chapter which had to be removed, one page was left blank. It was felt that this solution was prefereable to renumbering the pages.

Editor

argues, should be disposed of by penalties during the game, or by internal fine and suspension mechanisms. The more severe conduct[546] should be dealt with through the criminal justice system. The advantage of creating an overt policy of prosecuting only sports violence "above a certain level" (or, as Kuhlmann suggests, "in a certain category") avoids the pitfalls of "lumping all sports misconduct together."[547] Participants will more easily be able to distinguish between "criminal" and "part of the game" behavior. Further, "slippery slope"-type criticisms[548] can be more easily answered. Finally,

---

curred. Examples in this category are the two and three game suspensions meted out to Dennis Owchar of Pittsburgh and Bryan Watson of Detroit, respectively, for kicking with their skates, or the six game suspensions given to Don Saleski and Bob Kelly of Philadelphia for participation in a "massive gang-fight" earlier this hockey season. Some of the conduct in this category gets more serious, such as the breaking of Chris Oddleifson's jaw by Keith Magnuson's cast-encased fist. The Marichal-Roseboro bat-swinging incident discussed above must be listed here, noting that a civil suit was brought there resulting in an out-of-court settlement. Also included in this category is the Maki-Green stick-swinging hockey fight. Wisconsin Law Review, *supra*, at 782-83.

546 The third category of sports conduct is confined to sports whose intrinsically brutal nature has made complete state statutory control commonplace. Boxing and wrestling are traditionally so controlled. The purposes of such legislation are "...First, the desire to prevent as far as possible certain brutal and degrading features which have in the past sometimes attended such contests, and, second, to promote and protect such contests when conducted within the legitimate scope of a sport." Because the state has assumed such control, it likewise must assume the responsibility, if any is to be found, for injuries that occur within the rules of the state regulatory agency. *Id.* While the category structure is indeed laudible, Kuhlmann's placement *of* acts in each of the categories may be inappropriate. This paper has argued at numerous points that symbolic *criminal* enforcement is necessary for *some* of Kuhlmann's "category two" conduct, given the ineffectiveness of *intra*-league deterrence mechanisms.

547 *Id.*, at 787.

548 Boston Bruins' General Manager Harry Sinden's comment is an illustrative example of such an argument: "If they convict Forbes, think of what could happen to football players who hit the quarterback after the whistle or to baseball players who slide into second base with their spikes high and cut another player." *Sports Illustrated* 16 (January 27, 1975).

society in general, and sports fans[549] in particular will be able to draw a more definitive line as to what sports violence they will consider "criminal."

E. The Degree of Deference Paid to Other Dispute Resolution Mechanisms. This is perhaps the most significant factor because it engenders the most diverse perceptions of the prosecutorial role in controlling "during the game violence." Though the prosecutor's perception of his role is critical, the amount of deference also depends upon the mechanism to be deferred to. Hence, this factor focuses upon the nature of the prosecutorial inaction in deference to: (A) civil mechanisms; (B) game officials; (C) league fine and suspension mechanisms; and (D) legislation.

1. Deference to Civil Mechanisms. Some commentators argue that tort remedies are most efficient in compensating the injured sports victim and deterring future exceptionally severe violence. The great economic motivation involved in professional sports operates to lessen the sense of caution and innocence of motive that are characteristic of strictly leisure activity, such that the doctrine which initially shielded the innocent now protects those with more specious motives. Professional players also are in a better posi-

---

549 Prosecutors seemingly must not allow fans' perceptions to completely control their decisions. First, the spectators who influence the decision to investigate are likely to have strong home team loyalty and their concern will be triggered by who is injured rather than the nature of the conduct which caused the injury. American Criminal Law Review, *supra*, at 244. Second, defense attorney Meshbesher notes that, though the public may agree that violence need be controlled, it may disagree on court intervention as a remedy: "Public opinion polls in Canada regularly show majority sentiment that violence in hockey is disliked. However, interpreting opinion regarding the appropriate remedy for violence is less clear-cut. Shortly after the *Forbes* case ended in a hung jury, Mid-Continent Surveys of Minneapolis included an inquiry on fighting in professional sports in its statewide survey. Respondents in the probability sample preferred league discipline over court punishment 61% to 26%, with 5% suggesting both." Hallowell and Meshbesher, Trial, *supra*, at 28.

tion to pay for the injuries they cause.[550] From this perspective, sports violence cases may be uniquely suited to a civil solution. Some district attorney offices have noticed the inherent "efficiency" of the civil remedy. The office policy of the New York County District Attorney, for example, is not to bring a charge if a civil suit is pending.[551]

However, most of those responding shared a contrary view. Of eleven respondents who commented upon their "willingness to allow injured players to pursue remedies through the civil court system" one would accord complete deference, two would grant some deference, and nine would not defer at all.[552] Prosecutor Flakne "viewed this possibility [civil recovery by Boucha] as merely an option available to the injured party [to pursue independently on his own]."[553] Oakland District Attorney Jensen viewed the civil remedy as influential, but not dispositive in his decision to prosecute, calling it one of many "correlative social control processes."[554]

2. Deference to Game Officials. There is almost unanimous agreement on this factor. Much violence, including some which is intentional, may not justify any greater penalties than those which are imposed in the context of the competition itself. For example, offensive holding in football and intentional fouls in basketball normally only require action by the game of-

---

[550] Georgia Law Review, supra, at 390.

[551] Especially if a party seeks a criminal complaint to further "civil collection purposes."

[552] See Appendix M.

[553] Survey response to Question I(b)(5). (Received December 4, 1978.)

[554] Survey response to Question I(b)(5). (Received December 6, 1978.)

ficials.[555] Deference to "during the game" penalties for relatively minor sports violence has numerous advantages. The officials have broad discretion to impose penalties against a player or his team for any misconduct during the game. Such penalties, when compared to those given perpetrators for the same conduct outside the sports context, are minor. At best, the player may be suspended from the game and fined. However, the punishments are quick and certain. This is thought by some criminologists to be more effective in deterring undesired behavior than is the imposition of severe penalties.[556] Maricopa County (Phoenix) Attorney Hyder urged that "non-exceptional acts of sports violence should be excluded from consideration of criminal prosecution simply because such conduct can be adequately penalized under the rules of the sport."[557]

However, most everyone agrees that "during the game" penalties are ineffective for the exceptionally severe acts of sports violence that the criminal justice system would be concerned with. Clearly, fifteen yards and loss of down or two minutes in the "penalty box" can do little to deter what has been characterized as criminal hehavior. Furthermore, game referees are not very efficient policemen. Some referees admit only assessing penalties for

---

555 Though not advocating total deference, courts at least recognize that these mechanisms exist. The Hackbart court stated (435 F.Supp. at 354) that "the rules were enforced by six officials on the playing field. The primary sanction for a violation was territorial with the amounts of yardage lost being dependent upon the particular infraction. Players were also subject to expulsion from the game and to monetary penalties imposed by the league commissioner."

556 Michigan Law Review, supra, at 175.

557 Cover letter to survey. (See note 511, infra.)

one-quarter of the 70 infractions usually seen in a game.[558]

3. Deference to League Fine and Suspension Mechanisms. After describing these mechanisms in detail, Chapter II concluded that they were ineffective deterrents that should not be exclusively relied upon. Hence, Packer's sixth criteria suggests that the criminal sanction is appropriate in this context, since "there are no reasonable alternatives to the criminal sanction for dealing with it [sports violence]."[559] However, prosecutors have different perceptions concerning the level of deference that they should accord to these mechanisms. Of the twelve prosecutors who responded on the subject,[560] nine would not "defer at all to the leagues' internal fine and suspension mechanisms," two would defer somewhat, and two would defer completely. Elaborative comments suggest that there may be three separate views of deference in this context. These views are described below.

a. Complete deference. Though only two responding prosecutors said they would always defer, as a practical matter "this is the largest reason for the lack [of NFL] prosecutions."[561] There are many policy arguments used to justify this deference. First, while criminal prosecution may be in-

---

558 Criminal Law Quarterly, *supra*, at 432. One illustrative example occurred in a 1978 Super Bowl playoff game between the Pittsburgh Steelers and the Denver Broncos. Steeler defensive tackle "Mean" Joe Greene had frequently complained to the officials that Bronco guard Paul Howard had been repeatedly holding him on plays. Receiving little sympathy from the officials, "he took matters into his own hands. Or fists. Mean Joe leveled Howard with a devastating bolo punch to the solar plexus. Astonishingly, Greene's punch escaped the eyes of only six people--the members of Barth's [officiating] crew." Sports Illustrated 14 (January 2, 1978).

559 Packer, *supra*, at 296.

560 See Appendix M.

561 Personal interview with Ed Garvey, NFLPA Executive Director. (See note 152, *infra*.)

frequent at best, the internal mechanisms have the advantage of ongoing supervision as part of a rational (in theory) enforcement strategy When the law is idle, however, the league has "by default had exclusive authority."[562] Second, the league is theoretically capable of assessing more enlightened punishment because it is more sensitive to its players' actions. For example, it is claimed that hockey administrators know better than anyone what conduct is unreasonable in the heat of a hockey game. They also know what risks the players in fact assume because of their close contact with the history of the game and the players themselves. For these reasons, it is reasonable to assert that the policing of hockey is best left to the specialists.[563] [564] Third, the league has interests that are not likely to be considered fully in a public enforcement action. Concern for preserving the athletic contest as the primary focus of the fans' attention, concern for the individual club's responsibility to pay the medical expenses of players, and concern for the cost of crowd control are matters which are not typically taken account of in public prosecutions.[565] Fourth, a league system is likely to be more even-handed, since it relies upon central administration, and thus avoids the variance

---

562 Wisconsin Law Review, <u>supra</u>, at 783.

563 Id., at 784. Courts have deferred to the knowledge of "private organizations" in many contexts. For example, a federal court recently justified its refusal to overturn a suspension of a boxing license by stating: "To implement its various objectives, the Commission is entitled to wide freedom both for expert technical controls and for more romantic, even mid-Victorian judgments of moral, quasi-aethetic value." <u>Ali v. Division of State Athletic Commission</u>, 308 F.Supp. 11, 16 (S.D.N.Y. 1969).

564 But closely related to the second argument.

565 William and Mary Law Review, <u>supra</u>, at 729.

which might be reflected in the enforcement practices of individual prosecutors.[566] Fifth, the league mechanism is, in theory, a much more efficient punishment system than is the cumbersome and sometimes tedious criminal justice system. Oakland District Attorney Jensen argues that "the discipline structure of the league involved is a far more efficient control mechanism than the criminal justice system--barring a culpable homicide."[567] King County (Seattle), Washington Prosecuting Attorney Christopher Bayley agrees: "Criminal prosecution is an extremely limited role and other mechanisms are certainly the most effective way of dealing with sports violence (e.g., sanctions, fines, etc.)."[568] In short, though these five arguments may be less effective as a practical matter, they are used on a theoretical level by those who wish to justify complete deference to internal fine and suspension mechanisms.

---

566 Id.

567 Survey response to Question II(b)(5). (Received December 6, 1978) A corollary to this is the realization by legal authorities and the parties involved that the victim and offender have a continuing relationship. The prosecuting authorities may not wish to strain the relationship between neighbors or among family members by giving undue advantage to one party, particularly where a civil remedy is available. Thus, as in an assault and battery case between spouses, the authorities may feel prosecution would only exacerbate the hostility between athletes who must complete against each other at regular intervals. Wisconsin Law Review, supra, at 781. One of the policy reasons for such concern about the effect of a prosecution on the nature of the continuing relationship is the recognized societal value in maintaining such relationships (e.g., marriage). In the case of hockey fights, the question becomes whether the prosecuted player's team will again play in the jurisdiction which brought the indictment (assuming for the moment an "away" game for the defendant). The effect of a successful prosecution on league harmony is difficult to predict. But as an indication, one must note that Boston Bruin General Manager noted during the Forbes trial that, "[I]f Forbes is convicted of anything, we'd have to think twice about letting Bobby Orr, Phil Esposito and all of our other players ever skate in Minnesota again." Sports Illustrated 16 (January 27, 1975).

568 Survey response to Question III. (Received December 12, 1978)

b. "Selectively" defer to those mechanisms that work adequately; "symbolically intervene" in situations where they do not. On a practical level, the prosecutor takes into account the effectiveness of the sport's internal policing regulations. If a league or the governing body of the sport imposes a strict penalty upon the offending parties, this may act as a deterrent to similar conduct in the future, and the state may thus choose not to exercise its authority under the criminal justice system.[569] The argument states that though there are times when the criminal sanction is inappropriate, there are other times when it is both warranted and beneficial. The dispositive factor in this analysis is not the effectiveness of the criminal law in this context. Rather, it is the prosecutor's perception of the efficacy of the given fine and suspension mechanism. The Michigan Law Review supports the "selective deference" view: "The extent to which the state should demand a certain standard of behavior in athletics depends in part, however, on the ability of leagues and associations to regulate their own sports."[570] From this perspective, criminal prosecution is based upon the philosophy that self-regulation may not be adequate to protect professional athletes. "It is by no means certain...that private organizations themselves are capable of adequately protecting societal interests without judicial or other government involvement." Judicial intervention into the area of sports can be based on the "recognition that the sports establishment is often unable, or unwilling, to provide justice to players injured by adversaries playing outside the rules of the game."[571] This "symbolic intervention" has the

[569] J. Love, "Criminal Law: Consent as a Defense to Criminal Battery--The Problem of Athletic Contests," 28 Oklahoma Law Review 844 (1975).

[570] Supra, at 175.

[571] Schuett, Nebraska Law Review, supra, at 1138.

advantage of increasing the deterrent effect of the criminal sanction, since it would "let players know that they're not immune from the courts."[572] Further, the continual threat of "distasteful"[573] court intervention might spur professional sports to develop more effective methods of self-regulation.[574]

c. No deference whatsoever. The overwhelming majority (nine) of responding prosecutors advocated this policy. However, the respondents must only mean that they would not include this factor in a formal list of conditions,[575] since comments in other parts of their surveys indicated that they would avoid prosecution of "merely technical offenses."[576] In any event, there are four theoretical policy arguments advanced for the proposition that no deference will be accorded. First, it is inappropriate to place lawmaking power in any hands other than the legislature's. The argument maintains that the legislature, as representatives of the people, decides what conduct shall be considered criminal. To allow a private, profit-seeking group to make such decisions is tantamount to a grant of a part of the state's jurisdiction, using that word in a conceptual sense.[577] Second, Prosecutor Flakne argues that to suggest that the governing body of a particular sport determine appro-

---

572 Telephone interview with NHL Executive Vice-President Brian O'Neill. (See note 195, infra.)

573 See Chapter I.

574 Georgia Law Review, supra, at 392.

575 Oakland District Attorney Jensen suggested that internal mechanisms may be implicitly considered, even if not "technically part of the charge decision." Survey response to Question I(6)(5). (Received December 6, 1978.)

576 That would, presumably, be handled internally or not at all.

577 Wisconsin Law Review, supra, at 784.

priate sanctions for a quasi-criminal or criminal act would be tantamount to "granting the board of directors of General Motors jurisdiction over the determination of guilt or innocence and the appropriate punishment for one of their employees who, while on the job, killed his foreman. It would seem that if violence in sports is to be curtailed, the only effective remedy lies with the state, where the capability of meting out effective deterrent sanctions exists."[578] Third, on a factual level, Flakne and others argue that internal fine and suspension mechanisms can never deter sports violence to the extent that the criminal sanction is able to:

> It is ludicrous to think that anything short of criminal sanctions will deter conduct that is criminal in its character. Therefore, prosecutors and courts throughout this country must take a firm, consistent stand on the issue of violence in sports in an attempt to ameliorate this perplexing problem and its pervasive ramifications on our society. [579]

Fourth, even if these procedures were effective, some prosecutors argue that since the purpose of a prosecution would be to deter <u>all types</u> of criminal behavior, the impact of the internal mechanism could never be sufficiently broad. Maricopa County (Phoenix) Attorney Hyder urges that "there should be no question but that criminal prosecution must take an active role in controlling exceptionally severe acts of sports violence just as it must assume such a role in any act of violence off the field. The role or reason is much broader than mere protection of an individual athlete or the integrity of the sport; it must serve as a deterrent to all criminal aggressors."[580] As is

---

578 Flakne and Caplan, Trial, <u>supra</u>, at 33-34. Flakne reiterated the argument on survey response to Question I (b)(5). (Received December 4, 1978.)

579 <u>Id.</u>, at 35.

580 Cover letter to survey received January 9, 1979.

true on the other end of the deference spectrum, these four arguments are used on a theoretical level by those who wish to justify a policy of absolutely no deference to internal fine and suspension mechanisms.

4. Deference to Legislative Action. This argument suggests that sport is such a unique social activity that the legislatures must not have intended to police it through traditional criminal law statutes. Hence the prosecutor must wait for the legislature to pass laws specifically controlling sports violence. The Hackbart court agreed with this hypothesis, but on "efficiency grounds" as well. The court noted the lack of an identifiable code of conduct for professional football players, the substitution of "the morality of the battlefield for that of the playing field" in professional football, the ambiguity and difficulty of applicability of NFL rules of play, the speed of the game, the fine-line distinction between acceptable and unacceptable conduct, the problems in establishing causation, the probable volume of litigation, and the danger of conflicting standards in different jurisdictions as factors making adequate review by the judiciary impracticable. The court analogized to legislative action in the area of safety in the coal mining and railroad industries, maintaining that legislative bodies can act more rapidly and with greater specificity than can courts in such areas.[581]

However, this argument is rarely used by prosecutors, since it is, in essence, an assault upon their own power. Furthermore, on a policy level, judicial inaction will not necessarily force the legislature into action, especially in such a controversial area as regulation of professional sports.

---

581 Georgia Law Review, supra, at 389.

Bills regarding professional sports have had little success in Congress.[582]

F. Prosecutorial Evaluation of Problems of Judicial Intervention Into Sports Violence. Survey responses indicate that prosecutors envision four specific problems in deciding to bring charges in a specific sports violence incident: (A) problems of judicial expertise; (B) problems of jurisdictional non-uniformity; (C) problems of assembling the case; and (D) problems of producing a guilty verdict.

1. Problems of Judicial Expertise. The same commentators who argue that internal mechanisms possess more expertise to regulate players with whom they are familiar,[583] argue that the courts are not familiar enough with the problem to regulate it. One commentator notes: "The task is too complex for the courts; the piecemeal solutions tolerated by the present legal framework provide no answer to the conflicts and tensions."[584] Another suggests that "a lack of judicial expertise in the affairs of professional sports may easily lead to decisions which would obscure rather than clarify the limits of disciplinary discretion held by professional sports organizations."[585] Ronald I. Meshbesher, after condluding his successful defense in the Forbes case, explained the difficulties of sports violence regulation in the context

---

582 Capetta, Connecticut Law Review, supra, at 374. The article concludes: "Until Congress decides to involve itself in this field, the courts have little choice but to entertain actions...The feared inequality of application may be an incentive to Congress to take over this area, or to the teams and the leagues themselves to lobby for and accept legislative or administrative regulation." Id.

583 See text surrounding note 563, infra.

584 Suffolk University Law Review, supra, at 95.

585 Georgetown Law Journal, supra, at 793.

of a "normal criminal trial":

> Putting extreme cases aside, as in other specialized activities, sports conduct is not straightforward and easily understandable to those unacquainted with the nuances of play. Not surprisingly, the jury in the Forbes case split on several points and both attorneys expended considerable time examining witnesses on the definition of "normal" hockey play: ways of carrying the stick, body contact, language use, and more. Testimony on the context of the sport was offered (although an expert witness for the defense was not permitted to testify concerning the effect of the intense emotional processes on a player in competitive contact sport), including a crucial issue of whether the incident in question occurred in or out of the game. In the end, several jurors voting for conviction pointed with confidence that the incident was technically "out of play" as a "clincher" in their argument, and had it been in play, they would have been reluctant to convict regardless of the extent of injury. Likewise, prosecution counsel in the 1976 Maloney hockey trial in Toronto noted that the jury had difficulty making the decision.[586]

The Hackbart[587] court was sensitive to this problem. After an extensive discussion of the difficulties described by Meshbesher above, the court concluded that determining liability for sports violence is "a task for which the courts are not well suited."[588]

2. Problems of Jurisdictional Non-Uniformity. The diverse response from surveyed prosecutors suggests that conduct which will be condemned in one jurisdiction will go unprosecuted in another. Further, there is a high probability that different courts would set variant standards for their particular jurisdictions.[589] As in earlier contexts, both situations seem to violate

---

586 Halowell and Meshbesher, Trial, supra, at 29.

587 435 F.Supp. 352 (D.Colo. 1977).

588 Id., at 258. However, the court hastened to add that this dictum should not be construed as precedentially forclosing the possibility of a court remedy in future cases, either civil or criminal. "This conclusion that the civil courts cannot be expected to control the violence in professional football is limited by the facts of [this] case." Id.

589 Capetta, Connecticut Law Review, supra, at 374.

Packer's fourth criteria of "even-handed and nondiscriminatory enforcement."[590] If the result is that enforcement is inconsistent and ambiguous, a number of harms might follow. Such a result may open the floodgates of litigation, breed inconsistent results, mislead juries, allow the loss to fall upon the wrong person, discourage people from participating, and bury important policy questions.[591] Further, it may be argued that the league's cohesiveness and success depend on disciplinary control of misconduct in the arena. League solidarity might quickly disintegrate if differential treatment of similar conduct were to occur in different jurisdictions.[592] After evaluating these arguments and experiencing them first hand in the Forbes defense, Meshbesher concludes that some uniform policy is required: "Although several cases of assault in hockey remain to be tried and although there is some indication that criminal law intervention has influenced rule changes in the sports, we argue that sporadic criminal prosecutions are not an effective long-term solution and that the peculiar characteristics of criminal law and procedure reduce its effectiveness as an initial response to sports violence problems."[593]

---

590 Packer, supra, at 296. See text surrounding note 534, infra.

591 L. Goldstein, "Participant's Liability for Injury to a Fellow Participant in an Organized Athletic Event," 53 Chicago-Kent Law Review 108 (1976).

592 Wisconsin Law Review, supra, at 785. However, the argument is easily answered. The very economic considerations which stimulate the league's desire for internal control necessarily add an element of self-interest which may well be inconsistent with an unbiased penal process. For example, some observers feel the game profits from some violence and to crack down would hurt the league financially. Also, in the interest of solidarity, the league president's office may refuse to take severe action against only one club involved in an incident, even when the attack is particularly one-sided. Id.

593 Halowell and Meshbesher, Trial, supra, at 28.

3. Problems of Assembling the Case. Some prosecutors suggest that the most difficult part of a sports violence prosecution is amassing the available witnesses and evidence. Oakland District Attorney Jensen suggests that "availability of evidence, testimonial or otherwise, is a necessary part of the [sports violence] charging decision."[594] However, this process is frequently hampered by "the lack of cooperation from league officials,"[595] coaches, and players. Some of the prosecutors surveyed (three of the eleven responding on this issue) felt that a decision to prosecute would be influenced by "pressure from players, teams, or leagues to keep such cases out of the criminal courts."[596] Most (eight), however, perceived this as a minor or inconsequential issue. Harris County (Houston) District Attorney Vance was most vehement, suggesting that there is "no pressure. [I] never talked to anyone even casually about this."[597]

Specifically, a brief analysis of the relative availability of each component of a sports violence case would be instructive.

a. Victim as Complaining Witness. Though some prosecutors have suggested that they would go forward without the consent of the victim,[598] most said they would not.[599] San Diego District Attorney Miller, in describ-

---

[594] Survey response to Question I(6)(2). (Received December 6, 1978.)

[595] San Diego County District Attorney Edwin L. Miller. Survey response to Question I(6)(4). (Received December 26, 1978.)

[596] See Appendix M.

[597] Survey response to Question I(6)(4). (Received December 28, 1978.) See the Paiement-Polonich case study, suggesting that the NHL office was "extremely helpful" to the Wayne County Prosecuting Attorney's office.

[598] See the Paiement-Polonich case study following Chapter IV.

[599] Houston District Attorney Vance calls the victim's availability "the most important factor." (Survey response to Question I(6)(2).) (Received December 28, 1978.)

ing his office's minor league hockey and college basketball prosecutions, noted that "all cases involving these types of charges turn on the agreement of the victim to testify. In both of these cases, the victims were willing and signed the criminal complaint." He concludes later in the survey that "as in any act of violence involving one on one confrontation, the prosecutor can only proceed with the cooperation of the victim. Criminal prosecution can only be successful in assisting in the control of any "personal" violence--whether on the sports field or the city street--when the victim agrees to cooperate."[600] The sports victim is apparently perceived by prosecutors to be a cooperating individual. Most prosecutors (eight of eleven who responded to this question) thought such victims would be "willing to testify"; only two did not. Interestingly, one of the two was Oakland District Attorney Jensen, whose office had jurisdiction over the much-publicized George Atkinson-Lynn Swann altercation.[601] His perceptions suggest the importance of the complaining victim:

> George Atkinson hits Lynn Swann, great furor. Chuck Noll refers to Atkinson as "criminal element." Interesting aside [is that] no one ever approaches us re: possible criminal charge, which is not to say that we would have filed. Follow up: Atkinson sues Noll for slander, major trial results in defense verdict...We have never had a case presented to us by a law enforcement agency or by a citizen complaint. 602

b. Spectators as Complaining Witnesses. It is interesting to contrast the "passive" role of Oakland District Attorney Jensen (wait for the

---

600 Survey response to Questions I(b)(2) and III. (Received December 26, 1978.)

601 See text surrounding note 103, *infra*.

602 Survey responses to Question I(a) and I(b). (Received December 6, 1978.)

victim to seek out the prosecutor) to the more active role of offices such as Flakne's in Hennepin County (Minneapolis).[603] For the more "active" offices which would proceed even if the victim fails to come forward, at least two prosecutors commented upon the value of encouraging spectators to affirmatively complain. There are problems with this approach, however, Moore notes in another context[604] that "Alarmed citizens may make honest errors. Malicious citizens may harrass others by filing false complaints." American Jurisprudence, Trials, in its seminal article on sports injury cases maintains that spectator witnesses are, for the most part, ineffective: "If the injury was received during a game, the spectators are all potential witnesses, although they seldom prove effective on the stand. Few have any real knowledge of the techniques and fine points of the game."[605]

c. Game Officials as Witnesses. The officials in charge of the game can often make effective witnesses, as two did in the Forbes prosecution. The Am Jur article suggests that "these officials tend to make effective witnesses; one of them is usually in the area of the field where the injury occurred and in a position to see what happened, and they are all skilled in the techniques of the game and trained to spot infractions of the rules."[606]

---

[603] See the Paiement-Polonich case study, where the Wayne County Prosecutor suggested that he might proceed anyway, even though victim Polonich was "afraid" to sign a complaint.

[604] M. Moore discusses these problems with citizen complaints in drug law violations. Buy and Bust 157 (1977).

[605] "Contact Sports Injury Cases," 7 Am.Jur.Trials 227 (1964). The article advocates using sportswriters who, in addition to being more expert, "can also be helpful by giving leads as to coaches and scouts who were present as spectators."

[606] Id., at 228.

d. Team Coaches as Witnesses. Because of their expertise, the head coaches and their assistants may be very effective in presenting the nuances of the game. However, because they are part of the "sports establishment,"[607] they may either see nothing wrong in an act that is "just part of the game," or be altogether reluctant to testify. Generally, the most effective use of these witnesses is made by the defense. Indeed, the prosecution may find it difficult to obtain a coach who will be willing to testify on its behalf. Also, a coach may not testify since he could be civilly liable for negligence in many jurisdictions.[608]

e. Television Replays and Photographs as Demonstrative Evidence. With hundreds of photographs and perhaps a television record, there would seem to be no difficulty in establishing the act by the defendant. The Georgia Law Review argues that "the advent of televisicn with its thousands of witnesses and the instant replay with its preservation of the evidence mitigate in favor of courts' entertaining suits involving sports injuries."[609] If the television film discloses the mechanics of how the injury was incurred, a print of the film can be made for use in evidence. And enlarged, still prints can be made of the most pertinent pictures.[610] As for photographs, many pictures are taken that are never used. However, all photographs taken are usually kept on file, and they can all be examined.[611]

---

607 See text surrounding notes 134-135, infra. (Factor eight in Chapter I)

608 See Chapter IV.

609 Supra, at 390.

610 Am.Jur.Trials, supra, at 235.

611 Id., at 234.

4. Problems of Producing a Guilty Verdict. "Problems of proof" were mentioned by many prosecutors as the most significant reason for inaction. Of the thirteen prosecutors responding on this matter, seven maintained it is "a major problem," five suggested that it would not be.[612] The difficulty of applying the specific assault and battery elements and relevant defenses is the subject of Chapter IV. The point to consider here is that prosecutors and other attorneys familiar with the area perceive this as a major problem.[613]

The most significant problem perceived by attorneys was the difficulty in finding, and convincing the jury of, the line that separates tolerable aggressive hockey and football from actionable criminal conduct. Defense attorney Meshbesher describes the difficulty after dealing with it in the Forbes trial:

> A...problem with criminal court intervention involves the task of finding that line. The judge in Ted Green's 1970 trial for assault during a hockey game declared: "I do not think that any of the actions that would normally be considered assaults in ordinary walks of life can possibly be, within the context that I am considering, considered assaults at all. This does not justify a blanket exemption of sports from criminal sanctions. Cases such as the hockey stick-swinging death of Owen McCourt in 1907 demand legal scrutiny, but are fortunately rare. 614

---

612 One "wasn't sure."

613 For example, Bernard Carey, State's Attorney of Cook County (Chicago), Illinois suggests that proving "the requisite criminal intent" is the most difficult problem in prosecuting a sports violence case. While he "can imagine scenarios that might well result in a viable prosecution,...no such case" has come to his attention. (Letter received December 20, 1978.)

614 Halowell and Meshbesher, Trial, supra, at 28-29.

For example, many surveys attempted to list and evaluate each element of an assault and battery in this context. In every case,[615] the respondent listed the traditional elements, giving traditional legal definitions, without any attempt to recognize the unique conditions inherent in a sports violence case. Oakland District Attorney Jensen remarks that the problem "is [more] real [because] there is no established case law in the area."[616] Maricopa County (Phoenix) Attorney Hyder refers to the "myriad of legal problems including consent, self-defense and assumption of the risk."[617] If attorneys have no real sense of the standards in the area, it is hard to expect juries to comprehend them. Meshbesher notes that, "even if the juror grasps the facts of a particular incident and understands the context of the sport, the legal system provides little clear-cut guidance for fitting the facts to the law."[618] Applying statutory definitions of intent to traditional sports activity is confusing and served as another point of contention to jurors in the *Forbes* trial. Yet the judge in the *Forbes* case refused a defense instruction which would have specifically cautioned the jurors to consider the context of the incident in determining criminal intent. In effect, the judge's charge, which stated the law of assault in accepted traditional terms, could result in the conviction of a boxer for hitting his opponent, since the court recognized no consent defense.

---

[615] For example, Allegheny County (Pittsburgh) District Attorney Robert E. Colville's response to Question I(b)(7). (Received December 11, 1978.)

[616] Survey response to Question I(b)(3). (Received December 6, 1978.) Chapter IV indicates that this is not entirely true.

[617] Cover letter to survey. (See note 511, *infra*.)

[618] Halowell and Meshbesher, Trial, *supra*, at 29.

A corollary problem is that even if the "guilt line" may be clearly drawn, a sports violence case is intrinsically difficult to win, given the "part of the game" mentality.[619] Shiela Brooks, NFLPA Staff Counsel, suggested that it would be "impossible to prove guilt beyond a reasonable doubt with all the problems going against you."[620] Ed Garvey, Executive Director of that organization, agrees: "It's so hard to prove the requisite elements that most prosecutors you talk to wouldn't even try to convince a jury."[621] Attorney Nick Buoniconti suggested that "the proof problem would be so immense in football that even a football-related death could go unprosecuted."[622] The Hackbart court has noted, in dicta, that the game of football is so aggressive that no standard of "reasonableness" can be applied.[623] These arguments go far to explain the fact that there have been no successful hockey prosecutions to date, though six have been attempted. In short, the difficulty of obtaining convictions further diminishes the practicability of a league's reliance solely on criminal enforcement. Not only is the legal standard unclear, but also there appears to be a propensity for juries, particularly those composed of avid fans, to accept the notion that violence and assaults are part of the game.

---

619 Chapter IV analyzes this problem in much greater depth. In the interest of completeness only, it must be noted that one commentator maintains that "elements of intent to injure or harmful result to the victim do not appear to present real problems of proof. As the cursory review of the available defenses indicates, there is no reason to expect these defenses to have much applicability in the typical sports fight." Wisconsin Law Review, supra, at 774.

620 Telephone interview. (See note 124, infra.)

621 Personal interview. (See note 152, infra.)

622 Personal interview. (See note 69, infra.)

623 Georgia Law Review, supra, at 388.

G. Prosecutorial Fear that Successful Prosecution Would Result in an Unmanageable Volume of Sports Violence Cases. Since most sports contact is technically actionable under traditional assault and battery statutes, some responding prosecutors (three) expressed the fear that "one successful prosecution would open the floodgates for complaints" against professional athletes. Thus, the argument continues, though certain selective sports violence prosecutions could be cost-effective, a massive effort could not be. The criminal law could not possibly intervene after every punch, must less keep track of all the technical assaults and batteries that occur.[624] As such, the argument concludes, the hazards of court incompleteness and delay makes the internal fine and suspension mechanism more attractive. One commentator agrees:

> League enforcement may in fact be preferable to that administered through the criminal process. The league is in a better position to define and enforce specific rules of conduct than are the court, from which standards could emerge only from a case-by-case interpretation. Also, the range of conduct that the league might wish to control may well include actions of a sufficiently minor nature that public prosecution would be unwarranted. Thus, a system of league control may be more encompassing than that which would be found on the public side. 625

However, the prosecutor who mentioned this argument did not consider it dispositive for two reasons. First, an effective policy of "symbolically enforcing" only the most excessive violations would, in addition to the numerous advantages mentioned previously, mitigate the "floodgates" argument. While technical violations do always exist, they need not be prosecuted. In essence, therefore, the prosecutor will require a higher level of violent

---

624 Wisconsin Law Review, supra, at 786. The Connecticut Law Review also worries about "the potential volume of litigation in this area." Supra, at 374. The Hackbart court also expressed a similar concern.

625 William and Mary Law Review, supra, at 729.

conduct before he files charges under the assault and battery statutes. The Georgia Law Review explains the result in the tort context. "The concern expressed over a possible 'floodgates' situation could be assuaged by requiring a greater showing of misconduct than ordinary negligence on the part of the defendant; the recklessness standard discussed in Nabozny, for example, could serve this purpose. However, to allow no recovery at all would render professional contact sports an unfortunate aberration in American tort law."[626] Second, it is argued that prosecutorial inaction now causes more cumbersome, complex cases later. The Criminal Law Quarterly forcefully urges that, "it is the purpose of the prosecutors to enforce the laws evenhandedly. By neglecting their duty to police the violence in sports the judicial system leaves itself open to having to decide complex questions of criminal liability that could have been avoided through adequate notice to fans, coaches and players. Crime in the sports arena cannot be ignored by those charged by the public with enforcing the law."[627]

H. Prosecutorial Evaluation of the Argument that Inaction Grants Implicit Criminal Immunity to Sports Participants. This "equal protection-type" argument has been advanced by those prosecutors and others who most strongly advocate prosecution of all excessively severe acts of aports violence. Prosecutor Flakne reiterates the argument he employed in the Forbes prosecution:

> The rationale in support of the encroachment of the criminal justice system into the world of sports is derived from the proposition that no particular segment

---

626 Supra, at 392.

627 Supra, at 452.

> of society can be licensed to commit crime with impunity. As Lord Justice Bramwell instructed the jury in Regina v. Bradshaw (Cox. C.C. 83, 1878), a criminal prosecution resulting from a death during the course of a soccer game:
> "No rules of practice of any game whatever can make that lawful which is unlawful by the law of the land...no persons can by agreement go out to fight with deadly weapons, doing by agreement what the law says shall not be done, and thus shelter themselves from the consequences of their acts." [628]

King County (Seattle), Washington Prosecuting Attorney Christopher T. Bayley agreed, arguing that "the fact that someone is a sports figure...does not immunize him from prosecution if there is a provable case arising from conduct on or off the field..."[629]

The argument is based upon the premise that "our society never intended to excuse unjustified brutality merely because it occurs on a playing field."[630] The Hackbart court recognized, however, that such a distinction apparently exists: "In the context of common community standards, there can be no question but that...[it]...would generate civil liability. It would involve a criminal sanction if the requisite intent were present. The difference here [was] that this blow was delivered on the field of play during the course of action in a

---

[628] Flakne and Caplan, Trial, supra, at 33. Defense attorney Meshbesher responded that: "The crucial difference making sports unique is that violence is intrinsic to sports activity in a way that makes legal intervention difficult." Halowell and Meshbesher, Trial, supra, at 27.

[629] Survey response to Question III. (Received December 12, 1978.)

[630] Hofeld, Trial Lawyer's Guide, supra, at 405. Even Clarence Campbell, former NHL President and constant critic of court intervention, agreed with his premise indirectly (though probably without knowing it): "Something must be done to control the violence in our game. I hear at least 10 discipline cases each week. And over the course of a season, I suspect I hear at least 10 cases where the civil authorities might think a crime was committed. Without doubt, this has been our worst year ever for sheer violence on the ice." Sports Illustrated 16 (November 17, 1975). William Hechter presented the following emotional appeal in Criminal Law Quarterly, supra, at 425: "Criminal liability for an athlete's actions should not stop as a player leaves the realm of ordinary

regularly scheduled professional football game."[631] The logical conslusion of the argument is that whether an incident occurred during a game should make no difference.[632] As a practical matter, however, it is a very real consideration. Therefore, this argument is most strongly advanced to suggest that the excessively violent participant should not be immune from prosecution merely because his conduct takes place during a sporting event.

I. Prosecutorial Perception of the Political Advantage to be Gained Through Such Prosecution. Clearly, this paper does not advocate this factor as a "rational" consideration. It is only suggested that it may be implicitly relevant to a prosecutor's charging decision. Any prosecutor who contemplated such a decision, at least in the near future, would be cognizant of the fact that he would receive tremendous publicity since such a prosecution, in all probability, would be the first of its kind in the jurisdiction. Defense Counsel Meshbesher[633] suggests that, "the criminal sta-

citizen and enters the realm of athletic competition. Dwight White, professional football player, does not receive a license to cause bodily harm as he dons a uniform inside the confines of the stadium, or does he? If citizen Pete Jackson can be sentenced to jail following the commission of an assault in his own home, why should he be punished, when at the same time a professional hockey player is receiving a standing ovation for attacking an opposing player during the course of the game?"

631 Hackbart, supra, at 358. The specific factual scenario is presented in Chapter IV.

632 The prosecution strategy in Forbes, according to Flakne, was to select jurors who were not hockey fans and who had no particular reverence for athletics in general. "The prosecution was predicated on the theory that the enforcement of criminal laws should not stop at the admitting gates of sporting events. Each prospective juror, when questioned by the State, indicated that if the elements of an assault were proven beyond a reasonable doubt, it would make no difference whether the assault took place during an athletic contest, in a bar, or in the street." Flakne and Caplan, Trial, supra, at 34.

633 Perhaps backhandedly criticizing Forbes' prosecution by Flakne, Halowell and Meshbesher, Trial, supra, at 29.

tutes, as currently written, are tailored to the complexity of an industrial, urban society and offer only the most abstract guidelines for defining crimes. A priori exemptions are unrecognized and the burden of decision-making goes to the prosecuting attorney or grand jury. As Binder correctly notes, this leaves any particular individual open to prosecution for the general conditions of the sports organization within which he participates. In short, if the public perceives a sport as overly violent and interest in 'cracking down' on violence is intense, the politically-beholden prosecutor will likely cooperate." There have been more specific criticisms. The American Criminal Law Review notes that "the tremendous publicity that has accompanied the Forbes, Green, and Maki trials suggests that indicting a professional athlete for assault may be a means for a local prosecutor to further his political ambitions."[634] Forbes prosecuting attorney Flakne has been accused of indicting Forbes to further his own political ambitions,[635] to which he responded that any conscientous county attorney would have been compelled to indict Forbes.[636] In short, though the extent of such influence

---

[634] Supra, at 244. It is interesting to note that almost all the prosecutors who responded on the matter (six of nine) indicated that the "extent of media coverage" would not influence their decision to prosecute in any way. Given the arguments in this section, it may be more appropriate to analyze these particular responses with the proverbial "grain of salt."

[635] Stan Fischler, in his column "Speaking Out on Hockey," suggested that "David Forbes, the Boston Bruins' forward, would not have been indicted on charges of aggravated assault had he done what he did to Henry Boucha in any other place but Bloomington, Minn. Forbes was nailed by an ambitious district attorney." Sporting News 22 (March 1, 1975).

[636] Sports Illustrated 18 (November 17, 1975). Frequently, these charges of political expediency are based on home town loyalties. For example, after Ontario Attorney General prosecution of three Philadelphia Flyers in Canada, the Philadelphia District Attorney termed the prosecution a "perversion of office" by Canadian officials. Winnipeg Free Press 69 (April 21, 1976). (For a discription of the incident, see note 19, infra.)

can never be known, it appears to be an implicit factor in the sports violence charging decision.

In conclusion, it is clear that though technical violations of the assault and battery statutes frequently occur during a normal game, a prosecutor should not be required to bring an indictment in each instance. However, there are some exceptionally severe instances of sports violence which call for such intervention. Unfortunately, survey responses indicate that there is extreme diversity in prosecutors' views of their role in this area. Accordingly, this Chapter has attempted to identify nine characteristics and factors which influence a prosecutor's charging decision in the hopes of clarifying a presently confusing and ambiguous situation.

## IV) ANALYSIS OF LEGAL ELEMENTS OF ASSAULT AND BATTERY, AND THE RELEVANT DEFENSES EMPLOYED IN PREVIOUS SPORTS VIOLENCE CASES.

This Chapter assumes that a prosecutor, based on his evaluation of the factors in Chapter III, has chosen to activate the criminal justice system. Once the indictment has issued and trial preparation has begun, the most critical issue becomes an analysis of the elements of and defenses to an assault and battery case in the sports violence context.

As has been suggested by numerous prosecutors in Chapter III, the law in this area is extremely ambiguous and diverse. Common law is not well-developed. Federal legislation in the sports area is limited to prohibition of bribery;[637] and state legislation is virtually non-existent. From this perspective, any sports violence cases have significant precedential value. The first modern hockey assault cases under Canadian law were the Green and Maki indictments in 1969,[638] discussed in Chapter I.[639] Following the 1970 acquittals, Attorney General McMurtry "wanted to avoid such prosecutions but couldn't due to the clarity of the law on this matter."[640] As a result of this policy, "close to 100 convictions"[641] have been secured on the amateur

---

637 18 U.S.C. §224.

638 See notes 77-82, infra.

639 The defendants were acquitted in both cases. See Regina v. Green, 16 D.L.R.3d 137 (1970); Regina v. Maki, 14 D.L.R.3d 164 (1970).

640 The account was given by the Attorney General's brother, William, in a telephone conversation (see note 112, infra). Attorney General McMurtry eventually agreed with the policy of wholesale prosecution, finally arguing that "a criminal offense is a criminal offense"--a statement which Chapter III proponents of "symbolic enforcement" would find hard to accept.

641 Id.

level since 1969. In the United States, the seminal prosecution was the 1974 case of State v. Forbes.[642] The incident occurred on January 4, 1975 in a game in Minneapolis between the Boston Bruins and the Minnesota North Stars. Forbes apparently checked Boucha against the boards with his elbows up, and Boucha retaliated by punching Forbes who fell to the ice. Both players were sent off the ice for seven minutes each in penalties. The players apparently exchanged remarks from their adjacent penalty boxes. When they returned to the ice, Boucha was skating ahead of Forbes who allegedly made another remark and then took a swing at Boucha. Although missing with his gloved hand, Forbes did strike Boucha with the butt end of his stick, and after Boucha fell to the ice covering his seriously injured face, Forbes jumped on Boucha punching him until the two were separated by a third player.[643] Approximately 25 stitches were used to close the stick-inflicted cut next to Boucha's right eye. Double vision prompted X-rays and the need for surgery to repair a small fracture in the floor of the right eye socket.[644] Because of the egregious character of the widely publicized incident, Forbes was prosecuted under the Minnesota criminal assault statutes. The question of his culpability, however, was not resolved. The jury could not agree upon a verdict, and Prosecutor Flakne declined to retry the case.[645]

Flakne articulated his reasons for not reindicting Forbes in his 1975

---

[642] No. 63280 (Dist.Ct.Minn.) (July 19, 1975).

[643] Wisconsin Law Review, supra, at 771.

[644] Sports Illustrated, supra, January 27, 1975, at 17.

[645] Michigan Law Review, supra, at 148.

Trial article:

> In subsequent interviews with the jurors, it was determined that at the time when they became unable to reach a verdict the division was nine to three in favor of an assault conviction. We decided not to retry the Forbes case for two reasons: (1) We felt that by taking the Forbes case to trial we had put the sports world on notice that acts involving intention to cause serious bodily injury to another will not be tolerated in our jurisdiction and, (2) There was the likelihood of ending up with another deadlocked jury.

In his announcement to the press, however, Flakne suggested that his decision did not mean complete immunity for the athlete, warning that "we shall see more of this."[646] Despite the hung jury and subsequent non-reindictment, the case was significant in American sports law, for it "focused public and legal attention on the issue of violence in sports."[647]

Given the recent emphasis on court resolution of egregious sports violence cases, it is important to explore the elements of the respective cases for the prosecution and defense. They will be analyzed in the following manner: (A) Assault, battery, and the problems of establishing "intent"; (B) the consent defense; (C) the "assumption of risk" defense; (D) the "provocation" defense; (E) the "involuntary reflex" defense; (F) self defense; and (G) the "social utility" defense. Finally, section (H) analyzes the prospect for legal liability through intentional tort, negligence, respondeat superior, and criminal conspiracy theories.

A. Assault, Battery, and the Problems of Establishing "Intent".

Under Canadian law, the definition of assault is: A person commits

---

646 Criminal Law Quarterly, supra, at 431.

647 Schuett, Nebraska Law Review, supra, at 1129.

an assault when (a) without the consent of another person or with consent, where it is obtained by fraud, he applies force intentionally to the person of the other, directly or indirectly.[648] The common assault section states further that: (2) Every one who unlawfully causes bodily harm to any person or commits an assault that causes bodily harm to any person (a) is guilty of an indictable offence and is liable to imprisonment for five years; or (b) is guilty of an offence punishable on summary conviction. In Canada, any blow struck in anger or which is intended or likely to do corporal hurt is a criminal assault.[649]

Many American jurisdictions have similar statutes. In Minnesota, for example, assault is the intentional causing of fear in another of immediate bodily harm, or the intentional attempt to inflict bodily harm upon another.[650] David Forbes was charged with violation of the statute against aggravated assault. Minn. Stat. §609.25, Aggravated assault states: Subdivision 1. Whoever assaults another and inflicts great bodily harm may be sentenced to imprisonment for not more than ten years or to payment of a fine of not more than $10,000, or both. Subdivision 2. Whoever assaults another with a dangerous weapon but without intent to inflict great bodily harm may be sentenced to imprisonment for not more than five years or to payment of a fine of not more than $5,000, or both.[651]

As the statutes suggest, the prosecutor must prove that the indicted athlete either intended the act or intended the bodily harm. In either case, intent is "not only the most decisive element, but is also the most difficult

[648] Criminal Code, R.S.C., 1970 c. C-34, s.244. Section 245 states that assault is an indictable offense punishable by imprisonment for five years, or punishable on summary conviction.

[649] Criminal Law Quarterly, _supra_, at 429.

[650] Minn. Stat. §609.22, 1971.

[651] Most jurisdictions have a statute which proscribes aggravated batteries.

to prove."[652] In some cases, intent is not a significant problem. For example, in the Forbes case intent is a necessary element of aggravated assault in Minnesota often presumed by the nature and probable consequences of the defendant's act.[653] Furthermore, even though this element does not require special proof in Minnesota, there is evidence that could support such a finding in the Forbes case. A witness, employed by the arena, stated that while the players were in their respective penalty boxes, "Forbes held up a clenched fist and yelled over at Boucha, 'I'll get you, but it won't be with this. It'll be with my stick; I'll shove it down your throat.'"[654] In some jurisdictions, intent is not an element of assault and/or battery. In such a case, the basic rule is that "an averment of intent is not necessary when not specifically made an element of the offense or when it may be inferred from the act itself...."[655]

However, in jurisdictions where "intent" is critical, it is the most difficult element to prove in a sports violence case for three reasons. First,

---

Although many of these only use the term aggravated assault (in connection with a special intent, to murder, or a special instrumentality, a dangerous weapon), assault in these contexts means assault and battery. See, e.g., N.Y. Penal Code §120.10 (McKinney 1975). But see Cal. Penal Code §§ 240, 242, 245 (West 1970) (Assault and battery treated as separate crimes).

652 Personal interview with Nick Buoniconti. (See note 69, infra.)

653 State v. Peters, 274 Minn. 309, 143 N.W.2d 832 (1966). Reasoning from the case, the Criminal Law Quarterly notes that there appears to be no legal reason why players cannot be charged, tried and convicted of aggravated assault when they attack with full knowledge of the injuries that can occur from their violence, and the serious injuries inflicted were intentional. Supra, at 433-34.

654 Wisconsin Law Review, supra, at 773.

655 6 C.J.S. "Assault and Battery" §106 (1937).

"[t]he number of objective indications available to evaluate the mental state of the participant in this context is limited."[656] For example, criminal charges for intentionally throwing at a batter are nearly impossible to formulate due to the difficulty of proving intent on the part of the pitcher.[657] Second, the "assaulting" athlete may not possess the requisite mens rea. The popular view is that people participate in athletics out of love for the game, not out of a malicious desire to harm an opponent. It is not unlikely that courts embraced this view and presumed that participants possess an intent consonant with the idea of the game.[658] This presumption is significant: If the courts had instead assumed that the participants possessed intent to injure, convictions for sports conduct would have been more frequent.[659] Third, since physical intimidation is seen by those who would serve on juries as "just part of the hockey or football game,"[660] it would be difficult to prove that the athlete specifically intended to harm his opponent. These difficulties do

---

[656] Schuett, Nebraska Law Review, *supra*, at 1134.

[657] Criminal Law Quarterly, *supra*, at 442, suggests a potential solution, at least for the baseball problem. "Don Drysdale was given the green light to strike the batter if his catcher flicked his fingers. Such a signal, especially if on film, could aid plate umpires and prosecutors in acting against the pitcher, catcher and manager through conspiracy statutes."

[658] "[I]f a man is playing according to the rules and practice of the game and not going beyond it, it may be reasonable to infer that he is not actuated by any malicious otive or intention, and that he is not acting in a manner which he knows will be likely to be productive of death or injury." *Regina v. Bradshaw* (1878) 14 Cox Crim. Cas. 83, 85.

[659] Michigan Law Review, *supra*, at 172.

[660] See Chapter I, §A. See *N.Y. Times*, July 19, 1975, at 17, col. 3, quoting a *Forbes* juror: "Three of us...did not feel he [Forbes] intended to inflict any bodily harm."

not make a guilty verdict impossible. It is merely suggested that only the exceptionally severe incident will be appropriate to pursue in a jurisdiction in which intent must be specifically alleged.

B. The Consent Defense[661]

That "athletes willingly consent to all contact incident to a game" is the most common and productive argument that the athlete-defendant may use. As with other elements of traditional assault and battery, the precise requirements of consent vary inter-jurisdictionally. For example, Oakland District Attorney Jensen suggests that the label "mutual combat" is "more apropos"[662] in his jurisdiction. However, in most other jurisdictions, the general rule is that both participants are guilty of the offense and may be prosecuted. This approach makes sense when one considers that

---

[661] The consent defense is strikingly similar to consent to an intentional tort. In both the criminal and the tort setting, the factfinder must look at all the evidence to determine whether the victim in fact consented. This similarity is important because much more treatment has been accorded actual consent issues in civil tort cases than in criminal cases. Since the issue of the party's subjective state of mind is the same, the resolution of problems concerning actual consent that arise in the civil context applies equally to those problems that arise in a criminal trial.

This is not to say that the law of consent is identical for both civil and criminal cases. While the substantive issue of whether consent existed is the same, the effect of that consent, if present, may be different, since the state has an interest in criminal cases that is absent in civil cases. Theoretically, the civil tort case involves the interests of only the two parties before the court; the only question is whether the plaintiff has incurred an injury for which the defendant should have to compensate him. If the plaintiff actually consented, little reason exists to make the defendant compensate the plaintiff. The common-law maxim volenti non fit injuria expresses the idea that a willing party is not injured. Generally, then, in a torts case, the court should not be concerned with "effective consent" matters, which, because of the interests of the state, are present in a criminal case. Michigan Law Review, supra at 150. This is the only significant difference, however. Accordingly, tort case law and treatise law will be used frequently in this section to clarify the confusing application of this defense to the sports violence case.

[662] Survey response to Question I(b)(3). (Received December 6, 1978)

the purpose of the criminal law to deter such conduct is certainly not diminished by the concerted occurrence of two crimes. Some jurisdictions do not allow the consent defense at all. In the most notable instance, the trial judge in Forbes instructed the jury that "no one could consent to an assault either explicitly or implicitly."[663]

Case law in this area is extremely unclear. The recognition of the consent defense in the sports context dates back at least as far as 1934, when an English court noted that, "[Sports is one of the] well established exceptions to the general rule that an act likely or intended to cause bodily harm is an unlawful act."[664] Since that time, most courts have treated this issue as one to be decided on a case-by-case basis. In Agar v. Canning, the most notorious "provocation defense" case, the Manitoba Queen's Bench articulated the ambiguous view that many courts hold:

> [A] little reflection will establish that some limit must be placed on a player's immunity from liability. Each case must be deicded on its own facts so it is difficult, if not impossible, to decide how the line is going to be drawn in every circumstance. 665

Though some jurisdictions adopt the case-by-case approach as in Agar, many courts have attempted to carve out rational tests for the application of the consent defense to sports violence indictments. It is appropriate to mention seven such approaches.

1. The "scope of consent" test. This theory suggests that though a player will consent to his participation in a given sporting event, he does

---

663 American Criminal Law Review, supra, at 236.

664 Rex v. Donovan, 2 K.B. 498, 508 (1934).

665 Agar v. Canning, 54 W.W.R. (n.s.) 302, 304 (Q.B.) (Man.), aff'd, (1960) S.S.W.W.R. (n.s.) 384 (C.A.).

not consent to conduct which goes beyond a certain level of violence. Stated another way, participation in the game is seen as implying consent. However, it has also been said that "[t]he defendant's privilege is limited to the conduct to which the plaintiff consents, or at least to acts of a substantially similar nature."[666] Thus, if athletic participants do not engage in intentional conduct which is markedly different from that to which plaintiff consented or apparently consented, they will not be liable in assault and battery for resulting accidental injuries under this test. Although no American cases involving the scope of consent in professional sports have been reported, two Canadian trial court opinions have been published.[667] Both attempt to define the scope of actual consent that can be inferred from an individual's participation in a professional hockey game. Each player consents to such physical contact as is normally and properly incident to the game. The defendant thus must show that the supposedly wrongful act took place during the normal flow of the game. In deciding this, the jury should consider whether the sport was "contact" or "noncontact," the type of rules involved, and whether the infraction was of a type that is reasonable expected to occur during an average game.[668]

The most significant problem plaguing the "scope of consent" test is finding the threshhold of violent conduct above which a player does not consent. The Michigan Law Review agrees in substance, maintaining that, "scope of consent analysis has only limited utility since it is extremely difficult

---

666 W. Prosser, Torts §18, at 103 (1971).

667 Regina v. Green (1971) 16 D.L.R.3d 137 (1970); Regina v. Maki (1971) 14 D.L.R.3d 164 (1970). For a description of the incident, see notes 77-82, infra.

668 Oklahoma Law Review, supra, at 845.

to draw a fine line delineating the conduct to which the victim is, in fact, willing to acquiesce."[669] Additionally, the author argues that scope of consent provides little assistance in explaining the outcome in situations where the victim voluntarily undertakes an activity involving definite risks of injury because his desire to achieve a certain end or goal outweighs his desire to avoid the harm associated with the goal's attainment.[670] In other words, since the number of objective indications available to evaluate the athlete's mental state is limited, a factfinder may only be able to infer intent to participate in the game itself. While the factfinder would have to conclude that the athlete therefore consented to all acts associated with the game, he actually may have not so consented.[671] The line drawing problem has been recognized by many, including the Ontario court in dicta in Regina v. Green:

> One now gets the most difficult problem of all, in my opinion: since it is assumed and understood that there are numerous what would normally be called assaults in the course of a hockey game, but which are really not assaults because of the consent of the players in the type of game being played, where do you draw the line? 672

---

669 Supra, at 153.

670 Id., at 153-54.

671 The Michigan Law Review, supra, at 156, explains in the context of football. "In professional sports, the only information that can be considered in determining the scope of consent is participation in the game. The anomalous result is that a player may often have a strong desire that his opponent not engage in certain conduct; yet, the player may be held to have consented to the conduct. For example, if A is running with the football and B tries to tackle him, A may find the tackle most undesirable, especially if he is injured. However, this anomaly may be explained by saying that when a person participates in a game, he consents to his opponent's hitting him in certain ways, even though he may wish to avoid such contact at a given point in the course of the game."

672 16 D.L.R.3d 137, 142 (1970).

2. The "rules of the game" test. The Restatement of Torts[673] provides the most clear definition of this test. Taking part in a game manifests a willingness to submit to such bodily contacts or restrictions of liberty as are permitted by its rules or usages. Participating in such a game does not manifest consent to contacts which are prohibited by rules or usages of the game if such rules or usages are designed to protect the participants and not merely to secure the better playing of the game as a test of skill. This is true although the player knows that those with or against whom he is playing are habitual violators of this rule. The test implies that the setting, consisting of the rules and customs of the game, determines if plaintiff's participation in the game can reasonably be interpreted as consent to bodily contact. Thus, the argument goes, participating in a game does not manifest consent to acts which are prohibited by the rules and customs of the game, especially if such rules are designed to protect players from harm.[674] On a practical level, therefore, a hockey player would not consent to conduct prohibited by the minor-major-match-misconduct penalty structure contained in the NHL Rulebook.[675] Hence, acts such as spearing,[676] unnecessary roughness,[677] fighting,[678] and slashing with a stick,[679] are not consented to under this theory. In football, "uncon-

---

673 Restatement (Second) of Torts §50, Comment 6 (1965).

674 Comment, "Torts--Participant in Athletic Competition States Cause of Action for Injuries Against Another Participant," 42 Missouri Law Review 348 (1977).

675 See text surrounding notes 292-311, infra.

676 Rule 45(a).

677 Rule 84.

678 Rules 54 and 66.

679 Rule 45.

sented to" conduct would include that which violates the rule prohibiting a player from "striking, swinging, or clubbing on the head, neck or face with the heel, back, or side of the hand, wrist, forearm, elbow, or clasped hand."[680] Also applicable is Rule 12, §2, art. 15: "There shall be no unsportsmanlike conduct. This applies to any act which is contrary to the generally understood principles of sportsmanship."

There appears to be a significant dispute concerning the validity of this test. Some courts and commentators have suggested that the rules of the game should be the absolutely definitive standard of conduct to which a player consents. Professor Beale stated as early as 1878 that, "[i]n a football game, for instance, each player consents in advance to such injuries as he may suffer, so long as they are inflicted by one acting within the rules of the game; but an injury caused by unfair play is not consented to."[681] The *Wisconsin Law Review* agrees, noting that, "[t]hus, because [o]ne who enters into a sport, game or contest may be taken to consent to physical contacts consistent with the understood rules of the game, aggravated fighting in the athletic arena would appear to be without the aid of the defense under traditional rules."[682] Prosecutors Flakne and Caplan agree that this standard should govern sports violence cases, despite the fact that the consent defense was not allowed in the *Forbes* case itself. Flakne states:

> In theory, the rules, regulations, and equipment of contemporary significant body contact sports are designed

---

680 Rule 12, §2, art. 1, part c. *Official Rules of Professional Football.*

681 Beale, "Consent in the Criminal Law," 8 *Harv. L. Rev.* 317, 323 (1895), citing *Regina v. Bradshaw* (1878) 14 Cox Crim. Cas. 83.

682 *Supra*, at 775.

> to avoid serious danger to life or limb. Whether the defense of consent then may be raised successfully should be dependent on whether the injuries were occasioned through an accident while the actor was in compliance with the rules of the game or whether the injuries were inflicted under such circumstances that they tend to show a definite resolve on the part of the actor to cause a serious injury to another. If the attendant circumstances tend to show that the actor went beyond the scope of the rules of the game and purposefully injured or attempted to injure his opponent, the defense of consent should be unavailable. [683]

At least one court has adopted the strict interpretation of the rules of the game test. In Nabozny v. Barnhill,[674] an Illinois Appellate Court held that when athletes are engaged in athletic competition, the teams are trained and coached by competent personnel, a recognized set of rules governs the play, and a safety rule is contained therein which is primarily designed to protect players from injury, a player is liable for a deliberate, wilful, or reckless violation of said rule which causes injuries. Judge Adesko, speaking for the court, stated that one of the educational benefits of organized athletic competitions to youth is the development of discipline and self control and that this could best be accomplished by abiding by the rules of the game. He then cited and relied upon Section 50, comment b of the Restatement as standing for the proposition that such rules are designed both to secure the better playing of the game as a test of skill and to protect participants from serious injury.[685]

---

683
Flakne and Caplan, Trial, supra, at 35.

684
31 Ill. App, 3d 212, 334 N.E.2d 258 (1975). The facts of the case are described in text surrounding note 776, infra.

685
Chicago-Kent Law Review, supra, at 104.

By basing its decision on violation of a safety rule, the Nabozny court barred actions in which the act complained of is nothing more than a violent or forceful collision, wholly proper under the rules of the game. While such a collision, were it to occur outside the context of a contact sport, might properly be actionable, within such a context, it could not be so characterized. Inclusion of this condition requiring defendant's conduct to be in violation of a safety rule of the sport assured that such conduct would be wrongful in the context of the particular sport.[686]

Some other courts and commentators have argued that the rules of the game should not be a factor in determining consent. At least two cases have ignored the consent defense even when the conduct was within the rules. In R. v. Moore[687] the deceased was killed in a soccer match after being hit from behind during a game. The incident occurred where the ball was being played, and the defendant was found guilty or manslaughter. The Canadian court stated that the "rules of the game were quite immaterial, and it did not matter whether the prisoner broke the rules or not. Football was a lawful game, but it was a rough one, and persons who played it must be careful to restrain themselves so as not to do bodily harm to any other person. No one had a right to use force which was likely to injure another, and if he did use such force and death resulted the crime of manslaughter had been committed." In R. v. Bradshaw,[688] two soccer teams were playing

---

686 Though the case attempts to formulate a black letter "rules of the game" standard, its precedential value for consent in the criminal sports violence context may be doubtful. First, the case dealt exclusively with consent to intentional torts. Though the law is quite similar, the difference described in note 661, infra, must be remembered. Second, dicta in the opinion casts doubt over whether each of the three Nabozny criteria would be dispositive if standing alone.

687 14 T.L.R. 229 (1898).

688 14 Cox C.C. 83 (1878).

according to the "association rules." One player charged the other, they collided and death resulted. The defendant was charged with manslaughter and was acquitted by the jury. However, the jury instructions were as follows:[689]

> No rules or practice of any game whatever can make that lawful which is unlawful by the law of the land; and the law of the land says you shall not do that which is likely to cause the death of another. For instance, no persons can by agreement go out to fight with deadly weapons, doing by agreement what the law says shall not be done, and thus shelter themselves from the consequences of their acts.

From an opposite perspective, other cases have suggested that the conduct may have been consented to even if it violated a safety rule. The Green court clearly expressed the opinion that blows in violation of the rules, such as Green's blow to Maki's face, were consented to, at least where they were common and did not create a high risk of serious injury.[690] One commentator states that in games with considerable contact, such as football, "the consent by the players to the use of moderate force is clearly valid, and the players are even deemed to consent to an application of force that is in breach of the rules of the game, if it is the sort of thing that may be expected to happen during the game."[691]

Finally, other courts and commentators have carved out a middle ground position: that the rules of the game are merely one factor in the totality of circumstances to be analyzed to determine whether consent existed. In

---

[689] Criminal Law Quarterly, supra, at 443-44.

[690] 16 D.L.R.3d, at 140-41.

[691] Williams, "Consent and Public Policy," Criminal Law Review 81 (1962).

Tavernier v. Maes,[692] an action was brought by a participant in a family softball game on an improvised field for injuries sustained when he was struck by defendant who was sliding into second base. The California court suggested that there are many hazards which develop from player errors which cannot be classified as negligent and that the known customs of the game must play some part in determining whether conduct is or is not negligence. Rather, in order to determine whether a participant's conduct amounts to careless disregard for the safety of others, the jury must consider not only the rules and nature of the particular game but also the skill of the players and the risks which normally attend playing that game.[693] One commentator has proposed a two-pronged test combining the major elements of both the "rules" and "scope" tests: "In viewing the act, consideration should be given to whether it was in violation of a rule of the game, and, if so, whether the act was of a type that occurs regularly during the normal course of the contest."[694] The Michigan Law Review explains the advantages of such an approach over the more inflexible polar positions:

> The first approach--that the rules of the game delineate the scope of actual consent--appears too narrow. Strict reliance on all rules of the game is unreasonable because some rules are designed not to protect the players but instead to make the game more exciting or competitive, such as the rule in football prohibiting a player from crossing the line of scrimmage before the ball is hiked. As the Restatement (Second) of Torts recognizes, it would be inappropriate to assert that an injury caused by the player who is offside exceeds the scope of the injured player's consent simply because a rule has been violated. Furthermore, some infractions of the rules occur quite frequently and are not thought by the players to be serious. It may not be improper to consider such violations as part of the game; thus, a player may be deemed to have consented to such actions although a rule designed to protect the players has been violated. 695

---

692 242 Cal.App.2d 522, 51 Cal.Rptr. 575 (1966).

693 Chicago-Kent Law Review, supra, at 101.

694 Oklahoma Law Review, supra, at 843.

695 Supra, at 158.

3. The "magnitude of the act" test. This approach argues that the participating athlete consents to "reasonable" action on the part of another player, regardless of whether the conduct was within the scope of the rules,[696] or the consequences which follow from such conduct. The "reasonableness" standard appears to have been implicitly adopted in Maki dicta.[697] The judge maintained that a player does not consent to being viciously attacked with a hockey stick. The commission of such an act with a malicious intent is not, at least in the view of this judge, properly a "part of the game." He stated: "[A]ll players, when they step onto a playing field or ice surface, assume certain risks and hazards of the sport, and in most cases the defense of consent as set out in s.230 of the Criminal Code would be applicable. But...there is a question of degree involved, and no athlete should be presumed to accept malicious, unprovoked or overly violent attack." In People v. Fitzsimmons,[698] defendant Fitzsimmons struck and killed his sparring partner during an 1895 public boxing exhibition. The defendant claimed that he was engaged in a lawful contest of power and skill, and not in the misdemeanor forbidden by statute. The judge, in his final instructions to the jury, stated "that in any athletic contest, exhibiting powers of skill, there is necessarily involved an element of danger."[699]

The judge in the Fitzsimmons case clarified the consent issue by breaking it down into two questions for the jury to consider. The first was whether the deceased in fact consented to receive the blow and, second, whether a person may in fact legally consent to such a blow. He pointed out that a

---

[696] Though "rules of the game" advocates would argue that the rules are critical in defining reasonable conduct in this context.

[697] 14 D.L.R.3d at 167. It is only dicta because Maki was acquitted not as a result of his consent defense but because his act was considered to be in self-defense.

[698] 34 N.Y.S. 1102 (1895).

[699] Criminal Law Quarterly, supra, at 442-43.

football team may now lawfully engage in a game, "...with the idea that the result may terminate in the death or serious injury of one-half of them; but...the practices of the game are reasonable, are consented to by all engaged, are not likely to induce serious injury, or to end life, if then, as a result of the game, an accident happens, it is excusable homicide...and the defendant is presumed...to intend the ordinary and probable consequences of his acts."

4. The "magnitude of the harm" test. This approach argues that the participating athlete consents only to acts during a game which have no potential for serious bodily harm; all others are actionable. The English Courts generally employ this test. In the earliest English case, R. v. Coney,[700] Judge Stephen stated in 1882 that, "in cases where life and limb are exposed to no serious danger in the common course of things, I think that consent is a defense to a charge of assault, even when considerable force is used, as, for instance, in cases of wrestling, single-stick, sparring with gloves, football, and the like; but in all cases the question whether consent does or does not take from the application of force to another its illegal character, is a question of degree depending upon circumstances." Courts considering assaults in athletic contests ruled that defendants who acted in a manner that was intended or was likely to cause serious injury to another would lack a valid consent defense and would be guilty of assault.[701] The definition of "serious injury" was open to question, however. The 1934 English case of R. v. Donovan[702] developed an extremely broad definition of

---

[700] 8 Q.B.D. 534, 549 (1882).

[701] Michigan Law Review, supra, at 171.

[702] 2 L.B. 498 (1934).

"serious injury," holding that consent would not be a defense to blows intended to interfere with the health or comfort of the victim in more than a transient or trifling way.

Case law in many jurisdictions[703] has adopted much of the English approach that determines the nature of the consent from the seriousness of the injury. Prosecutor Flakne noted that the Minnesota case law governing Forbes provided that "when great bodily harm or death results, consent is not a viable defense."[704] In fact, where the assaultive behavior has resulted in death, the defense of consent has never been invoked successfully. Thus, where a suicide pact was carried out and one of the participants lived, the survivor was charged with murder.[705]

There are a number of problems with the "magnitude of the harm" test. First, the standard requires a player, not motivated by any malicious intent, to evaluate at his own peril the dangerousness of any act before undertaking it. Making the players accountable in this way would probably reduce the frequency of serious injury; however, it could alter drastically the manner in which games are played. "Having competitive, vigorous contact games may well be incompatible with asking players continuously to evaluate the harmful potential of their conduct."[706] Second, the vagueness of the serious injury test makes it susceptible to overly broad interpreta-

---

[703] Commonwealth v. Farrell, 322 Mass. 606, 78 N.E.2d 697 (1948); People v. Lenti, 44 Misc.2d 118, 253 N.Y.S.2d 9 (1964).

[704] Survey response to Question I(6)(3). Received December 4, 1978.

[705] R. v. Alison, 8 Car. and P. 418, 175 E.R. 557 (1838). Flakne and Caplan, Trial, supra, at 35.

[706] Michigan Law Review, supra, at 176.

tion "wholly unrealistic in the context of contemporary sports."[707] For example, if "serious injury" were defined as it was in Donovan, the consent defense would become inapplicable to common practices in most contact sports because contact sports involve the risk of broken bones and other injuries clearly more than "transient or trifling." Third, the "magnitude of the harm" test may not reflect reality in that players may, in fact, willingly entertain the threat of serious injury as "part of the game." While no one "consents" to a serious injury, the problem becomes significant in a case such as New England Patriot Darryl Stingley's, where he sustained a paralyzing injury from contact within the scope of the rules.[708] Flakne notes that, "as a practical matter in contemporary body contact sports, the risk of broken bones and other types of serious injuries is ever present."[709] Hence, a "magnitude of harm" standard may effectively eliminate the consent defense.

5. The "forseeability" test. This approach suggests that the injured player consents only to those acts (test three) or harms (test four) which

---

707 American Criminal Law Review, supra, at 243-44. The article notes that this vagueness can be corrected. It advocates limiting the definition of serious injury to death or maiming. "This will provide athletes with notice of what type of behavior will cause the intervention of the criminal law, reduce the likelihood that prosecutorial discretion will be influenced by extraneous factors, and allow behavior common to a sport to be protected although it may pose a threat of minor injury." Supra, at 247.

708 Stingley was injured and left essentially paralyzed from the neck down in a collision with Oakland safety Jack Tatum last August 12. Though Oakland D.A. Jensen noted that "consensus from the media was that Tatum was not at fault" (see note 530, infra), the Washington Post notes that Stingley is considering suit against the rule structure of the league itself for permitting such contact. "Stingley Weighs Suit Against NFL," Washington Post (February 9, 1979). If such a suit were successful, Attorney Nick Buoniconti predicted that it might "condemn football for good." Personal interview (see note 69, infra).

709 Flakne and Caplan, Trial, supra, at 35.

were reasonably forseeable when he entered the game. This is the position adopted by the drafters of the Proposed Federal Criminal Code (PFCC)[710] and the Model Penal Code.[711] The PFCC Working Papers suggest that the goal of their standard is to "specifically provide a defense to criminal prosecution whenever the injury inflicted or risked is a 'reasonably forseeable hazard' of a sports competition...."[712]

However, this test may not be the definitive solution to the problem. Most importantly, because of the pressures described in Chapter I, a "non-violent" athlete might enter a game knowing the potential harms, yet be powerless to do anything about it. Surely, he cannot be deemed to have "consented" to exceptional violence just because he is able to "forsee" it. For example, one commentator notes that "because of its commercial nature, professional football is not the same game it was in years past."[713] The

---

[710] §1619. Consent as a Defense.

(1) When a Defense. When conduct is an offense because it causes or threatens bodily injury, consent to such conduct or to the infliction of such injury by all persons injured or threatened by the conduct is a defense if

....

(b) the conduct and the injury are reasonably foreseeable hazards of joint participation in a lawful athletic contest or competitive sport.

Final Report of the Natl. Commn. on Reform of Federal Criminal Laws, §1619, at 182 (1971).

[711] (2) Consent to Bodily Harm. When conduct is charged to constitute an offense because it causes or threatens bodily harm, consent to such conduct or to the infliction of such harm is a defense if:

....

(b) the conduct and the harm are reasonably forseeable hazards of joint participation in a lawful athletic contest or competitive sport....

Model Penal Code, §2.11(2)(b). It is difficult, however, to understand why the provisions require that both the conduct and the harm be forseeable. If the defendant's conduct was reasonably forseeable, it would seem undesirable to assert that the injured party's consent did not extend this far simply because the forseeable conduct resulted in an unforseeable injury, such as a fluke injury resulting from a legitimate tackle. Michigan Law Review, supra, at 158.

[712] 2 Working Papers of the Natl. Commn. on Reform of Federal Criminal Laws 851 (1970).

[713] Schuett, Nebraska Law Review, supra, at 1132.

Hackbart court began its analysis by stating that "this case must be considered in the context of football as a commercial enterprise."[714] As one note has stated:

> The type of conduct that a participant can reasonably expect to occur in some of today's professional sports markedly differs from the type of conduct he could have reasonably expected in the days when the participants played for the love of the game. At that time there was not the strong motivation to win that exists in professional sports today. A participant could expect that fellow players would conduct themselves in a manner that was in keeping with the letter and the spirit of the rules. Today, the economic rewards or losses from winning or losing encourage players to adopt the attitude that one must do almost anything to win. 715

Thus, the fact that a player enters a game dominated by violent behavior does not necessarily mean that he consents to it.[716] The American Criminal Law Review reaches the same conclusion using different terminology. The author argues that, "even if consent were recognized as a possible defense to hockey assaults, a victim might argue that there was no valid consent in fact because it was obtained under duress" created by social custom rather than force.[717] "Duress might apply to hockey fights because it has been argued that in modern hockey players are forced to fight when challenged or risk being branded as cowards by both their peers and spectators. If a court adopted this view of duress, it could negate the consent as a defense, sub-

---

714
435 F.Supp. at 354.

715
Michigan Law Review, supra, at 159.

716
There is precedent for the proposition that consent to certain conduct when engaged in with a particular intent or purpose is not consent to the same acts carried out with a different intent or purpose. See Agar v. Canning (1965) 54 W.W.R. (n.s.) 302, 304 (Q.B.) (Man.), affd., (1966) 55 W.W.R. (n.s.) 384 (C.A.).

717
A situation similar to that described in early English "dueling" cases.

jecting the defendant to criminal sanctions."[718] The Michigan Law Review argues that the "forseeability" approach would be an appropriate standard if coupled with the element of "malicious intent": "There are certain kinds of conduct that a player expects to take place and that society chooses not to punish. Yet if this same conduct is undertaken with a malicious intent it is better to criminalize the conduct. For example, it is certainly foreseeable that a batter in baseball may be hit by a pitch. However, if a pitcher, motivated by a malicious desire to injure, intentionally hits a batter and causes serious harm, the pitcher should be criminally liable."[719]

6. "Effectiveness of consent" test. Case law in many jurisdictions suggests that even if a victim actually consents to the infliction of harm, his consent is not "effective" because he is powerless to waive the interests that the state has in controlling serious crime.[720] The argument implies that in a criminal case, the state may possess interests, for instance, the preservation of healthy citizens, that are stronger than the individual's own interests in being free to allow any intrusions that he wishes (i.e., to give effective consent). Although an individual can waive his own interests, he cannot waive those of the state.[721] In the Forbes case, the State requested and was granted an instruction that, with respect to the crime of aggravated assault, one cannot consent either expressly or by implication to

---

[718] Supra, at 245.

[719] Michigan Law Review, supra, at 175.

[720] For this reason, some suggest that the consent defense is more readily available in civil actions. Judge Hawkins stated in R. v. Coney, supra, that, "It may be that consent in all cases be given so as to operate as a bar to a civil action; upon the ground that no man can claim damages for an act to which he himself was an assaulting party." But one cannot contract the rights of the state away. Criminal Law Quarterly, supra, at 446.

[721] Michigan Law Review, supra, at 162.

be a victim of the crime. In his memorandum justifying such a request, Prosecutor Flakne relied upon State v. Fransua,[722] where the court stated: "Whether or not the victims of crimes have so little regard for their own safety as to request injury, the public has a stronger and overriding interest in preventing and prohibiting acts such as these, we hold that consent is not a defense to the crime of aggravated battery...irrespective of whether the victim invites the act and consents to the battery."

Of course, if the state's interest were to predominate in every class of crimes, there could be no consent defense in criminal law. This defense, therefore, is effective only if its existence sufficiently satisfies the state's interests in making the conduct criminal.[723] Assault during a sporting event appears to be in the class of crimes where consent may be "ineffective." Factor one in Chapter III emphasizes the societal harms to uncontrolled sports violence beyond any injury to a single participant.[724] Hence,

---

722
510 P.2d 106 (Ct.App.N.M. 1973).

723
If the predominant state interest is, for example, protecting the individual from unwanted acts that cause the individual harm, the consent of the "victim" should be a complete defense. Accordingly, consent is a complete defense in prosecutions for rape or larceny, since giving it "destroys the otherwise antisocial character of the accused's act." On the other hand, if making an act criminal is intended to protect society rather than individuals, consent is irrelevant, as in the case of treason and tax evasion.

Between these two classes of offenses lies a third category where the interest in protecting individuals against harm-causing acts is accompanied by a state interest in prohibiting antisocial behavior. The victim can consent and thereby satisfy the state's interest in protecting individuals from unwanted intrusions. His consent, however, cannot satisfy any other interests of the state. Thus, the question in this type of crime is whether the particular conduct so infringes these other societal interests that the perpetrator should be punished, notwithstanding the victim's consent. Michigan Law Review, supra, at 163.

724
Spectator violence; negative influence on children; societal violence. See text surrounding notes 478-490, infra.

if the victim consents, the state interests in preventing unwanted intrusions is satisfied, but the interest in protecting the well-being of society's members might not be met and, accordingly, the victim's consent might not be effective.[725]

7. An attempt at consensus: which specific acts are "consented to" in hockey and football? The six diverse approaches are at least an attempt in the right direction away from decisional ambiguity. However, given the problems with each respective "test," it is appropriate to explore the court holdings and commentator conclusions with respect to the specific types of sports violence.

In hockey, the Green court emphasized that, "No hockey player enters

---

725 There are two problems with placing "sports violence" cases in the class of crimes where consent is ineffective. First, the "social utility" of sport may outweigh any "societal harms to uncontrolled sports violence" such that consent should operate to provide implicit immunity in most cases. Second, there is some support for the position that the individual's right to make informed decisions causing harm only to himself is inviolable (see, e.g., People v. Smallwood, 52 Misc.2d 1027, 277 N.Y.S.2d 429 (Ct. Spec.Sess. 1967). Some courts, rather than defining the interest as a "societal right to protect its citizens," pose the problem in "breach of the peace" terms. This was the position taken by the Maryland Court of Appeals in Taylor v. State, 214 Md. 156, 159; 133 A.2d 414, 415 (1957). The Court noted that, "A criminal assault which tends to bring about a breach of the public peace is treated as a crime against the public generally, and therefore the consent of the victim is no defense. On the other hand, a criminal assault which is not accompanied by the threat of serious hurt or breach of public peace is treated as a crime against the person, and the consent of the person assaulted is held to be a good defense..." An Ontario Appellate Court agreed in R. v. Gillin (1948), 93 C.C.C. 1, 7 C.R. 103 (Ont.C.A.), affd 94 C.C.C. 337 (1949) S.C.R. 658, holding that a player's consent to participate in the sport cannot take away the basic criminal nature of the act as the consent can in no way affect the rights of the public, and as the assault was a breach of the peace the consent of the person struck is immaterial.

onto the ice of the National Hockey League without consenting to and without knowledge of the possibility that hs is going to be hit in one of many ways once he is on that ice."[726] The key, therefore, is finding the line where consent ends and criminal liability begins. Normal "incidental" contact which is "truly" part of the game has been held to be consented to. An example is the Green case itself, where Boston Bruin Ted Green was charged with assault for hitting "Maki with his glove" before Maki felled Green with his stick.[727] In acquitting Green, the judge stated that, "I think within our experience we can come to the conclusion that this is an extremely ordinary happening in a hockey game and the players really think nothing of it. If you go behind the net of a defenceman, particularly one who is trying to defend his zone, and you are struck in the face by that player's glove, a penalty might be called against him, but you do not really think anything of it; it is one of the types of risk one assumes."[728] One case even suggests that "a normal hockey fistfight" may be consented to, given the frequency with which they occur. In R. v. Starratt,[729] the Ontario Court of Appeals indicated that the force of a fight "does not exceed that authorized by the other player." However, if, for example, a player "deliberately cross-checks [another player] across the mouth area breaking his nose,"[73] this would seem to go beyond the spirit of Starratt. The Criminal Law Quarterly attempts to "draw the line" in the hockey context:

---

[726] 16 D.L.R.3d 137, at 140.

[727] The incident is more fully described in text surrounding notes 77-82, infra.

[728] Id.

[729] (1972), S.C.C.C.2d 32, (1972) 1 Q.R. 32 (C.A.).

[730] An example given by an NHL player of something that he "would not consent to." Confidential survey received February 15, 1979.

> Though no athlete could be presumed to consent to being violently attacked during the course of a game, no hockey player enters onto National Hockey League ice without the knowledge that he may soon be hit. He accepts it as an inherent risk, and consents to his being assaulted by participation in the contest. Unprovoked savage attacks resulting in serious injury appear to be the only level of violence that may be subject to prosecution. [731]

The "savage attack" that seems to meet universal hockey condemnation is stickswinging. Chapter I notes that this may indeed be the only "on the ice" act that is considered "illegal" by the hockey establishment.[732] In the _Maki_ stickswinging prosecution, the judge acquitted Maki based on self-defense. However, he found the consent defense inapplicable to stickswinging, stating that "no athlete should be presumed to accept malicious, unprovoked, or overly violent attack."[733] No attempt was made to define "overly violent attack" because the violent nature of stickswinging was not seriously disputed. The _Criminal Law Quarterly_ agrees, arguing that, "There is no doubt as to the high degree of harm that can result from one player assaulting another with a razor-sharp hockey stick. Clearly, this is significant force which goes beyond that to which any player would willingly consent."[734] In fact, the one factor that makes an attack in hockey appear criminal, according to NHLPA Managing Officer Simpson, is that "all of the players have dangerous weapons in their hands."[735]

---

[731] _Supra_, at 430-31.

[732] See text surrounding notes 81-84, _infra_. In fact, "normal hockey brawling etiquette calls for the discarding of the weapon before a fight..." Flakne and Caplan, Trial, _supra_ at 34-35.

[733] 10 C.R.N.S. at 272.

[734] _Supra_, at 432.

[735] Telephone interview to NHLPA office, Toronto, Canada. (January 11, 1979)

In football, as in hockey, the "criminal liability line" is difficult to draw. Former All-Pro defensive tackle Alan Page explains: "If there is an invisible line on the playing field which you might cross and then be subject to prosecution, it is a very fine line. Professional football is basically a game of violence, and it is condoned; it's part of the game. Placing that line to halt unnecessary violence is going to be difficult." Page continued that, "if violence were ever to get out of hand, I think you would have to prosecute...because even though it's a game that you do voluntarily, I don't think you consent to [aggravated assault]."[736] "Incidental" contact such as an exceptionally violent tackle or block seems to be consented to. Perkins elaborates: "The violent tackle which wins applause on the football field would be a battery if practiced on an unwilling citizen on the street. This is because the player by entering the contest consents to such physical contact as is properly incident to the game."[737] For example, former star linebacker Nick Buoniconti suggests that "all wide receivers take the chance that they'll be 'clotheslined' coming across the middle; but everyone assumes it's a normal occupational hazard."[738]

However, there are certain acts which are not consented to. When the "clotheslining" coming across the middle of the field is coupled with a forearm blow to the head, players refer to it as a "cheap shot." Receiver Lynn Swann, hit in such a fashion by Oakland Raider George Atkinson in the 1975 AFC Championship Game, remarked that, "I almost retired from football after

---

[736] Criminal Law Quarterly, supra, at 439.

[737] R. Perkins, Criminal Law 109 (2d ed. 1969).

[738] Personal interview. (See note 69, infra.)

that season. It wasn't the intimidation, it was the unnecessary brutality. I couldn't see playing a game and risking my life."[739] Similarly, football players cannot be held to have consented to contact after the whistle signals an end to the play. In Hackbart, the complainant was hit in the back after the play had ended. In that case, Dale "Hackbart would not reasonably expect to experience forcible contact when the action on his end of the field had ceased."[740] In commenting upon the incident, the District Court judge seemed to have expanded the notion of consent in this context, suggesting that, "[t]he record...reflects that what he did is, unfortunately an example of the excesses of violence which have become expectable as a result of the style of play in the NFL." Even if such conduct is expectable, it does not necessarily follow that it should be tolerable, nor can it be said that consent to such conduct exists in every case.[741] The Criminal Law Quarterly agrees that "late hits" are not consented to: "Where a player makes a tackle after the official has whistled the play to stop, he may be acting outside of the rules of the game to the extent that his conduct may make him criminally liable. Surely, no player consents to late hits particularly when they are calculated to do him great bodily injury which may shorten his life."[742] Finally, one author argues that an exceptionally severe clip cannot be consented to even if it occurs before the whistle ends play: "A football player, by the fact of his participation, apparently

---

739 Marantz, Boston Globe (January 18, 1979), supra.

740 Schuett, Nebraska Law Review, supra, at 1134.

741 435 F.Supp. at 357.

742 Supra, at 437.

consents to the normal intentional contact incident to the game but does not consent to an intentional 'clip' which is a violation of a rule designed primarily to protect players from serious harm."[743]

In conclusion, the defense of player consent, through willing participation in the game, stands as the legal barrier to prosecution under these statutes. Otherwise there would be no contact sports. However, when a player crosses that invisible line and intentionally inflicts injury that no player would consent to, he must be held criminally liable.[744] The previous seven sections have attempted to clarify where this line has been, and should be, drawn.

C. The "Assumption of the Risk" Defense.

Technically, assumption of risk means that the plaintiff, in advance, has given his consent to relieve the defendant of an obligation toward him, and to take his chances of injury from a known risk arising from what the defendant is to do or leave undone.[745] Though traditionally employed only as a defense to civil liability,[746] the doctrine has heretofore been implicitly applied in criminal matters as well. Oakland District Attorney Jensen remarked that "assumption of risk is a civil issue, not a criminal [one], but in a pragmatic sense any reasonable jury would include this issue in

---

743 Missouri Law Review, supra, at 349.

744 Criminal Law Quarterly, supra, at 433.

745 W. Prosser, Handbook of the Law of Torts, §68 (4th ed. 1971).

746 In the Forbes case, for example, the defense had requested and was denied an instruction on the assumption of risk by virtue of its sole applicability to civil law. Flakne and Caplan, Trial, supra, at 34.

their thinking."[747]

In most respects, this doctrine is similar to the consent defense. Hence, in most jurisdictions, the case law and policy arguments presented in Chapter IV, §B, will be appropriate concerning "assumption of risk"[748] as well. However, there are some differences. The *Second Restatement of Torts* differentiates the two defenses by indicating that assumption of the risk is consent to conduct which is merely negligent, whereas consent is used in reference to conduct which is *intended* to invade the interests of the plaintiff.[749]

In applicable jurisdictions, the question of whether the injured participant "assumed the risk" of violent contact frequently dominates the entire case. An injury that gives rise to litigation is likely to be extremely serious, so that it can be argued that it was not one of the risks inherently involved in the game; it was an extraordinary risk. Even if it is accepted as an inherent risk, the matter of the player's knowledge

---

[747] Survey response to Question I(6)(3). Received December 6, 1978.

[748] In some jurisdictions where the assumption of risk defense is applied only in limited instances, the defense used in the remaining instances is *volenti non fit injuria*. *Wood v. Postlethwaite*, 6 Wash.App. 885, 496 P.2d 988, 992 (1972). There is no distinction between the principles underlying this defense and those underlying the defense of assumption of risk, as both defenses require knowledge and appreciation of danger and a voluntary exposure thereto. *Bailey v. Safeway Stores, Inc.*, 55 Wash.2d 728, 349 P.2d 1077, 1078-79 (1960). University of Missouri-Kansas City Law Review, *supra*, at 1212.

[749] §50, comment 6 at 86 (1965). With respect to injuries caused by the intentional conduct of others, it seems proper to speak in terms of consent; with respect to injuries caused by the unintentional or inadvertent conduct of others, it seems proper to speak in terms of assumption of risk. Some courts have considered the entire problem as one of assumption of risk: "Generally, the participants in an athletic event are held to have assumed the risks of injury normally associated with that sport." *McGee v. Board of Education*, 226 N.Y.S.2d 329, 331, 16 App.Div.2d 99, 101 (1962). Michigan Law Review, *supra*, at 156.

concerning the risk is still of the utmost importance.[750] Since the defense is so important, it is appropriate to analyze it on a general level.

Assumption of the risk takes two forms in sporting events. When the plaintiff voluntarily enters into a game knowing and appreciating the risks involved in the sport he is deemed to *impliedly* agree to relieve the defendant of his duty to the plaintiff.[751] In effect, the defendant is granted an immunity from liability. This form of assumption of the risk is most commonly encountered in the cases and is referred to as *implied* assumption of the risk. The other form of assumption of the risk is where the plaintiff is aware of and voluntarily encounters a risk created by the existing negligence of the defendant. In both forms a subjective test is used to determine whether the plaintiff knows and appreciates the risk, but his testimony on this matter will not be conclusive.[752] As with the consent defense, early decisions attempted to distinguish between injuries that are an expected part of the game and those that would not ordinarily be anticipated to result from

---

750
7 Am Jur Trials, *supra*, at 219. In fact, the *Am Jur Trials* sample defense opening in a sports violence case makes "assumption of risk" the focal point of the attorney's strategy. For example, the following passage appears, in similar form, four times in a four page opening statement:

> Plaintiff fully knew the nature of the game of football; he knew it was a strenuous bodily contact sport; he knew persons playing the game might be injured, and in the game he could expect to tackle and be tackled. He knew that he might be one of those injured, and injury could involve broken bones, including the vertebrae. Knowing all these things, plaintiff willingly and gladly played football. *Id.*, at 257.

751
*Restatement (Second) of Torts*, §496C (1965).

752
*Crane v. Kansas City Baseball Co.*, 168 Mo.App. 301, 153 S.W. 1076 (K.C. Mo.App. 1913).

engaging in athletic competition.[753] Generally a participant in a lawful game or contest assumes the dangers inherent in that game or contest with consequent preclusion from recovery for injury or death resulting therefrom. But he does not assume the risk of injury resulting from negligence, though, of course, he may be precluded from recovering because of his own contributory negligence. Nor does the voluntary participant assume the extraordinary risks of the game or contest unless he knew of them and voluntarily assented to them.[754] The difficulty of ascertaining "what risks an athlete assumes" is as large a problem as it is with the consent defense.[755] The *Missouri Law Review* correctly notes that prior case law and attempts at codification "merely establish labels which are used to support the court's ultimate decision that the particular risk has or has not been assumed by the plaintiff. No analysis is supplied to guide future decisions. Thus, a case by case approach is necessary to determine what risks are 'forseeable' or are 'inherent' or 'ordinarily incident' to that sport."[756]

---

753 See, e.g., *Tavernier v. Maes*, 242 Cal.App.2d 532, 51 Cal.Rptr. 575 (1966) (baserunner sliding into fielder at base); *Benedetto v. Travelers Ins. Co.*, 172 So.2d 354 (La.App. 1965) (injuries sustained when bat slipped from defendant's hands); *McGee v. Board of Educ.* 16 A.D.2d 99, 226 N.Y.S.2d 329 (1962) (teacher helping with baseball practice hit by ball); *Gordon v. Deer Park School Dist. No. 414*, 71 Wash.2d 119, 426 P.2d 824 (1967) (involving injuries sustained when bat slipped from defendant's hands). Schuett, Nebraska Law Review, *supra*, at 1131.

754 "Liability for Injury to or Death of Participant in Game or Contest," 7 *American Law Reports* 2d 704, 706.

755 Ed Garvey, NFLPA Executive Director calls the "line drawing" problem "the major reason why legal controls don't work in this area." Personal interview (see note 152, *infra*.).

756 *Supra*, at 351. One commentator attempted to develop a list of "determinants" which would help to assess the vitality of the "assumption of risk" defense in each case. His list includes the following: the rules and customs

Realizing that a case by case approach may be "the law" in this area, it is appropriate to discuss the "assumption of risk" cases which represent the most significant precedent in each respective sport.

In football, the watershed case is Hackbart v. Cincinnati Bengals, Inc.[757] decided in 1977 by the Federal District Court of Colorado. On September 16, 1973, the Cincinnati Bengals were playing the Denver Broncos in Denver. Plaintiff Dale Hackbart, a thirteen-year veteran playing free safety for the Broncos, was covering the defendant Charles "Booby" Clark, a first-year fullback for the Bengals, who had gone out for a forward pass. The pass was intercepted by another Denver player who began to run the ball upfield. Hackbart tried to block Clark and fell. While Hackbart, who was resting on one knee, watched the play move upfield, Clark approached him from behind and struck him with a forearm to the back of the head. There was no apparent provocation for the attack other than frustration at the outcome of the play. The force of the blow knocked both players to the ground. Although a specific NFL rule prohibits the striking of an opponent's head or neck with the forearm, elbow, or hand, Clark was not penalized or disqualified because the game officials did not observe the contact. Hackbart and Clark went to the sidelines and both played the rest of the game. Hackbart later began to feel pain, but did not report the injury to a doctor until after he had played two more games and had been released by the Broncos. The painful condition

---

of the game, the specific game involved, the ages and physical attributes of the participants, their respective skills at the game and their knowledge of its rules and customs, their status as amateurs or professionals, the type of risks which inhere in the game and those which are outside the realm of reasonable anticipation, the presence or absence of protective uniforms or equipment, the degree of zest with which the game is being played, "and doubtless others." Georgia Law Review, supra, at 385.

[757] 435 F.Supp. 352.

was later diagnosed as a neck injury.[758] The Court held that a professional football player is not bound by a duty of care for the safety of other players. Further, even if such a duty of care existed, consent and assumption of the risk are valid defenses to allegations of reckless misconduct or negligence and would preclude recovery. Liability could not be imposed because Hackbart had assumed the risk of the injury he had suffered. The court found neither Clark nor the Bengals liable to Hackbart for any damages incurred due to the injury.[759] In holding that "assumption of the risk" precluded liability in this context, the Court noted that, "[t]he level of violence and the frequency of emotional outbursts in NFL football games are such that Dale Hackbart must have recognized and accepted the risk that he would be injured by such an act as that committed by the defendant...."[760] The holding in <u>Hackbart</u> has been strongly criticized in recent publications. First, assumption of the risk requires that the party have knowledge of the risk that he assumes. Although players obviously are aware of the risk of injury resulting from play among professional football players, it is "incongruous to suppose knowledge or expectation of gratuitous violence unrelated to the progress of the game."[761] Second, one of the essential requirements of this defense is that the plaintiff's choice to incur the risk be voluntary and that the plaintiff make some manifestation of his freely given consent.[762]

---

758 Capetta, Connecticut Law Review, <u>supra</u>, at 365-66.

759 The <u>Hackbart</u> decision was litigated solely on the issue of liability. The issues of causation and damages were reserved pending resolution of the liability issue. Because of the court's finding of no liability, the other issues were never litigated. <u>Id.</u>, at 373.

760 435 F.Supp. 352, 356.

761 Georgia Law Review, <u>supra</u>, at 389-90.

762 This argument is similar to the one made as a criticism to the "forseeability" approach to the consent defense. See text surrounding notes 713-718, <u>infra</u>.

A consideration which clearly indicates that a pro football player's choice to incur the risk may not be voluntary is the economic pressure exerted by a threatened loss of employment. The Connecticut Law Review notes that, "The pressure on players to maintain their jobs is obviously enough to force them to assume the risk of injury and to play with pain. The choice does not seem voluntary in that they would almost assuredly desire to play football and not be required to risk injury if that combination were available."[763] Third, the Court noted in dicta that "[t]he character of NFL competition negates any notion that the playing conduct can be circumscribed by any standard of reasonableness."[764] Some commentators have suggested that this statement is tantamount to giving NFL players a "free rein"[765] in continuing to play violently. One commentator emotionally argues that the Hackbart dicta "has in effect exempted professional football players and their teams from...liability under traditional concepts of...law for recklessly or negligently caused injuries."[766]

In hockey, the most influential "assumption of risk" case is Agar v. Canning[767], decided in 1965 by the Manitoba Queen's Bench. The plaintiff was struck by a hockey stick in the face. The court found the defendant liable despite evidence which proved provocation.[768] Though the court spoke in terms

---

763 Supra, at 372.

764 435 F.Supp. at 356.

765 Schuett, Nebraska Law Review, supra, at 1133.

766 Capetta, Connecticut Law Review, supra, at 365.

767 (1965) 54 W.W.R. 302 (Man.Q.B.) affd 55 W.W.R. 384 (C.A.).

768 See text surrounding notes 783-787, infra.

of risks "consented to," the issue presented to it was the validity of "assumption of the risk" in the hockey context. In its decision, the court relied on the following rationale: "Hockey necessarily involves violent bodily contact and blows from the puck and hockey sticks. A person who engages in this sport must be assumed to accept the risk of accidental harm and to waive any claim he would have apart from the game for...enjoying a corresponding immunity with respect to other players....But a little reflection will establish that some limit must be placed on a player's immunity from liability. Each case must be decided on its own facts so it is difficult, if not impossible, to decide how the line is to be drawn in every circumstance. But injuries inflicted in circumstances which show a definite resolve to cause serious injury to another, even when there is provocation and in the heat of the game, should not fall within the scope of implied consent. I have come to the conclusion that the act of the defendant in striking plaintiff in the face with a hockey stick, in retaliation for the blow he received, goes beyond the limit marking exemption from liability."[769]

In baseball, the leading case is <u>Bourque v. Duplechin</u>,[770] a 1976 Louisiana case. The case involved a softball game in which the participants were sponsored by business establishments. The plaintiff, a twenty-two year old second baseman, sued for negligence when a member of the opposing team, running from first to second base, deviated from the baseline to run into the plaintiff and in so doing, brought his arms up under the plaintiff's chin. The court found that the defendant "was under a duty to play softball in the

---

769 Agar, <u>supra</u>, at 304.

770 331 So.2d 40 (La.App. 1976).

ordinary fashion without unsportsmanlike conduct or wanton injury to his fellow players. This duty was breached by defendant, "whose behavior was, according to the evidence, substandard and negligent."[771] The court stated that the second baseman may have assumed the risk of being spiked while standing near the base, but did not assume the risk of contact that was so far away from the base as to be a violation of a duty to play the game in the ordinary manner.[772] Though the court's holding seems critical only for professional baseball, broad dicta in the case is applicable to all professional sports:

> A participant in a game or sport assumes all of the risks incidental to that particular activity which are obvious and forseeable. A participant does not assume the risk of injury from fellow players acting in an unexpected or unsportsmanlike way with a reckless lack of concern for others participating.[773]

In basketball, the noteworthy case is the 1965 Illnois case of <u>Griggas v. Clauson</u>.[774] An amateur basketball player brought suit when an opponent struck him in the head with his fist. The court, although mainly addressing whether the damages awarded were excessive, found the jury's verdict was supported by the weight of the testimony and affirmed a judgment for the plaintiff, despite an "assumption of risk" argument.

Finally, in <u>Nabozny v. Barnhill</u>,[775] the Illinois Appellate Court attempted to expand a "soccer violence" holding into one applicable to all sports.

---

771 Schuett, Nebraska Law Review, <u>supra</u>, at 1130.

772 Bourque, <u>supra</u>, at 42.

773 <u>Id.</u>, at 42.

774 6 Ill.App.2d 412, 128 N.E.2d 363 (1955).

775 31 Ill.App.3d 212, 334 N.E.2d 258 (1975).

During the course of the game, the defendant, a forward, kicked the plaintiff goalkeeper's head, causing severe injuries. The plaintiff had been within the penalty area at all times and the game was being played under organizational rules which prohibit contact with a goalkeeper who is in the penalty area and in possession of the ball.[776] The Nabozny court set out the following requirements for recovery for the type of risks assumed:

> [W]hen athletes are engaged in an athletic competition, all teams involved are coached by knowledgeable personnel, a recognized set of rules governs the conduct of the competition, and a safety rule is contained therein which is primarily designed to protect players from serious injury, a player is then charged with a legal duty to every other player on the field to refrain from conduct prosecribed by a safety rule.[777]

The court suggests that in a sporting event the risk of defendant's negligence can be assumed by the plaintiff in the proper circumstances but not the risk of defendant's recklessness.[778] In its opinion, the court intimated that the Nabozny rule should be applied broadly to all sports. It noted that, "We have carefully drawn the rule announced herein in order to control a new field of...litigation."[779] One commentator has criticized the Nabozny rule, suggesting that a rigid application could lead to "the overly simplistic rule that athletes assume the risk of injuries suffered during their participation in athletic contests of all kinds."[780]

---

776 Schuett, Nebraska Law Review, supra, at 1130.

777 Nabozny, supra, at 215.

778 Missouri Law Review, supra, at 353.

779 Trial Lawyer's Guide, supra, at 386.

780 Id., at 393.

In conclusion, the "assumption of the risk" defense is a confusing concept. This is especially true in the sports context, given (A) the unprincipled interchange of civil and criminal doctrine, and (B) the difficult line drawing problems. Some courts have perceived this problem. The Illinois Supreme Court explained that "[t]he expression 'assumption of risk' is a very confusing one. In application it conceals many policy issues and it is constantly used to beg the real question. Accurate analysis...would probably be advanced if the term were eradicated."[781] In fact, some jurisdictions have held the defense inapplicable to all sports injury cases.[782]

D. The "Provocation" Defense.

The argument that the defendant was "provoked into retaliation" may be unimportant in the professional sports violence context. First, many jurisdictions do not recognize the defense. In Agar v. Canning,[783] for example, Judge Bastin held that a "retaliatory blow, struck by the defendant in anger during the course of a hockey game, even though provoked by the plaintiff, went beyond the immunity conferred on players and was actionable."[784] Furthermore, provocation by words is rarely available as a defense absent some statutory authorization. Typically, Minnesota has no statutory authorization creating such a privileged use of force.[785] The common law basis for this

---

781 Barnett v. Fritz, 248 N.E.2d at 115 (1969).

782 See, e.g. Carey v. Toles, 7 Mich.App. 195, 151 N.W.2d 396 (1967).

783 See text surrounding note 768, infra.

784 Agar, supra, at 304.

785 Wisconsin Law Review, supra, at 774.

rule was the belief that peace and order are adversely affected when individuals take the law into their own hands to right their own wrongs.[786] Second, in those jurisdictions that do recognize the provocation defense, it is considered only in mitigation, not guilt or innocence.[787]

E. The "Involuntary Reflex" Defense.

This defense was successfully employed by Meshbesher in the Forbes case.[788] It argues that since athletes are trained "from age four" that violence is "part of the game," such violence is the product of an instinctive reflex action without the necessary mens rea.[789] There are good reasons for the success of this defense. First, as §A of this Chapter indicates, intent is a difficult element to prove in sports violence cases even without the "reflex" argument as a complicating factor. Second, Chapter

---

786 Criminal Law Quarterly, supra, at 453.

787 This is said to have been derived from Lord Abinger's statement in Fraser v. Berkeley, (1836), 7 Car. + P. 621, 173 E.R. 272, that: "The law I think would be an unwise law, if it did not make allowance for human infirmities; and if a person commit violence at a time when he is smarting under immediate provocation, that is a matter of mitigation."

788 Hallowell and Meshbesher, Trial, supra, at 29.

789 The Michigan Law Review states this defense partially in consent terms: "It appears that whenever a player's actions are closely related to the playing of the game (i.e., are 'part of the game'), his instinctive reactions should not expose him to liability. This result is consistent with the rationale for having 'part of the game' as the standard. In other words, if society wants the game to be played in a certain manner, society must accept certain unavoidable deviations such as instinctive reactions. As illustrated by these cases, one can determine that players' instinctive reactions are protected because either (1) players consent to the instinctive reactions of others, or (2) if the action were instinctive, the perpetrator lacks the requisite intent." Supra, at 162.

I(A)(5)[790] documents the argument that sports violence is taught and accepted by its participants as non-criminal at a very early age. Prosecutor Flakne noted that "during the course of the Forbes trial, it became apparent that a myriad of psychological and sociological pressures exist which are imbued at the earliest possible moment in the young athlete who engages in a body-contact sport. He is taught from the outset to intimidate his opponent and to precipitate physical altercations rather than to avoid them."[791] Allan Caplan, associate prosecutor in the Forbes case, suggested that the defense was prepared to elicit testimony from experts in the field of sports psychology to the effect that these athletes are "capable of only an involuntary response; that they are incapable of forming criminal intent."[792] Third, given the high pressured, emotional nature of the sports in question, the atmosphere is conducive to a player "losing control." In hockey, dicta in Agar v. Canning suggests that courts are aware of these pressures: "The conduct of a player in the heat of the game is instinctive and unpremeditated and should not be judged by standards suited to polite social intercourse."[793] In the Green case, the judge found that Green's swinging his stick at Maki was "instinctive" and that Green "had no intent to commit an assault."[794] In football, the Hackbart case[795] re-

---

[790] See text surrounding notes 109-121, infra.

[791] Flakne and Caplan, Trial, supra, at 34.

[792] Telephone interview with Allen Caplan; Hennepin County Attorney's Office, Minneapolis, Minnesota (January 12, 1979). Caplan noted that the defense was precluded from calling this expert as a witness, however,

[793] Agar, supra, at 304.

[794] 16 D.L.R.3d at 142.

[795] Described further in text surrounding notes 757-766, infra.

ferred to the "controlled rage" that each player is taught to cultivate. Augmenting this, in the court's opinion, were the emotional reactions from the crowd, the abrupt changes in relative position, and the physical shock of the violent contacts which created an atmosphere conducive to emotional outbursts.[796] Nick Buoniconti notes that a football player's reactions are "so instinctive that he usually doesn't think about what he's doing."[797]

This defense has not been limited only to the traditional "contact sports." In R. v. Leyte,[798] a handball player broke his opponent's nose during the course of a swing. In acquitting the defendant, the Ontario court maintained that, "Players of a competitive sports like handball are deemed to consent to the instinctive reactions of other players closely related to the play of the game. Bodily contacts arising from these instinctive reactions will not be declared assaults unless it can be demonstrated that the assaulting player's reaction was not a normal occurrence under the circumstances, and that the reaction was not during the game."[799]

The "involuntary reflex" defense has been employed successfully in a number of sports contexts. While Attorney Bob Woolf cynically states that the "heat of the game has always been a kind of moral defense in sports to

---

[796] Georgia Law Review, supra, at 388.

[797] Personal interview (see note 69, infra.).

[798] (1973), 13 C.C.C.2d 458 (Ont.Prov.Ct.Crim.Div.).

[799] Given the wide application of the defense, it seems that there would be little chance for liability. However, where there is a significant time interval between the termination of play and the blows struck, and where the players by their conduct have after the stoppage of play ceased to be aggressive to that their subsequent actions should no longer be instinctive, then the players cannot be deemed to consent to assaults at that stage. Michigan Law Review, supra, at 162.

excuse bad manner and irrational acts,"[800] the defense is nevertheless a viable one.

F. Self Defense.

A gamesman acting in self-defense to ward off an unlawful attack is not guilty of assault or battery. The rule that a person who finds himself assaulted may answer the force with force was fashioned to protect a victim from injury for as long as the apparent danger is present.[801] In R. v. Maki[802] and R. v. Green,[803] both defendants were acquitted on the basis of self-defense. The Green trial judge stated in his oral opinion that "the blow struck by Mr. Green was struck almost immediately after the blow--the much more serious blow in my opinion, the spearing--which had been struck at him by Mr. Maki. I do not think that Mr. Green was doing anything more in the circumstances than protecting himself."

However, in most cases, self defense cannot be relied upon by the defendant. First, the defendant is limited to force roughly equal to that used toward him. The force used in self defense must be no greater than was reasonably necessary to accomplish the lawful purpose of self-protection. Self-defense is not proper if the blow was unnecessarily severe and vindictive ra-

---

[800] Woolf, Behind Closed Doors, supra, at 141.

[801] Criminal Law Quarterly, supra, at 450.

[802] (1970) 14 D.L.R.3d 164 (Prov.Ct.). See text surrounding notes 77-82, infra.

[803] (1970) 16 D.L.R.3d 137 (Prov.Ct.).

ther than preventitive,[804] and the use of excessive force may constitute an assault, if it goes beyond the "necessary for the purpose" test.[805] Hence, in cases where the retaliatory response is so much more severe than the initial incident (Forbes' reaction to Boucha's contact, for example[806]), self defense is not applicable. Furthermore, if dicta in Hackbart is to be believed[807] self defense is inapplicable to football as well.

The second reason for the limited force of self defense is that the rule requires the absence of provocation on the defendant's part; the actual and honest belief that he was about to be placed in immediate danger of death, or great bodily harm, necessitating his action and the existence of reasonable grounds for the defendant's fears.[808] In this context, the problem is one of proof. Since subjective intent must be explored, the same "intent" problems prevail as those discussed in §A of this Chapter.

Third, the "self defending" athlete may use force only when retreating or avoiding the danger is unreasonable. Hence, when a player has the "option" of walking away from a fight, self defense will not excuse him if he chooses to "stand up" to the opponent.[809]

---

804 R. v. Kinman (1911), 18 C.C.C. 139, 16 B.C.R. 148 (C.A.); Nykolyn v. The King (1949), 94 C.C.C. 145, 8 C.R. 7 (1949) S.C.R. 392.

805 Criminal Law Quarterly, supra, at 429-30.

806 Associate Prosecutor Caplan suggested that the Forbes scenario was "the best set of facts you could have for the prosecution." (Telephone interview. See note 792, infra.) For a factual description of the case, see text surrounding notes 642-647, infra.

807 Professional football is a "commercial enterprise" whose most distinguishing feature is "violent physical behavior" accompanied by "reckless abandonment of self-protective instincts." Hackbart, supra.

808 Criminal Law Quarterly, supra, at 451.

809 It would be interesting to explore how a court would analyze McMurtry's argument that a player is "socially required" to stand his ground and fight or

G. The "Social Utility" Defense.

This argument suggests that since the sport performs a vital function in society, a "limited immunity" should be accorded its participants. The Michigan Law Review advocates this theory under the German name "Sozialadaquanz." This approach recognizes that if society wants the game to be played in a certain way, it must tolerate certain harms. It follows that if society does not choose to accept these harms, it may demand that the game be played in a different way. Thus, if a player possesses an attitude consistent with the ideal of the game, then any injury he causes his opponent while playing is justified, and the player whose conduct caused the injury would have a defense.[810] The theory continues that without this protection the fear of criminal liability might deter individuals from engaging in ac-

face rejection from teammates, opponents, coaches, and spectators. Hence, it might be argued that retreat would be "unreasonable" in this context.

810 Michigan Law Review, supra, at 177. The note explains its theory in the context of what is or is not "part of the game." It suggests that, "as a general matter, members of society must tolerate certain inconveniences to sustain a modicum of social order. Similarly, the athlete is a member of a smaller society or 'the game,' and he is expected to suffer certain inconveniences (injuries) so that the game may be played. The game, however, is a part of the larger society, and it must necessarily conform to the standards of that society...Any player's conduct that is not consistent with society's notions of how the game should be played should not be considered 'part of the game.' Thus, this concept can serve as a standard for defining the scope of a participant's consent: An athlete consents only to that conduct which is part of the game. Such an approach is in accord with the notion of Sozialadaquanz. The athlete who participates in the game must tolerate certain inconveniences or injuries so that the game may be played in the manner that society demands or allows it be played...foreseeability approach is undesirable, 'part of the game' should be understood as including only conduct that either is consonant with the ideal of the game or is an unavoidable concomitant of playing the game with an attitude that is consistent with society's standards as to how the game should be played should not be a part of the game."

tivities that produce benefits which outweigh their harmful effects.[811] The Michigan Law Review provides a football-related example: "To hold the tackler strictly accountable for such conduct would prevent football from being played with the vigor society desires. On the other hand, if requiring the player to consider the results of his acts will not change the way the game is played, then society may properly hold the player criminally responsible."[812]

The critical component of this theory, therefore, is the analysis of whether the benefits to society from sports outweigh the societal interest in protecting persons from the intentional infliction of injuries. This issue was first explored in the context of whether a given sport was "lawful" or not. An 1876 case, Commonwealth v. Collberg,[813] used such reasoning to declare the sport of boxing illegal and, therefore, its participants guilty of assault regardless of any defenses they may have had. However, the concept of professional sport has changed dramatically in the 103 years

---

[811] American Criminal Law Review, supra, at 237.

[812] Supra, at 177. Some commentators have phrased this theory in terms of "consent." The Nebraska Law Review, supra, at 1135, notes that, "One possible reason why consent has been deemed effective more frequently in sports than in other contexts is that athletic events have beneficial aspects that justify society's toleration of certain injuries."

[813] 119 Mass. 350 (1876). "The common law recognizes as not necessarily unlawful, certain manly sports calculated to give bodily strength, skill and activity, and 'to fit in time of need.' Playing at cudgels or foils, or wrestling by consent, there being no motive to do bodily harm on either part, are said to be exercises of this description...But prize fighting, boxing matches, and encounters of peace, and are unlawful when entered into by agreement and without anger or mutual ill will....If one party license another to beat him, such license is void because it is against the law." Id., at 353.

since Collberg.[814] One commentator, discussing sport in another context, nevertheless notes that, "Sports and sports teams serve an important function in the community: spectator sports provide recreation and relaxation in a unique combination of theatre and amusement. Identification with a particular city's team can be a bond that cuts through traditional social barriers such as race and social status. A successful sports franchise can benefit the overall community, both socially and economically through the unity that it provides, and the commerce that it attracts." Another commentator argues that professional sporting events "add texture to the monotonous routines of daily living and a sense of community identity to our increasingly mechanized, mobile, and fragmented society."[815] It cannot be denied that sports performs somewhat of a "vital societal function."

However, the argument that the value of sport should mean criminal immunity for its members is open to serious question. First, as Chapter III, §1 suggests,[816] there are significant societal harms to the violent manner in which sports are currently played which seem to justify prosecution rather

---

814 Nelson, Connecticut Law Review, supra at 256, arguing the value of sport to develop the concept of sport as a "public utility" for antitrust purposes.

815 Suffolk University Law Review, supra, at 48. There are other arguments advanced in support of this proposition. The Michigan Law Review observes that, "Sports help maintain the citizenry's physical fitness, provide an outlet for frustrations and aggressive tendencies, satisfy the need and desire of people to prove their self-worth, provide for recreation and the pleasureable use of leisure time, and, at least with regard to team sports, train individuals to sacrifice themselves for the good of the group." Supra, at 174. Klein notes that it "has become more than a game. It has become a cult. A religion. An obsession." (Pro Football Mystique, supra, at 4.)

816 See text surrounding notes 478-490, infra.

than immunity. Second, this approach is harmful in that it grants immunity to players who maliciously intend to injure, but do so within the rules of the game. It is arguable that the rules delineate what society considers to be within the spirit of the game. According to this argument, rules that are designed to prevent injury automatically designate how much injury society will tolerate.[817] Thus, conduct--regardless of the intent with which it is undertaken--is immune from liability. The Criminal Law Quarterly notes, in support, that, "There is no socially useful element to an unprovoked, premeditated assault, even though it took place during the course of a sporting event. A hockey game may be socially useful, but any assault is not, and public acceptance of violence is no justification for its continuance."[818]

## H. Alternative Liability Through Tort, Respondeat Superior and Criminal Conspiracy.

In addition to the elements and defenses involved in assault and battery discussed in A through G above, a participant may be held directly or indi rectly responsible through three alternative theories.

First, the injured player may sue in tort, based on either intentional assault and battery, or unintentional negligence. San Diego District Attorney Edwin L. Miller suggests that if a complainant "has enough of a case" to seek a criminal response, he most surely has an action in tort.[819] Though

---

817 Michigan Law Review, supra, at 178.

818 Supra, at 450.

819 Survey response to Question I(6)(6). Received December 26, 1978. Of course, the "internal pressures" described in Chapter I, §B are relevant here.

the tort law may not be an "effective, widespread deterrent to violence in sports,"[820] it has been used periodically by players who are insensitive to the pressures described in Chapter I. The most notable example was the 1970 suit between John Roseboro and Juan Marichal, professional baseball players for the Los Angeles Dodgers and San Francisco Giants, respectively, for injuries arising out of an altercation during a game in which Marichal hit Roseboro over the head with a baseball bat.[821] More recently, tort suits have been launched somewhat successfully in all sports (as the cases described in the "assumption of the risk defense" suggest).[822] Ed Garvey, NFLPA Executive Director, argues that the tort law should be the main judicial control "over this type of activity."[823]

Second, a coach may be liable under a respondeat superior, vicarious liability, or principal/agent approach. Chapter I, §8 describes the pres-

---

820 Wisconsin Law Review, supra, at 775.

821 The incident occurred on August 22, 1965. Over the course of a weekend series between the Los Angeles Dodgers and the San Francisco Giants, harsh words had passed between Roseboro, the Dodger catcher, and members of the Giants. On Sunday (the 22nd), Roseboro threw the ball back to the pitcher (Sandy Koufax) and in so doing, nicked Marichal's ear (Marichal was batting at the time). Marichal supposedly said "What do you do that" [sic] and then, so Marichal claims, Roseboro "came at him." Marichal then struck Roseboro over the head with his bat, causing some considerable injury. N.Y. Times 20 (August 24, 1965).

Marichal was fined $1,750 by the league and suspended for eight playing dates. Roseboro filed suit against both Marichal and the San Francisco club for $110,000 damages. N.Y. Times 24 (September 2, 1965). The case was settled out of court, reportedly for $7,500. N.Y. Times 45 (February 6, 1970). Wisconsin Law Review, supra, at 775.

822 See text surrounding notes 745-782, infra.

823 Personal interview. (See note 152, infra.)

sures coaches use to encourage conformity to the generally accepted standard of violent behavior.[824] Thus, liability under one of these theories is indeed plausible.[825] In Hackbart, the defendant advanced this theory. In denying the claim, the court noted that

> Liability of the defendant Cincinnati Bengals, Inc. is based upon a contention that the Bengals failed to instruct and control their rookie fullback. The record, however, reflects that what he did is, unfortunately, an example of the excesses of violence which have become expectable as a result of the style of play in the NFL. The question of liability of the employer under the doctrine of respondeat superior is not presented because Charles Clark is not liable to the plaintiff.[826]

Hence, the District Court seemed to have left the door open for future liability of coaches under one of these theories.

Third, it is possible that teammates, coaches, or owners who encourage violent conduct could be liable under applicable criminal conspiracy doctrines.[827] Such conspiracies apparently do not require that serious injury

---

824 See text surrounding notes 134-135, infra.

825 Former All-Pro Alan Page describes what the argument would be like: "Certainly in college, and even in some professional teams, the coach does everything he can to get players in an emotional pitch, which on occasion leads them to do things they might not normally do, and might not really want to do." Criminal Law Quarterly, supra, at 439. Some have even suggested that a coach has a duty to instruct in line with the "safety rules of the game," one criteria for liability in the Nabozny decision. See, e.g., Langerman and Fidel, "Responsibility is Also Part of the Game," Trial, supra at 24.

826 435 F.Supp. at 357.

827 Most states have conspiracy statutes which would be applicable. See, e.g., Minn.Stat.Ann. §609.175(2)(1964): "Whoever conspires with another to commit a crime and in furtherance of the conspiracy one or more of the parties does some overt act in furtherance of such conspiracy may be sentenced as follows:...(3) If the crime intended is any other felony or a gross misdemeanor, to imprisonment or to payment of a fine of not more than one half the imprisonment or fine provided for that felony or gross misdemeanor or both." Under this statute, the question would be whether someone else on the

or bodily harm results before leaving the conspirators subject to criminal prosecution. A coach or owner who so conspires with a team to harm an opposing player is clearly subject to criminal sanctions. In Pinkerton v. United States,[828] the Supreme Court reiterated that "The criminal intent to do the act is established by the formation of the conspiracy. Each conspirator instigated the commission of the crime....The rule which holds responsible one who counsels, procures, or commands another to commit a crime" is himself responsible. The overt assault on the ice against another, is the remaining essential ingredient of the crimes of conspiracy under law.[829] Though no such cases have yet been tried, there are indications that the elements of liability may be present. One commentator notes an allegation that in the early 1950's the players on some of the professional teams would all contribute to a pool that would go to the individual who forced the quarterback of the opposing team to be removed from the game.[830] During the Forbes trial, Prosecutor Flakne stressed that Boston's Bobby Schmautz "skated by the

---

team had conspired with Forbes to commit the crime of assault and battery, the overt act in furtherance of the conspiracy having been accomplished by Forbes. While there is no evidence of any such conduct in the Forbes case, it is not so unlikely that players are encouraged to perform conduct on the playing field or in the rink that is unquestionably beyond the rules of the game. Wisconsin Law Review, supra, at 776.

[828] 328 U.S. 640 (1946).

[829] Criminal Law Quarterly, supra, at 435. During one NHL violence investigation, there may have been a "conspiracy" of another sort. Ontario Attorney General Roy McMurtry ordered that videotapes of the Toronto-Philadelphia brawl be turned over to authorities for the possible charging of coaches and fans who might have encouraged the violence. Upon inspecting these league tapes, Roy McMurtry said: "Parts of the Maloney tape have been erased. I don't know if it's deliberate." Id., at 435-36.

[830] 7 Am.Jur. Trials, supra, at 238.

[penalty] box and said tc the defendant, "Get him the first chance you get, buddy."[831] In short, when players, coaches, or owners overtly conspire to do injury to the opposition, they may be liable under applicable conspiracy statutes.

---

[831] Criminal Law Quarterly, *supra*, at 436.

## CASE STUDY: OCTOBER 27, 1978 PAIEMENT-POLONICH STICKSWINGING INCIDENT: AND SUBSEQUENT INVESTIGATION BY THE WAYNE COUNTY (DETROIT) PROSECUTING ATTORNEY'S OFFICE

One of the implicit themes of this paper is that all of the interrelated considerations discussed in the four chapters are relevant in <u>every</u> exceptionally severe case of sports violence. Accordingly, one recent hockey incident and the subsequent six-week prosecutorial investigation will be explored in the hopes of demonstrating the practical workings of each of the four chapters.

Much of the information was provided through correspondence with Wayne County Chief Assistant Prosecuting Attorney Dominick R. Carnovale. Despite refusing all comment on the Paiement-Polonich incident in his <u>initial</u> survey response,[832] Carnovale subsequently forwarded relevant Press Releases concerning his office's investigation.[833] Finally, after a telephone interview,[834] Carnovale forwarded a copy of the investigative report prepared by his office.[835] Using these and other materials, this paper will attempt to present a detailed account of the proceedings in the following manner: (A) the incident and its aftermath; (B) Chapter I issues: the league reaction; (C) Chapter II issues: internal fine and suspension proceedings; (D) Chapter III issues: the reasons behind the decision not to prosecute; (E) Chapter IV issues: the applicable law.

---

[832] December 6, 1978.

[833] December 21, 1978.

[834] January 24, 1979.

[835] January 29, 1979. (A copy of this correspondence appears as Appendix Q.)

A. The Incident and Its Aftermath.

During the second period of a hockey game between the Colorado Rockies and the Detroit Red Wings on October 25, 1978 at Olympia Stadium in Detroit, Red Wing player Dennis Polonich came into possession of the puck in the vicinity of the Red Wing net. (A diagram appears as Appendix R.) He attempted to clear the puck up the ice, and in so doing his stick struck Rockies player Wilf Paiement in the face. Paiement then swung his stick like a baseball bat and struck Polonich on the bridge of his nose, dropping him to the ice. Polonich was rendered semi-conscious by the blow. The Officials Report to the League President noted that Polonich "lay there in a pool of blood." Polonich was given an immediate Rule 58C major high sticking penalty by the referee. Paiement was given a Rule 49 ten minute match penalty for intentional injury to an opponent. The extent of the injuries vary depending upon which news account is read. The Detroit Free Press deals only with the Detroit player's injury, saying that he suffered a broken nose and, as a result, "has had one hospital stay so far and is expected to undergo two more operations, one at the end of the season and another when he ends his career. Polonich missed the next eight games, returning to action Wednesday in Atlanta wearing a wire cage to protect his face."[836] The (Denver) Rocky Mountain News' account of the injury was that "Paiement suffered a badly bruised lip. Polonich suffered a badly broken nose and needed 12 stitches on his face."[837]

---

[836] T. Henderson, "Prosecutor Studies Case Against Wilf," Detroit Free Press (November 18, 1978).

[837] F. Pietila, "Rockies' Paiement Doesn't Regret Incident With Detroit's Polonich," Rocky Mountain News 110 (October 27, 1978).

B. Chapter I Issues: The League Reaction.

Most members of the "hockey establishment" publicly expressed displeasure over the incident. Paiement himself remarked, "I figure if I have to play and take those sticks in the face, I'll quit. If they want to fight, I'll fight. He's been using his stick in the past."[838] Detroit coach Bobby Kromm was quoted as saying, "He [Paiement] swung his stick like a baseball bat. He should be suspended for at least a year. He has done it before--he did in Europe (two years ago)--and there is no room for actions like that in hockey."[839] Retaliation, however, was expected to occur on the ice rather than through the judicial process. Colorado Coach Pat Kelly indicated that "Polonich is the type of kid that's always in trouble (830 penalty minutes the last three seasons). He runs around a lot. He's given the stick to a lot of guys in this league. He's a small guy. Maybe he feels no one should bother him. But there's an old motto, he who lives by the sword dies by the sword."[840]

As expected, most of the hockey "family" disdained the idea of a criminal prosecution. Polonich, "who promised blood revenge at one point,"[841] was against criminal prosecution of Paiement. Polonich was expected to file a civil suit to insure payment of his medical expenses. But, as the Detroit News indicated, "hockey sources say he is opposed to criminal prosecution because of the possible effects on his NHL career. "He still has to make his living in this league, so he doesn't want to be known as the guy who put

---

838 Id., at 110.

839 Id.

840 Id.

841 Henderson, Detroit Free Press, supra.

Paiement behind bars," said one hockey source."[842] The owners were also against prosecution. Interestingly, even Bruce Norris, the owner of the Red Wings, was vehemently opposed to prosecution even though his team would lose Polonich's services for eight games. Said Norris: "We like to see the league be the instrument through which punishments are meted out and leave the outside, outside."[843] Detroit General Manager Ted Lindsay publicly "demanded prosecution," prompting additional statements by Norris that this "type of thing should be kept within the family."

Though many hockey insiders were opposed to prosecution, they were "very cooperative once the investigation started."[844] The Detroit Management gave the prosecutors "anything they asked for." The league itself was apparently cooperative as well. The Wayne County Prosecuting Attorneys' December 13, 1978 intra-office memorandum (hereinafter "Memo") suggested that, "Mr. John Ziegler, President of the NHL, has been cooperative during the investigation. He has forwarded to us a copy of a report of the incident from Referee John McCauley, who was within a few feet of the two players when the incident occurred (see Appendix S). Mr. Ziegler has also made available for our viewing and copying the Rockies' videotape."[845]

---

[842] V. Kupelian and R. Roach, "Cahalan Checking Paiement Incident," <u>Detroit News</u> 1C (November 17, 1978).

[843] Henderson, Detroit Free Press, <u>supra</u>.

[844] Telephone interview with Assistant Prosecuting Attorney Carnovale. (January 24, 1979)

[845] <u>Memo</u>, at 5-6.

C. Chapter II Issues: Internal Fine and Suspension Proceedings.

There were two hearings convened by Brian O'Neill, NHL Executive Vice-President; one on October 27, 1978 and the other on November 6, 1978. In attendance at the first hearing were player Wilf Paiement, Ray Miron - Colorado Rockies General Manager, Referee John McCauley and the Referee-in-Chief - Scotty Morrison. The second hearing was held in order to review the final medical report and to hear the oral testimony of the injured player Dennis Polonich who was unable to attend the first hearing. In attendance at the second hearing besides Polonich and Paiement were Red Wings General Manager Ted Lindsay, Ray Miron, Armand Pohan and Aldo Guidolin all of the Colorado Rockies, as well as Referee John McCauley and Referee-in-Chief Scotty Morrison. Also in attendance was Bill Watters, Mr. Paiement's representative.

The facts were elicited by videotape, oral testimony, and the Officials' Report to the League President, completed by the game referee, John McCauley. (This report appears as Appensix S.)

There were a number of punishments assessed, in addition to the "during the game" penalties mentioned earlier. Paiement was "fined the maximum amount permitted under the rules--$500" and was suspended for fifteen games beginning November 7, 1978. The record shows that Paiement's suspension of 15 games was the second-longest given for player violence in the history of the National Hockey League. It's one game less than the record suspension given to Boston's Eddie Shore 45 years ago when his stick nearly killed Toronto's Ace Bailey, Sr. Paiement's suspension was longer than the 11-game suspension given Wayne Maki 10 years ago "when he tried to split Ted Green's skull." Paiement's suspension was quite a bit longer than the 10-game suspension given to Detroit's Bryan (Bugsy) Watson two years ago. That one came after Watson, with stick in fist, hit Chicago's Keith Magnuson from the blind side with a "sucker punch" that broke Magnuson's jaw.[846] Also, since Polonich "had publicly vowed to seek personal revenge, the NHL banned Paiement from the remaining games between the two teams, on November 29 and February 25."[847]

In addition to these punishments, Executive Vice-President O'Neill issued a deterrence warning to the rest of the league in his three-page written decision on November 7, 1978 (hereinafter "Decision"). (This decision appears as Appendix T.) He stated:

> This suspension represents approximately 20% of the playing season and is one of the severest disciplinary actions imposed in the League's history for an on-ice altercation. Each player and Club must take note that stick-swinging will bring a forfeiture of the privilege of playing. This is the first incident of a deliberate injury to an opponent in several years and we trust all players will learn that there is not to be another.

In its Decision, the NHL advanced three reasons justifying its "sentence" of Paiement. First, in his testimony Paiement stated that he thought that Polonich had deliberately struck him in the mouth with his stick and that he immediately retaliated. The videotape showed Polonich's stick striking Paiement but it "cannot be determined whether it was deliberate."[848] Second, Paiement "has not received any previous match penalties and that in four seasons in the League has not been noted as a player who uses his stick against his opponent."[849] Third, the Decision refers to the fact that Polonich's injur-

---

846 J. Lapawrite, "A Little Advice for Wings: Let Bygones Be Bygones," Detroit Free Press (November 12, 1978).

847 Kupelian and Roach, Detroit News, *supra*, at 3C.

848 *Decision*, at 2.

849 *Id.*

ies were not extraordinarily severe.[850]

Reaction by the "hockey establishment" to the NHL's sentence was predictably diverse. Detroit Red Wings Owner Norris and General Manager Lindsay both thought the punishment was extremely lenient, especially for "a two-handed baseball swing."[851] The Colorado management, on the other hand, thought the punishment was extraordinarily severe, since "Paiement was provoked by Polonich."[852]

D. <u>Chapter III Issues: The Reasons Behind the Decision Not to Prosecute.</u>

The Wayne County Prosecuting Attorney's Office began an investigation after receiving an oral complaint from a fan who attended a game. Prosecuting Attorney William L. Cahalan indicated that, "It was brought to our attention and we felt this was the type of case we should investigate."[853]

A December 19, 1978 Press Release from the Office of the Prosecuting Attorney spoke of the completion of a "thorough and complete investigation." (A copy of the Press Release appears as Appendix U.) The Press Release suggested that "not only was Mr. Polonich interviewed, over 150 contacts were made, thereby locating a large number of eye witnesses who also were inter-

---

850 <u>Decision</u>, at 3-4. "A full report on the physical condition of Dennis Polonich was received on November 6th by attending Physician Dr. John H. Finley of Detroit. The report describes the injury in detail and states that he is recovering satisfactorily. Polonich was discharged from hospital after three days and following additional tests was given permission to skate on November 2, 1978. The doctor indicated, also, that if there are no delayed abnormalities Polonich could return to play with facial protection sometime between November 8 and November 15, 1978.

851 Lapointe, Detroit Free Press, <u>supra</u>.

852 Henderson, Detroit Free Press, <u>supra</u>.

853 V. Kupolian, "Wilf Will Not Be Prosecuted," <u>Detroit News</u> 8D (December 20, 1978).

viewed and interrogated. Videotapes were reviewed and the records of the National Hockey League disciplinary proceeding against Mr. Paiement were obtained and evaluated." The Prosecuting Attorney concluded that "after a careful review of this investigation, we have decided that no criminal charge will be brought against Mr. Paiement." The following factors were somewhat influential in this decision:

1. The extent of media coverage and public awareness. The game itself was televised in Denver, but not in Detroit.[854] However, the Detroit media covered the incident extensively.[855] Assistant Prosecutor John Thomson, who was in charge of the investigation, noted to the press that "This is a thing which got a lot of publicity, so the consequences take on a little different flavor than just an ordinary punch in the mouth by a guy in a saloon."[856] During the investigation, the media editorialized on the appropriateness of a potential indictment. One critic predicted that an indictment of Paiement would "open the floodgates":

> Last week, Wayne County Prosecutor William Cahalan said he's investigating a vague, anonymous complaint that felonious-assault charges be brought against Paiement, who used his stick to break the nose of Polonich because Polonich used his stick to cut Paiement's face. Enough of this. If the legal threats keep up, they could result in a circus worse than the McMurtry prosecutions two years ago in Ontario. 857

---

854 Memo, supra, at 2.

855 Four news articles describing the incident appeared in the two major Detroit newspapers within a two day period after the game.

856 Henderson, Detroit Free-Press, supra.

857 Lapointe, Detroit Free-Press, supra.

Another critic referred to the investigation as "a political crusade":

> A player for the home team, Polonich of the Red Wings, had been injured seriou sly by a player of a visiting team, Paiement of the Colorado Rockies. Although Polonich provoked the attack, and although Paiement was suspended for 15 games, even harsher punishment was demanded by Polonich and Red Wing officials. An eye for an eye or a broken nose for a broken nose, or something like that.

2. Availability of evidence: complaining victim; witnesses; and demonstrative evidence. The victim, Dennis Polonich was interviewed in the office of his attorney, Mr. Brian Smith, on November 17, 1978. He had no recollection of being hit during the game. His memory stopped sometime shortly before being hit and resumed during the administration of first aid. He could not testify of his own knowledge who it was that hit him. Furthermore, Polonich, through his attorney, expressed some reluctance to sign a complaint based upon the fear of retaliation by other players during upcoming games. It was agreed that this decision did not need to be made at that point and that the investigation would proceed. He did indicate he would sign if it were necessary. According to Assistant Prosecutor Thompson, "his lack of memory would require him to sign the complaint on information and belief, though anyone with personal knowledge may sign with legal effect."[858] Prosecuting Attorney Cahalan told the media that "if Polonich isn't interested in pursuing a criminal complaint, prosecution would be difficult, but not impossible. We couldn't do much if we have to subpoena Polonich into court and Polonich doesn't want to be subpoenaed into court. If the guy who got hit doesn't want (to prosecute)...if he doesn't make a good witness, you ain't gonna win the case."[859]

858 Memo, supra, at 2.

859 Henderson, Detroit Free-Press, supra.

The investigation attempted to locate other witnesses. The General Manager of the Red Wings, Mr. Ted Lindsay, was interviewed at Olympia on November 20, 1978. He saw the incident in question. He stated that he had never seen a more vicious and wilful blow. He described the initial contact between Polonich and Paiement as more or less normal.[860] Lindsay stated that he could not understand why Polonich did not make some defensive move while Paiement swung his stick like a baseball bat into Polonich's face, as he thought the two men were face to face at the time Paiement's blow was struck. Furthermore, Lindsay provided a list of season ticket holders for the seats in the vicinity. Approximately 150 people were contacted. Of these 150 contacts, 26 persons saw the event to one degree or another and of the 26, perhaps six persons saw and recalled enough to be useful as witnesses. Many of the season tickets were owned by companies who provided customers and friends with the tickets. A significant percentage of the tickets were three and even four times removed from the original holders. Assistant Prosecutor Thompson noted that "the degree of success achieved in reaching these witnesses was a good indication of the magnitude and difficulty of the res gestae problem in this case."[861] One fan was so appalled that he had called Ted Lindsay after the game to volunteer his assistance. He was approximately 30 years old and "obviously a devoted Red Wings fan."[862] He recalled the incident in great detail though significantly different than the other versions. He believed that Paiement had swung his stick like a baseball bat

---

860 Memo, <u>supra</u>, at 4.

861 <u>Id.</u>, at 5.

862 <u>Id.</u>

from Polonich's blind side after being ticked on the chin by Polonich's stick.[863] The logistical resource problem of locating witnesses was noted as "an impediment to a successful prosecution of this case."[864]

Finally, the investigation attempted to obtain demonstrative evidence that could be used at trial. Detroit television cameras missed the Paiement-Polonich incident. However, the Red Wings videotaped the game for coaching purposes. The footage, however, did not show Paiement swinging his stick at Polonich. The Assistant Prosecutor examining the footage noted that it was, at best, inconclusive:

> As the puck was cleared by Polonich, the camera followed the puck and even in slow motion Polonich and Paiement are lost to view before they collide. It is clear however that the collision was imminent and unavoidable. Polonich could be seen raising his stick as they move closer to each other, though whether in a natural follow through or in a deliberate attempt to fend off Paiement is open to question.[865]

The investigators were unable to view the film from Denver television but were informed that it also did not show more than the Red Wing film. The investigators also attempted to secure the prior testimony given at the NHL fine and suspension hearing; but, as the Memo indicates, "these hearings were not recorded in any way and thus there is no transcript of the testimony."[866]

3. <u>The prospects for success on the merits.</u> There were many problems perceived. First, because of the ambiguity of the law in this area, Prose-

---

863 <u>Id.</u>

864 <u>Id.</u>, at 10.

865 Memo, <u>supra</u>, at 3.

866 <u>Supra</u>, at 5.

cutor Cahalan told the media that "no jury would have convicted (Paiement)."[867] One of the major arguments in Thompson's memo to Chief Assistant Prosecutor Carnovale was that "in other jurisdictions, hockey players have been prosecuted, though none have been convicted."[868] Second, the argument that Paiement's action was "just part of the game" was given considerable weight. Cahalan informed the media that, "If this had occurred on the street, there would be no question about it. It's a question of whether an injury such as this--and the actions on the part of Paiement were offensive, no doubt about it--there's a question whether they were so far out of line, so far out of the game that they should be put in the criminal justice system".[869] The prosecutor said that although Paiement's action was beyond what is normal in hockey, it wasn't enough to merit prosecution. Many of the spectators interviewed also considered Paiement's action as within the bounds of normal hockey. Thompson suggested that many of the Olympia fans told him that Paiement over-reacted with a vicious swing of his stick. But also, according to Thompson, "People kept saying that s.o.b. (Polonich) got what he deserved."[870] In fact, this "part of the game" rationale appears to be the most significant factor in the Wayne County Prosecutor's decision not to indict Paiement. The intra-office memo concludes:

> I do not believe that our investigation has shown that Paiement's act is criminal. The provable facts do not show that Paiement's blow, while offensive,

---

867 J. Lapointe, "Paiement No Criminal," Detroit Free-Press (December 20, 1978).

868 Memo, supra, at 9.

869 Kupelian, Detroit News, supra, at 8D.

870 Lapointe, Detroit Free-Press, supra.

> rises so far above the level of violence prevalent in professional hockey games that it becomes transformed from a part of the game to an offense against the peace and dignity of the People of the State of Michigan. [871]

Hence, the office issued its December 19 Press Release in terms suggesting that little deterrence would result from an unsuccessful prosecution: "The decision whether or not to prosecute a player for acts committed during an athletic contest can be a difficult one to make. A prosecution which is not soundly based in law and fact would have no deterrent effect at all, and might even encourage more violence in contact sports such as hockey."

4. Deference to alternate dispute resolution mechanisms. Though apparently not formally considered in the intra-office memo or comments to the press, the prosecuting attorneys must have been aware that Polonich was expected to file a civil lawsuit to recover his medical expenses, since this was much publicized by the media. As for the league fine and suspension proceedings, the Memo explicitly argued that "the question of the sufficiency of the league disciplinary action is basically immaterial because a private organization does not have the authority to determine criminality."[872] As a practical matter, however, the memo did recognize that "the 'severe' penalty given Paiement by the League does detract from the power of a charge against him."[873]

---

871 Memo, *supra*, at 11.

872 *Id.*, at 10-11.

873 *Id.*, at 11.

5. <u>The "societal value" of prosecuting Paiement when balanced against other priorities competing for finite resources.</u> Given the large amounts of resources expended in witness location and evidence gathering, Prosecutor Cahalan determined that further proceedings would be, among other things, cost ineffective. Cahalan told the media that, "After thoroughly investigating this and talking to all the witnesses, we conclude that we will not recommend a warrant. We do not think that this is the type of case that belongs in the criminal justice system. This is not the type of case (to which) the resources of Michigan criminal justice system should be applied."[874] Cahalan seems to have decided that a six week "public" investigation coupled with a strongly worded press release, would serve somewhat of a symbolic deterrent function without the expense of a formal prosecution. Accordingly, after the Press Release announced the non-prosecution, it continued: "On the other hand, the operation of law does not stop at the ticket gates of any sports event in my jurisdiction. Even though this specific incident will not result in a criminal prosecution, everyone concerned should understand that criminal violence occurring during any sporting event will, if supported by fact and law, be prosecuted. Nonetheless, we are of the opinion that the evidence here will not support a criminal charge against Mr. Paiement."

E. <u>Chapter IV Issues: The Applicable Law</u>

The prosecution had considered charging Paiement with felonious assault. This offense, distinguished from the misdemeanor assault and battery, is defined as the inflicting of serious bodily injury with a weapon. Under Michi-

---

874 Kupelian, Detroit News, <u>supra</u>.

gan law, a conviction on the charge could warrant a sentence anywhere from probation to a four-year prison term. Factually, the Memo indicates that there was no question that Paiement struck Polonich. He apparently testified on his own behalf at the disciplinary hearing and admitted striking the blow. He admitted it was a two handed swing, though he denied using the degree of force attributed to it by the refe ree.[875]

Predictably, a major problem was proving that Paiement intended the act and/or the injury. Assistant Prosecutor Carnovale explained that none of the evidence "revealed whether he so intended."[876] The NHL "judges" faced the same problem, as "the disciplinary hearing decision said that it could not be determined if this high sticking was intentional."[877]

As for the consent defense, the Prosecuting Attorney employed the "magnitude of the harm" test. The Memo indicates as much:

> The seriousness of injury inflicted is a consideration in determining whether an act during a sporting event is criminal. In this case, while the treating physician stated in his report that this was the worst nose fracture he has seen in 18 years of treating hockey players, Polonich was playing again within approximately three weeks of the incident. He has played regularly since then, though wearing a protective face mask. Obviously the potential for serious injury existed in Paiement's blow, but the actual injury fell far short.

The unspoken implication of Assistant Prosecutor Thompson's statement is that Polonich could be deemed to have consented to conduct producing this type of injury.

---

875 Memo, *supra*, at 8.

876 Telephone interview (see note 844, *supra*.)

877 Memo, *supra*, at 7.

The "assumption of risk" defense was not considered explicitly in the Memo or elsewhere. However, Carnovale suggested that it would "undoubtedly be argued to a jury since any hockey players knows that if he hits, he'll be hit back."[878]

The provocation defense was a major consideration; especially since "Polonich's high stick immediately before Paiement's retailiation was severe enough to draw blood."[879] The Memo concluded that "it was in retaliation for this blow that Paiement struck Polonich with his stick."[880] Cahalan's characterization of this defense to the media suggests that Paiement could still have been held liable: "It is not enough for Paiement to claim he was provoked, he would also have to show that his baseball swing to Polonich's face was reasonable and necessary.[881] However, the character of the initial conflict is important both factually and legally. If the initial contact is viewed as a provocative and deliberate act, obviously any sympathy a jury might have for Polonich's injury is greatly diminished.[882]

Self defense was not deemed significant, given the degree of force that Paiement used. According to Cahalan: "The general principle is that you can use whatever force is necessary to protect yourself. If you use force beyond that which is necessary, if you use unreasonable force, then you'd be charged."[883]

---

878 Telephone interview (see note 844, <u>infra</u>).

879 <u>Id.</u>

880 Memo, <u>supra</u>, at 6.

881 Henderson, Detroit Free-Press, <u>supra</u>.

882 Memo, <u>supra</u>, at 7. The Memo also refers to Polonich as having a "general reputation of being a feisty, rough and tumble hockey player." <u>Id.</u>

883 Henderson, Detroit Free-Press, <u>supra</u>.

The "involuntary reflex" defense was a "significant consideration,"[884] according to Chief Assistant Carnovale. The Memo suggests that the prosecution placed great weight on the merits of this defense:

> In other prosecutions for similar incidents, part of the defense has been the notion that a hockey player is conditioned from boyhood to react to violence without even thinking. He is encouraged to meet aggression with aggression, face to face. Whatever the merits of this theory, a jury may be more sympathetic to a reaction to provocation.[885]

Finally, the "social utility" defense was suggested. The prosecution apparently considered whether the conduct of professional hockey players is "privileged" under state law and "whether it is appropriate for the prosecutor's office to become involved in this."[886] Implicitly arguing the general virtues of hockey, the Memo concluded that, at least so far as the Wayne County Office should be concerned, participants should be granted some tacit immunity. Thompson notes in his memo that, "There seems to me no question at all that the Prosecuting Attorney does have the duty and obligation to prosecute crimes committed by players which occur during sporting events in general. If, for instance, Paiement had drawn a pistol and shot Polonich, he would and should be prosecuted. Instead, however, the instant case involves an attack which occurred in the context of a not unusually violent hockey game. The response of Paiement was disproportionate to the provocation involved, but was it criminal?"[887]

---

884 Telephone interview. (See note 844, infra.)

885 Memo, supra, at 7.

886 Kupelian and Roach, Detroit News, supra.

887 Memo, supra, at 8.

## RECOMMENDATIONS

This paper has attempted to expose some of the more glaring deficiencies in the current structure of dealing with excessively severe acts of sports violence. In essence, the members of the sports establishment consider most severe acts "non criminal"; the private criminal lawmaking entrusted to internal fine and suspension structures may be deficient both in procedural regularity and deterrence capability; finally, the criminal justice system's attempt at intervention in this area has been plagued by inconsistent enforcement and ambiguous standards of proof. In attempting to deal with these problems, recommendations will be proposed in the following areas:

### A. Chapter I Issues: Internal Perceptions and Structure Based Upon Those Perceptions.

Any suggestions in this area are perhaps idealistic at best, given the "part of the game" dogma that is entrenched within the hockey establishment. However, a number of arguments could be used in an attempt to convince the "hockey powers" to reduce their zeal for violence. First, a surprising number of players (45 percent of those interviewed by Smith) would prefer "less fist fighting in games" while a greater number (82 percent) would prefer less "illegal stick-work."[888] McMurtry indicates that, "without exception," Canadian players who played certain games under less violent international rules suggested that they were "more rewarding experiences."[889] Second, it can be

[888] Smith, *supra*, at 15.

[889] McMurtry, *supra*, at 26-27.

empirically documented that "if [the establishment] continues to encourage the present trends in hockey where skill is secondary to physical intimidation, then it is likely that every other hockey nation will surpass North America in actual hockey skills."[890] Third, Attorney Bob Woolf and others have argued that, contrary to management perceptions, violence may not be critical to spectator attendance.[891] Fourth, even if violence were productive attendance-wise, this profit is more than outweighed by compensation to injured athletes. For example, in the 1973-1974 season, the estimated cost to the NFL's 20 teams in salaries and other compensation amounted to

---

[890] McMurtry, <u>supra</u>, at 21. Hopefully, the 6-0 humiliation of Team NHL by the Soviet All-Stars on February 11, 1979 will have a positive effect in this direction. The <u>Toronto Star</u> editorialized: "Now that the NHL has been suitably humbled, let's hope it learns something. In recent years NHL fans have been treated to mediocre hockey with players, coaches and club owners putting the stress in violence and muscle instead of team play and style..."

[891] B. Woolf, Behind Closed Doors, <u>supra</u>, at 147-48. He supports his position by arguing that"through the years, one of the least provocative teams in the league had been the Montreal Canadiens. Yet they seem to have won their share of Stanley Cups, and endured as the best gate attraction in the game." Washington General Manager McNab attempted a fan survey while General Manager of the Western Hockey League San Diego Gulls. The survey revealed that fans listed "skill and reflex action" as the primary reason for their return to see a second game. Tex Schramm, president of the Dallas Cowboys, speaking for the NFL: "I'm not sure the game is rougher today than it used to be. But the roughness is being talked about more. We're coming into an era when undue violence is repelling people. My friends in television and the movies tell me brutality isn't the salable quality it used to be. There has been a public reaction against an excess amount of violent scenes. Sports fans today differentiate between contact and brutality--and we're responding to this." Kindred, "Fans See Difference Between Contact, Violence," <u>Washington Post</u> D4 (March 31, 1979).

$17,600,000.[892]

If these arguments are persuasive enough to alter the "hockey establishment's" pro-violence perception, then a number of significant structural changes would be possible. First, a change in many of the existing "safety-oriented" rules of the game would be appropriate. In hockey, for example, McMurtry proposes the following: (a) increase the fighting penalties under Rule 54;[893] (b) introduce an automatic game misconduct or suspension for fighting so that "any player can [be justified] in refusing to fight" so that he doesn't lose face with his peers;[894] (c) change Rule 37d to allow all three "on the ice" linesmen and referees to assess infractions, thus reducing the chance of undetected retaliation; (d) upgrade referee standards so rules are consistently and completely enforced.[895] McMurtry concludes that, "the sooner steps are taken to see that fighting, intimidation and provocation of an opponent are no longer 'part of the game,' the healthier hockey will be."[896] If the rules are to be changed, permitting the players to participate in redrafting the rules defining punishable conduct will increase the respect for such rules. One NHL player responding to the survey advocated the creation of "a board to control procedures,"[897] while another

---

[892] Hofeld, Trial Lawyer's Guide, <u>supra</u>, at 401-02.

[893] McMurtry, <u>supra</u>, at 27. He notes the toughening of the rules in the Metropolitan Toronto Hockey Association in 1971. Since that time, the league had played 2,100 hockey games and "had only one incident which was actually called a fight." McMurtry concludes: "They learn very, very quickly when they are told 'No fighting,' and they have not fought."

[894] <u>Id.</u>, at 29.

[895] <u>Id.</u>, at 39.

[896] <u>Id.</u>, at 37.

[897] Confidential survey (received February 20, 1979).

argued for "increased input as a team."[898] The NFL has already developed a Joint Committee on Player Safety and Welfare for the purpose of deliberating on rules "that could adversely affect player safety."[899]

Second, the system should "increase its emphasis on skill development at lower age levels."[900] Coaches must be instructed that "there is a purpose to amateur hockey beyond that of training professionals."[901] McMurtry speaks of a "mandatory certification program;"[902] there is also a proposal to make the coach responsible for his players' actions through the fine and suspension mechanisms;[903] finally, one commentator suggests that "coaches who teach spearing and butting should be fired."[904]

Third, media support should be solicited in an effort to educate the American hockey public to be sensitive to the distinction between subtle skills and overt physical violence. McMurtry notes that, "Reform is never easy. It means changing the existing order--often at the expense of vested

---

898 Confidential survey (received February 17, 1979).

899 NFL Collective Bargaining Agreement, Article XI, Section 8.

900 McMurtry, _supra_, at 36.

901 _Id._ McMurtry suggests that there are some coaches who are "constructive voices in the wilderness." He mentions WHA Coach Billy Harris, who stated: "I tell my kids if a guy gets up there and high-sticks you, avoid trouble. Turn your back. Show some courage, but turn your back. Don't be afraid to be embarrassed. This is a way of showing some courage. You're not afraid to be embarrassed because it has been the thing to do for some thirty years. Turn your back on him. Let's change things."

902 _Id._, at 38.

903 _Id._, at 39.

904 Philo and Stine, Trial, _supra_, at 40.

interests and against the weight of entranched prejudices."[905] However, if the establishment could be convinced that sports violence is a criminal offense rather than an entertaining diversion, reform would be that much easier.

B. Chapter II Issues: Internal Discipline, Collective Bargaining and Players Association Protection.

Even though Chapter II exposes the various problems with the internal fine and suspension mechanisms, total elimination of their "sentencing" powers would be clearly unwise.[906] Partial reform is all that is called for. Though this paper has previously advocated due process and antitrust arguments as vehicles to improve current procedures, most commentators maintain that improvement will be attained only through the skillful negotiation of future Collective Bargaining Agreements. One note argues that, "The possibility of good faith collective bargaining appears to offer the only hope for resolution of the complex problems raised by player controls in professional team sports."[907] If this is an accurate appraisal of what the future holds for improvement of disciplinary mechanisms, three recommendations

---

905 McMurtry, supra, at 45.

906 California Western Law Review cryptically concludes that: "Any drastic changes in football's controls over its athletes might kill the sport. If a cure threatens to kill the patient, then the cure is of little avail." Comment, "Sherman Act: Football's Player Controls--Are They Reasonable?," 6 California Western Law Review 133, 145 (1969).

907 University of Pittsburgh Law Review, supra, at 670. The Valparaiso Law Review goes even further: "The next five years should provide the experience with which to improve any flaws that may be inherent in the new systems. Now that bona fide collective bargaining has occurred with respect to all the issues, it is hoped that the courts will never again have to intervene to protect the rights of the players." Supra, at 413.

can be suggested. First, the courts, in displaying an inclination for professional athletics to develop along more traditional freedom of contact lines, have provided a strong boost to the collective bargaining efforts. The judiciary is withdrawing cautiously, however, attempting to assure that the individual interests involved are adequately protected.[908] The courts should maintain their "theoretical" supervisory function each time a professional sport collective bargaining agreement is being negotiated.

Second, future negotiations must be geared toward insuring that each procedure contain some access to a neutral arbitrator. The Nebraska Law Review summarizes the argument introduced earlier, maintaining that "all issues subject to the grievance provisions must be finally resolved by an impartial third party, regardless of whether the dispute involves fines, suspensions, or the integrity of the game. The commissioner is not such an individual. Confidence in the system can only be gained when a player has the right to appeal to an impartial party; the simple fact is that the commissioner cannot be impartial."[909] Though the parties "should not shy away from grievance arbitration as a workable process for settling disputes in the professional sports industry, as its merits greatly outweigh its disadvantages,"[910] Buoniconti and others have noted that the system "will never be fair as long as the chief judge has conflicting interests."[911] Reform in this area is possible. For example, the freedoms won by other professional athletes in courts were won by baseball players through arbitration.[912]

---

[908] T. Gilroy and P.J. Madden, "Labor Relations in Professional Sports," 28 Labor Law Journal 768, 775-76 (1977).

[909] Gessford, Nebraska Law Review, supra, at 380.

[910] Id., at 382.

[911] Personal interview. (See note 69, infra.)

[912] Brody, Trial, supra, at 37.

Third, each league's Player's Association must negotiate zealously for the improvement of the fine and suspension procedures. It is obvious that professional athletes are no longer prepared to rely on the benevolence of club owners in obtaining better working conditions.[913] Hence, the unionized player associations, unlike the representative system, are theoretically more independent and tightly-knit organizations capable of affirmative action and economic tests of strength. In the last several years, they have made great progress in affecting league policy and negotiating terms and conditions of employment.[914] However, it has become apparent through surveys, interviews, and correspondence that the Players' Associations are not as concerned with player discipline as they are with "more important" issues of salaries, free agency, pension plans, and the like.[915] If it is true

---

913 Manitoba Law Journal, supra, at 376.

914 Gessford, Nebraska Law Review, supra, at 363. The National Football League Players' Association was recognized as the sole bargaining agent for the players by the NLRB pursuant to a consent election agreement on July 10, 1970. The National Labor Relations Act, 29 U.S.C. Section 158(d)(1970) forces an employer to bargain in good faith. In hockey, the NHL Players' Association has not obtained formal certification as of 1973 but rather has been granted recognition from all NHL teams and has negotiated a series of agreements with the league and teams covering matters of importance to players. The CFL Player's Association, although a functioning association is, according to one of its executive members, at least five years behind the NFL Player's Association in terms of relative strength to management, "but is moving toward closing this gap." Manitoba Law Journal, supra, at 375-76.

915 The NHLPA seemed only moderately interested in exploring this problem. I wrote to NHLPA Executive Director Alan Eagleson on November 10, 1978, asking him to comment on the various problems discussed in this paper. (The precise request appears in the letter, attached as Appendix V). Eagleson responded on December 1 that he "could not be of any further assistance." (Appendix W) However, on January 11, 1979, I secured permission from Managing Officer Simpson to use the NHLPA name on the player survey (see Appendix C). In practice, the NHLPA has little incentive to insure that egregious violations are fairly "tried" internally, since "they are opposed to such conduct themselves." (Telephone interview with NHL Executive Director O'Neill. See note 307, infra.)

that players are concerned but the associations may not be, it is possible that such a situation violates the union's duty of fair representation. Alternatively, it could be argued that such inaction violates the Constitution of the respective Players' Association. For example, the Constitution of the National Hockey League Players' Association (Appendix X) provides in Article II, Section 1(e) that "the Association...shall...develop such projects and enterprises which will bring further benefits to Members as individuals or to the Association as an entity."

If the internal disciplinary mechanisms were improved, either through application of antitrust or due process concepts or through the three recommendations suggested above, it would almost surely reduce the need for criminal law intervention.

C. Chapter III Issues: Symbolic Enforcement and Prosecutorial Consistency.

In most cases, the sports establishment is correct when it maintains that most disputes should be "kept within the family." However, on a theor-

---

The NFLPA has been unhelpful. After getting no response from an inquiry substantially similar to that of Appendix V, I telephoned the Washington office numerous times. Though the Washington meeting with Executive Director Garvey on November 23 was productive, the NFLPA has subsequently failed to send promised material. There is also a possibility that the NFLPA conducted a "freedom issue" survey shortly before I talked to them, yet this was never mentioned. Finally, though Garvey did agree to "sponsor" the survey on December 8, 1978, I was notified that it was not dispatched until March 3, 1979.

Judging from correspondence with the basketball (L. Fleischer) and baseball (M. Miller) Players' Associations, they seem unconcerned with these issues. In these cases, however, the unconcern can be attributed to the relative infrequency of sports violence in either sport.

etical level, the criminal law must stand ready to intervene, based on the argument that organized athletic competition does not exist in a vacuum. Rather, "some of the restraints of civilization must accompany every athlete onto the playing field."[916] On a practical level, the criminal law must intervene in the severe case where deterrence is critical[917] or where internal procedures fail.[918] What is clearly needed is cooperation between the public and private law-enforcing agencies in this context. Once it is accepted that neither internal nor legal control can be exclusively applied to all types of violence in the arena, a rational enforcement strategy can be developed that would accommodate the interests of all concerned.[919]

Plainly, however, to merely recommend that prosecutors "symbolically enforce" provides little guidance given the ambiguous nature of "prosecutorial discretion." If there is a problem of unbridled discretion in "traditional" prosecutorial charging decisions, it is even more significant in an evolving area such as sports violence where office policies have not yet been crystallized. "That some uncertainty is inevitable and has been held permissable should not obscure the dilution of this right that discretionary decision-making entails. At the least, this consideration requires that

---

[916] University of Missouri-Kansas City Law Review, _supra_, at 128.

[917] Since the criminal law "may be the only way to reach this conduct." Wisconsin Law Review, _supra_, at 788.

[918] Because "a sophisticated and well-tested system of protections is already built into the criminal procedure." _Id._, at 789.

[919] One commentator suggests that such cooperation is necessary for the players' benefit, a concept foreign to those in the "hockey family" who advocate complete internal deference: "Action by both the hockey establishment and the courts is necessary if professional hockey is to be played without subjecting the players to potential, unpredictable criminal liability for activities common to the sport." American Criminal Law Review, _supra_, at 246.

there be persuasive and substantial reasons for discretionary power and that it not be permitted to be exercised by default."[920] Accordingly, some accountability in this area is appropriate. First, prosecutorial offices should develop standards or guidelines involving their assessment of the relative merits of the "conditions" set out in Chapter III. Armed with experience gained from the Forbes prosecution, County Attorney Flakne argues that prosecutors should formulate "appropriate guidelines as to which acts should in fact be prosecuted."[921] In fact, Section 2.5 of the ABA Standards may require such a result:

> (a) Each prosecutor's office should develop a statement of (i) general policies to guide the exercise of prosecutorial discretion and (ii) procedures of the office. The objectives of these policies as to discretion and procedures should be to achieve a fair, efficient and effective enforcement of the criminal law.
> (b) In the interest of continuity and clarity, such statement of policies and procedures should be maintained in a handbook of internal policies of the office.[922]

---

920 Vorenberg, Duke Law Journal, supra, at 665.

921 Flakne and Caplan, Trial, supra, at 35.

922 Section 3.9 of the ABA Standards (Discretion in the Charging Decision) provides a suggested set of guidelines:

> Illustrative of the factors which the prosecutor may properly consider in exercising his discretion are:
> (i) the prosecutor's reasonable doubt that the accused is in fact guilty;
> (ii) the extent of the harm caused by the offense;
> (iii) the disproportion of the authorized punishment in relation to the particular offense of the offender;
> (iv) possible improper motives of a complainant;
> (v) reluctance of the victim to testify;
> (vi) cooperation of the accused in the apprehension or conviction of others;
> (vii) availability and likelihood of prosecution by another jurisdiction.

Second, if prosecutors fail either to develop or abide by such standards, it may be appropriate to seek legal remedy against the prosecutor based on (a) "abuse of discretion;"[923] (b) "selective enforcement;"[924] or (c) breach of duty"[925] theories. Admittedly, the law strongly favors the

---

[923] The law does not favor this position. In Manning v. District Court of Roxbury (Mass.S.C.Adv.Sh. 1977, p.749), a Fenway Park spectator sought an indictment after being struck in the head by a ball thrown by pitcher Ross Grimsley. The District Attorney refused to prosecute. The court held for the prosecutor, explaining that "a District Attorney has wide discretion in determining whether to prosecute an individual just as he has wide discretion in determining whether to discontinue a prosecution once commenced.... The plaintiff has no constitutional right to direct the conduct of a public prosecutor."

Former Circuit Judge Berger agreed in Newman v. U.S., 127 U.S. App. D.C. 263, 264, 328 F.2d 479, 480 (1967): "Few subjects are less adapted to judicial review than the exercise by the Executive of his discretion in deciding when and whether to institute criminal proceedings..."

[924] Theoretically, a prosecutor could be liable if he prosecutes sports violence cases "with an evil eye and unequal hand." (Yick Wo v. Hopkins, 118 U.S. 356, 1886). In practice, however, this doctrine has been applied only to the most egregious cases. Therefore, it may not be useful in requiring the development of workable guidelines. First, it has only been applied where a prosecutor has been overzealous, not if he is not aggressive enough (Oyler v. Boles, 368 U.S. 448, 1962). Second, "selectivity" in and of itself is insufficient. One must prove that the selection was deliberately "based on an unjustifiable standard such as race, religion, or other arbitrary classification." (U.S. v. Steele, 461 F.2d 1148, 1972). Third, there are substantial and legitimate interests underlying selective enforcement, such as (1) achieving general deterrence; (2) making better allocation of prosecutorial resources; (3) obtaining maximum results from prosecutorial efforts; (4) bringing test cases; and (5) taking the individual circumstances of offenses and offenders into account. Fourth, cases cloak the prosecutor with a presumption of enforcement in "good faith and in a nondescriminatory manner"; the suing plaintiff must reverse this presumption (U.S. v. Falk, 479 F.2d 616, 624, 1973). Fifth, those few who are prosecuted, such as Dave Forbes, might conceivably raise an equal protection argument if they can define the classification decision rule which has singled them out. However, in addition to proving the existence of other violators who remain free from prosecution, one must also show "that the selection of particular violators for arrest and prosecution from among a larger class of violators of the same criminal statute is the result of intentional and deliberate choice by law enforcement officers, and is not the result of 'mere laxity.'" Wisconsin Law Review, supra, at 778.

[925] A recent article has advocated liability for those government officials who were negligent in handling those entrusted to their care and, as a result,

prosecutor in each instance. However, if the threat of legal liability is a strong enough lever to induce a prosecutor to adopt and enforce precise standards, then it should not be dismissed out of hand.

D. Chapter IV Issues: Federal Sports Commission as A Solution to Statutory and Common Law Ambiguity.

While proceeding through the various elements of and applicable defenses to a sports violence assault and battery indictment, Chapter IV attempted to explore the problems inherent in each element and defense. In essence, the rampant ambiguities and line drawing problems suggest that the criminal justice system is attempting to meet a specific problem with a set of statutes that have, at best, only partial application.

---

caused harm to a third party. The argument is drawn from Restatement (Second) of Torts, §319 (1965): "One who takes charge of a third person whom he knows or should know to be likely to cause great bodily harm to others if not controlled is under a duty to exercise reasonable care to control the third person to prevent him doing such harm." Courts applying this principle have found actionable negligence in the negligent release of a dangerous prisoner on parole and negligent release from secure, court-ordered psychiatric confinement. In both cases the released prisoner murdered members of the public at large. The argument could, therefore, be made that a prosecutor would be liable to a victim who was attacked during a game, if the prosecutor had failed to indict for a previous attack. However, this novel argument is incompatible with case law, at least as currently developed. First, general sovereign immunity has been held dispositive in two cases (see Reiff v. Pennsylvania, 397 F.Supp. 343, E.D.Pa. 1975). Second, there have been no cases which have applied the doctrine specifically to the prosecutor's office--a doubtful proposition given the "prosecutorial immunity" espoused in Imbler and Newman, supra. Third, the litigator must contend also with the general rule that while public officials owe a duty to the general public, they owe no duty to a specific plaintiff. (Gerneth v. City of Detroit, 465 F.2d 784, cert.den., 409 U.S. 1109 (1973). See generally Carrington, "Victims' Rights Litigation: A Wave of the Future," 2 University of Richmond Law Review 447 (1977).

One significant solution to this and other problems appears to be a governmental sports agency which would have the power to oversee and regulate all aspects of sport.[926] There are a number of different proposals. Though the mechanics of such a system can be debated, the advantages common to all proposals are worth noting.

In the criminal context, there would be numerous advantages. First, the problem of discriminating individual liability from sports liability would not be eliminated, but would be less compelling in fact when the sport institution, through regulatory guidance, ceases to promote or tolerate questionable activity.[927] Second, Meshbesher argues that the difficulties of defining appropriate conduct would be reduced by forming a regulatory board

---

926 The Suffolk Law Review advocates the following system: The three commissioners would promulgate rules and regulations, hear all league-wide disputes, make all franchise decisions, and review all suspensions ordered by associate commissioners. The associate commissioners would arbitrate localized disputes and enforce their decisions with fines or suspensions. They would be dispatched to trouble spots, holding hearings or arbitrating disputes in private. The associates would thus be able to react to a situation immediately and effectively. Development by the associate commissioners of specialities in a particular sport, while beneficial in some respects, may be conducive to their "capture" by special interests. Therefore, specialization should probably be discouraged. By remaining general experts in all the sports, the associate commissioners may be better able to preserve their objectivity. Supra, at 83. Forbes defense counsel Meshbesher proposes a cooperative effort among the federal and state governments to establish either a federal sports commission, state sports commissions, or both. This approach would give primary review of sports-related matters to a regulatory board and provide for criminal sanction through referral of extreme cases only as a last resort. Halowell and Meshbesher, Trial, supra, at 32. McMurtry proposes a Council composed of "responsible persons with a solid representative background in hockey, coaching, physical education, sports psychology, health, and recreation." It should be answerable directly to the government, but "be separate from it." McMurtry, supra, at 41. NFLPA Executive Director Garvey advocates a system whereby the team or league files an individual complaint "before an arbitration panel or agency." Georgetown Law Journal, supra, at 796. The Nebraska Law Review suggests that federal and state sports commissions be created and given primary review of sports-related matters, with only extreme cases being referred to the judicial system. Supra, at 1139.

927 Halowell and Meshbesher, Trial, supra, at 32.

composed of knowledgeable representatives of the sport itself and of other sports-related fields.[928] The Georgetown Law Journal agrees, noting that "an agency could acquire greater expertise in the problems of professional sports than could the courts, for the sole function of the agency would be the regulation of such sports."[929] Third, an agency could impose uniform national regulation, thus avoiding possible inconsistencies inherent in judicial proceedings.[930] Fourth, even if civil or criminal sanctions would suffice under normal circumstances, the agency could provide the additional deterrent of imposing additional sanctions on the team for a player's violations.[931] Fifth, Meshbesher argues that the public policy issues and current ambiguities can be confronted head-on through legislative and administrative action with more effectiveness and justice.[932]

Furthermore, there are additional spinoff advantages that flow from administrative-type regulation in this context. First, such an approach

---

928 Id.

929 Supra, at 795.

930 Id. Meshbesher developes the advantages of such uniformity: By replacing sporadic and haphazard intervention of criminal law with an institutionalized process, disciplinary continuity could lead to increased deterrence and predictability. This would be partly a result of uniformity that can be secured through governmental response, and would alleviate the cynic's observation that several different assault laws apply to hockey--depending on the site of the contest. Halowell and Meshbesher, Trial, supra, at 32.

931 House Select Committee on Professional Sports, Inquiry into Professional Sports. Final Report, HR Rep. No. 1786, 94th Cong., 2d Sess (1976).

932 Halowell and Meshbesher, Trial, supra, at 32.

would be similar to the situation long established for other occupations, most notably the professions, "and would be long overdue recognition of the nature of sports as a business enterprise."[933] Second, an agency approach could reduce the "Chapter I, §A pressures" inflicted on players by the sports establishment by eliminating the need for an athlete to affirmatively initiate court action. Rather, under an agency approach, the club, league, or sport which has been damaged by an individual's alleged misconduct would bear the burden of initiating action, and would be required to file a complaint upon which the agency could take appropriate disciplinary action against an athlete.[934] Meshbesher suggests that "the administrative process provides the advantages of legal intervention while at the same time preserves that sense of uniqueness that sports officials demand."[935]

In recommending such a government sports agency, it must be realized that Congress has traditionally been opposed to such a proposal. The record of Congress provides evidence of a public "hands-off" policy toward the regulation of professional sport. Although numerous bills concerning professional sport have been introduced in the Congress in recent years, only two of those bills have been enacted into law.[936] In 1958, for example, a proposal which would have established an agency to regulate baseball was summarily rejected by Congress for several not entirely persuasive reasons. One reason was the expense of establishing another government agency

---

933 Id.

934 Georgetown Law Journal, supra, at 796.

935 Halowell and Meshbesher, Trial, supra, at 32.

936 Gonzaga Law Review, supra, at 66.

and of forcing the sport to follow new administrative procedures. A second, more serious objection was the belief that the various sports should be free to work out their own problems without governmental influence.[937] However, the knowledge of prior Congressional opposition should not deter future efforts at implementation, especially since the idea is an advantageous one.

Some of the proposed suggestions and recommendations run the predictable risk of being overly idealistic or impractical. Rather than creating a justification for instant rejection, such criticisms should serve to generate a more precise and detailed set of proposals. Clearly, professional sports violence has become a significant problem. Chapter I argues that the establishment will continue approving of such violence. Chapter II argues that violence will increase if internal fines and suspensions are the only deterrent. Chapter III argues that violence will continue unless prosecutors develop a forceful, consistent, and rational policy of symbolic enforcement. Chapter IV argues that violence will remain as long as criminal statutes are incapable of redrawing old lines to meet new situations. The Paiement-Polonich case study confirms the prior analysis.

Hopefully, this paper has provided some informational insight into a process which has heretofore lacked comprehensive study. Defense attorney Meshbesher, reflecting upon the system through his experience in the Forbes case, remarked that "increases in information and...research on the key ques-

---

937 Capetta, Connecticut Law Review, supra, at 374.

tions...would be beneficial to creating the informational basis necessary for effective policymaking."[938] If this paper has disseminated some of that information, it has largely satisfied its goal.

---

[938] Halowell and Meshbesher, Trial, *supra*, at 32.

....

The game started out all right, but before long it got rather bloody. This is when [my English visitors] both started asking questions.

"Is the object of the game to injure as many players on the other team as possible?" the husband asked.

"No, that is not the object of the game," I said.

The wife asked,"Do you get more points for breaking a man's leg or his neck?"

"You don't get points for breaking either his leg or his neck. You get penalized for it."

"Oh," said the husband. "What is the penalty?"

"Your team is penalized 15 yards."

"Do you mean to say that if you break an opponent's leg, you only get 15 yards against you?"

"What do you think he should get?" I said, trying to hold my temper.

"In England, I believe it's three years in prison," the wife replied.

"It's a game!" I said. "The men who play expect to have their legs broken. That's what makes it so exciting."

"How civilized," the wife said.

....

I couldn't keep my temper in any longer. "What do you think we are--barbarians?"

"Quite," the husband said.

--Art Buchwald, "Beginners Watching Football," Atlanta Journal and Constitution 21A (October 23, 1977).

## Athlete Surveys

Sent to players in the following sports:

National Basketball Association (245 players on the following teams):

Atlanta Hawks
Boston Celtics
Chicago Bulls
Cleveland Cavaliers
Denver Nuggets
Detroit Pistons
Golden State Warriors
Houston Rockets
Indiana Pacers
Kansas City Kings
Los Angeles Lakers
Milwaukee Bucks
New Jersey Nets
New Orleans Jazz
New York Knickerbockers
Philadelphia Seventy Sixers
Phoenix Suns
Portland Trail Blazers
San Antonio Spurs
San Diego Clippers
Seattle Super Sonics
Washington Bullets

National Football League (56 Player Representatives of the following teams):

Atlanta Falcons
Baltimore Colts
Buffalo Bills
Chicago Bears
Cincinnati Bengals
Cleveland Browns
Dallas Cowboys
Denver Broncos
Detroit Lions
Green Bay Packers
Houston Oilers
Kansas City Chiefs
Los Angeles Rams
Miami Dolphins
Minnesota Vikings
New England Patriots
New York Giants

New York Jets
Oakland Raiders
Philadelphia Eagles
Pittsburgh Steelers
Saint Louis Cardinals
San Diego Chargers
San Francisco Forty Niners
Seattle Seahawks
Tampa Bay Buccaneers
Washington Redskins

National Hockey League (425 players on the following teams):

Atlanta Flames
Boston Bruins
Buffalo Sabres
Chicago Black Hawks
Colorado Rockies
Detroit Red Wings
Los Angeles Kings
Minnesota North Stars
Montreal Canadiens
New York Islanders
New York Rangers
Philadelphia Flyers
Pittsburgh Penguins
St. Louis Blues
Toronto Maple Leafs
Vancouver Canucks
Washington Capitals

## Books/Reports

Anderson, J. (ed.). Economic Regulatory Policies (1976).

Asinof, E. Eight Men Out (1963).

Brief for Appellants NFL and Alvin Ray Rozelle. Mackey v. National Football League, 543 F.2d 606 (8th Cir. 1976).

Cahalan, William L. Press Release Concerning Wayne County Prosecuting Office Decision in Paiement-Polonich Incident (December 19, 1978).

Conacher, Brian. Hockey in Canada; The Way It Is (1971).

Fischler, S. Slashing (1975).

Greenwood, et al. The Criminal Investigation Process (1977).

Hearings on Organized Professional Team Sports Before the Subcommittee on Antitrust and Monopoly of the Senate Committee on the Judiciary, 85th Cong., 2d Sess. 423 (1958).

Klein, David. Pro Football Mystique (1978).

LaFave, W. Arrest: The Decision to Take a Suspect into Custody (1965).

Landry, F. and W. Orban (eds.). Ice Hockey: Research, Development and New Concepts (1979).

McCauley, John. Official's Report to the League President Concerning the Paiement-Polonich Incident (October 25, 1978).

McMurtry, William. Investigation and Inquiry into Violence in Amateur Hockey (1974).

Model Penal Code (1962).

Moore, Mark H. Buy and Bust (1977).

National Football League Collective Bargaining Agreement (1977).

National Hockey League Collective Bargaining Agreement (1978).

Official Rule Book of the National Hockey League (1978).

Official Rules of Professional Football (1975).

O'Neill, Brian. Decision on Paiement Match Penalty. Game #58. Colorado at Detroit (November 7, 1978).

Packer, Herbert. The Limits of the Criminal Sanction.

Parrish, Bernard. They Call It A Game (1974).

Perkins, R. Criminal Law (2d ed. 1969).

Proposed Federal Criminal Code. Final Report of the National Commission on Reform of Federal Criminal Laws (1971).

Prosser, William. Torts (1971).

Restatement (Second) of Torts (1965).

Schrag, C. (ed.). Crime and Justice American Style (1971).

Sobel, Lionel. Professional Sports and the Law (1977).

Steinmetz, S.K. and M.A. Straus (eds.). Violence in the Family (1975).

Thompson, John L. Internal Memorandum to Chief Assistant Prosecutor Carnovale Concerning the Polonich-Paiement Incident (December 13, 1978).

Woolf, Bob. Behind Closed Doors (1976).

Yiannakis, A., T. McIntyre, M.J. Melnick, and D.P. Hart (eds.). Sport Sociology: Contemporary Theories (1976).

## Cases

Agar v. Canning, 54 W.W.R. (n.s.) 302 (Q.B.Man.), affd., (1960) SS W.W.R. (n.s.) 384 (C.A.).

Ali v. Division of State Athletic Commission, 308 F.Supp. 11 (S.D.N.Y. 1969).

American Football League v. National Football League, 205 F.Supp. 60 (D.Md. 1962), affd, 323 F.2d 124 (4th Cir. 1963).

American League Baseball Club v. Chase, 86 Misc. 441, 149 N.Y.S. 6 (Sup.Ct. 1914).

American League of Professional Baseball Clubs, 180 N.L.R.B. 189 (1969).

Argersinger v. Hamlin, 92 S.Ct. 2006.

Bailey v. Safeway Stores, Inc., 55 Wash.2d 728, 349 P.2d 1077 (1960).

Barrett v. Fritz, 248 N.E.2d (1969).

Benedetto v. Travelers Ins. Co., 172 So.2d 354 (La.App. 1965).

Bernstein v. Alameda-Contra Costa Medical Ass'n, 139 Cal.App.2d 241, 293 P.2d 862 (Dist.Ct.App. 1956).

Blalock v. Ladies Professional Golf Association, 359 F.Supp. 1260 (N.D.Ga. 1973).

Bourgue v. Duplechin, 331 So.2d 40 (La.App. 1976).

Carey v. Toles, 7 Mich.App. 195, 151 N.W.2d 396 (1967).

Carroll v. Electrical Workers Local 269, 133 N.J.Eq. 144, 31 A.2d 223 (Ch. 1943).

Commonwealth v. Collberg, 119 Mass. 350 (1876).

Commonwealth v. Farrell, 322 Mass. 606, 78 N.E.2d 697 (1948).

Crane v. Kansas City Baseball Co., 168 Mo.App. 301, 153 S.W. 1076 (K.C.Mo. App. 1913).

Deesen v. Professional Golfer's Ass'n, 358 F.2d 165 (9th Cir. 1966).

Denver Rockets v. All-Pro Management, Inc., 325 F.Supp. 1049 (C.D.Cal. 1971).

Falcone v. Middlesex County Medical Soc'y, 34 N.H. 582, 170 A.2d 790 (1961).

Federal Baseball Club of Baltimore v. National League, 259 U.S. 200 (1922).

Flood v. Kuhn, 407 U.S. 258 (1972).

Fraser v. Berkeley, 7 Car. + R. 621, 173 E.R. 272 (1836).

Gardella v. Chandler, 79 F.Supp. 260 (S.D.N.Y. 1948).

Gerneth v. City of Detroit, 465 F.2d 784, cert. den., 409 U.S. 1109 (1973).

Gibeline v. Smith, 80 S.Q. 961 (Mo.App.).

Gordon v. Deer Park School Dist. No. 414, 71 Wash.2d 119, 426 P.2d 824 (1967).

Greene v. McElroy, 360 U.S. 474 (1959).

Griggas v. Clauson, 6 Ill.App.2d 412, 128 N.E.2d 363 (1955).

Hackbart v. Cincinnati Bengals, Inc., 435 F.Supp. 352 (D.Colo. 1977).

Haywood v. National Basketball Ass'n, 401 U.S. 1204 (1971).

Hurwitz v. Directors Guild, 364 F.2d 67 (2d Cir. 1966).

James v. Marinship Corp., 25 Cal.2d 721, 155 P.2d 329 (1944).

Joint Anti-Fascist Refugee Comm. v. McGrath, 341 U.S. 123 (1951).

Kansas City Royals v. Major League Baseball Players' Association, ___ F.2d ___ (8th Cir. 1976).

Kapp v. National Football League, 390 F.Supp. 73 (N.D.Cal. 1974).

McCune v. Wilson, 237 So.2d 169 (Fla.Sup.Ct. 1970).

McGee v. Board of Educ., 226 N.Y.S.2d 329, 16 App.Div.2d 99 (1962).

Mackey v. National Football League, 543 F.2d 606 (8th Cir. 1976).

Manning v. District Court of Roxbury (Mass.S.C.Adv.Sh. 1977, p.749).

Marjorie Webster Jr. College v. Middle States Ass'n, 302 F.Supp. 459 (D.D.C. 1969).

Matthews v. Eldridge, 242 U.S. 319 (1976).

Mechanical Contractors Bid Depository v. Christiansen, 352 F.2d 817 (10th Cir. 1965), cert. den., 384 U.S. 918 (1966).

Metropolitan Exhibition Co. v. Ewing, 42 F. 198 (C.C.S.D.N.Y. 1890).

Molinas v. National Basketball Association, 190 F.Supp. 241 (S.D.N.Y. 1961).

Nabozny v. Barnhill, 31 Ill.App.3d 212, 334 N.E.2d 258 (1975).

Nassau Sports v. Peters, 352 F.Supp. 870 (E.D.N.Y. 1972).

National Football League Management Council and the Constituent Member Clubs of the National Football League and National Football League Players' Association, 203 N.L.R.B. 165 (1973).

Newman v. United States, 127 U.S.App.D.C. 263, 382 F.2d 479 (1967).

Nykolyn v. The King (1949), 74 C.C.C. 145, 8 C.R. 7, (1949) S.C.R. 392.

Oyler v. Boles, 368 U.S. 448 (1962).

People v. Fitzsimmons, 34 N.Y.S. 1102 (1895).

People v. Lenti, 44 Misc.2d 118, 253 N.Y.S.2d 9 (1964).

People v. Smallwood, 52 Misc.2d 1027, 277 N.Y.S.2d 429 (Ct.Spec.Sess. 1967).

Philadelphia Ball Club v. Lajoie, 202 Pa. 210, 51 A. 973 (1902).

Philadelphia World Hockey v. Philadelphia Hockey Club, 351 F.Supp. 462 (E.D. Pa. 1972).

Pinkerton v. United States, 328 U.S. 640 (1946).

Radovich v. National Football League, 352 U.S. 445, reh. denied, 353 U.S. 931 (1957).

Regina v. Alison, 8 Car. and P. 418, 173 E.R. 557 (1838).

Regina v. Bradshaw, 14 Cox Crim Cas 83 (1878)

Regina v. Coney, 8 Q.B.D. 534 (1882).

Regina v. Cullen, 93 C.C.C. 1, 7 C.R. 103 (Ont.C.A. 1948), affd 94 C.C.C. 337, S.C.R. 658 (1949).

Regina v. Green, 16 D.L.R.3d 137 (Ont.Prov.Civ. 1970).

Regina v. Kinman (1911), 18 C.C.C. 139, 16 B.C.R. 148 (C.A.).

Regina v. Leyte, (1973), 13 C.C.C.2d 458 (Ont.Prov.Ct.Crim.Div.).

Regina v. Maki, 14 D.L.R.3d 164 (1970).

Regina v. Moore, 14 T.L.R. 229 (1898).

Regina v. Starrat, (1972), S.C.C.C.2d 32, (1972) 1 O.R. 32 (C.A.).

Reiff v. Pennsylvania, 397 F.Supp. 343 (E.D.Pa. 1975).

Reilly v. Pinkus, 338 U.S. 269 (1949).

Rex v. Donovan, 2 K.B. 408 (1934).

Robertson v. National Basketball Association, 389 F.Supp. 867 (S.D.N.Y. 1975).

Sanders v. International Ass'n of Bridge Workers, 130 F.Supp. 253 (W.D.Ky. 1955).

Silver v. New York Stock Exchange, 373 U.S. 341 (1963).

Smith v. Pro Football, 420 F.Supp. 738 (D.D.C. 1976).

State v. Forbes, No. 63280 (Dist.Ct.Minn.) (July 19, 1975).

State v. Fransua, 510 P.2d 106 (Ct.App.N.M. 1973).

State v. Peters, 274 Minn. 309, 143 N.W.2d 832 (1966).

Tavernier v. Maes, 242 Cal.App.2d 532, 51 Cal.Reptr. 575 (1966).

Taylor v. State, 214 Md. 156, 133 A.2d 414 (1957).

Tepler v. Frick, 204 F.2d 506 (2d Cir. 1953).

United States v. Falk, 479 F.2d 616 (1973).

United States v. Steele, 461 F.2d 1148 (1972).

United Steelworkers of America v. Enterprise Wheel and Car Corp., 363 U.S. 593 (1960).

Wood v. Postlethwaite, 6 Wash.App. 885, 496 P.2d 988 (1972).

Yick Wo v. Hopkins, 118 U.S. 356 (1886).

General Manager Surveys

Sent to the following Team Executives in the National Hockey League:

Allen, Keith. General Manager. Philadelphia Flyers.

Bastien, Baz. General Manager. Pittsburgh Penguins.

Fletcher, Cliff. General Manager. Atlanta Flames.

Francis, Emile. General Manager. St. Louis Blues.

General Manager. Buffalo Sabres.

Gregory, Jim. General Manager. Toronto Maple Leafs.

Grundman, Irving. Vice President. Montreal Canadiens.

Lindsay, Ted. General Manager. Detroit Red Wings.

McGuire, George. General Manager. Los Angeles Kings.

McNab, Max. General Manager. Washington Capitals.

Milford, Jake. General Manager. Vancouver Canucks.

Miron, Ray. General Manager. Colorado Rockies.

Nanne, Lou. General Manager. Minnesota North Stars.

Pulford, Bob. General Manager. Chicago Black Hawks.

Shero, Fred. General Manager. New York Rangers.

Sinden, Harry. General Manager. Boston Bruins.

Torrey, William. General Manager. New York Islanders.

## Interviews

Brooks, Shiela. National Football League Players' Association Staff Counsel. Washington, D.C. Telephone interview (November 11, 1978). Personal interview (November 23, 1978).

Buoniconti, Nick. Attorney and Former NFLPA President while a player with Boston Patriots and Miami Dolphins. Miami, Florida. Personal interview (January 3, 1979).

Caplan, Allan. Associate Prosecutor in Forbes case. Hennepin County (Minnesota) Attorney's Office. Minneapolis. Telephone interview (January 12, 1979).

Carnovale, Dominick R. Wayne County (Detroit), Michigan Chief Assistant Prosecuting Attorney. Detroit. Telephone interview (January 24, 1979).

Cohen, Jeff. Boston Celtics (NBA) Assistant General Manager. Boston, Massachusetts. Personal interview (February 9, 1979).

Fishkin, Ken. Attorney associated with sports attorney Bob Woolf. Boston. Telephone interview (November 15, 1978).

Gardner, Pierce. Washington Capitals (NHL) Public Relations Director. Landover, Maryland. Personal interview (February 3, 1979).

Garvey, Ed. National Football League Players' Association Executive Director. Washington. Personal interview (November 23, 1978).

Greeby, Ray. Major League Baseball Director of Player Relations. New York. Telephone interview (November 10, 1978).

McDonough, Will. Boston Globe sportswriter. Boston. Telephone interview (November 11, 1978).

McMurtry, William. Attorney and author of comprehensive Investigation and Inquiry into Violence in Amateur Hockey. Toronto. Telephone interview (January 12, 1979).

McNab, Max. Washington Capitals (NHL) General Manager. Landover, Maryland. Personal interview (February 3, 1979).

O'Neill, Brian. National Hockey League Executive Vice-President. Montreal. Telephone interview (January 11, 1979).

Rose, Peter. Major League Baseball Players' Association Associate Counsel. New York. Letter (December 7, 1978).

Simpson, M. National Hockey League Players' Association Managing Officer. Montreal. Telephone interview (January 11, 1979).

## Law Review Articles/Periodicals

Alyvia, K., "Professional Sports Contracts and the Player's Association," 5 Manitoba Law Journal 359 (1973).

Assault and Battery, 6 Corpus Juris Secundum 106 (1934).

Beale, "Consent in the Criminal Law," 8 Harvard Law Review 317 (1895).

Binder, Richard L., "Consent Defense: Sports, Violence, and the Criminal Law," American Criminal Law Review 235 (1975).

Brody, F., "Impact of Litigation on Professional Sports," 14 Trial 34 (1978).

Bulmer and Carmichael, "The National Labor Relations Board and the Duty to Bargain in Good Faith," in J. Anderson (ed.), Economic Regulatory Policies 135 (1976).

Burr, Keith J., "Player Control Mechanisms in Professional Team Sports," 34 University of Pittsburgh Law Review 645 (1973).

Capetta, John, "The Booby Trap: Does the Violent Nature of Professional Football Vitiate the Doctrine of Due Care in Participant Tort Litigation?," 10 Connecticut Law Review 259 (1978).

Carrington, F.G., "Victims' Rights: A New Tort?," 14 Trial 39 (1978).

Carrington, F.G., "Victims' Rights Litigation: A Wave of the Future," 2 University of Richmond Law Review 447 (1977).

Clark, W.J., E. Vaz, V. Vetere, and T.A. Ward, "Illegal Aggression in Minor Hockey: A Causal Model," prepared for F. Landry and W. Orban (eds.), Ice Hockey: Research, Development and New Concepts (1979).

Comment, "Assumption of Risk Defense," 7 American Law Reports 3d 1300 (1977).

Comment, "Contact Sports Injury Cases," 7 American Jurisprudence Trials 218 (1964).

Comment, "Not Quite Cricket," 6 Anglo-American Law Review 133 (1977).

Comment, "Sherman Act: Football's Player Controls--Are They Reasonable?," 6 California Western Law Review 133 (1969).

Comment, "Sherman Act and Professional Team Sports: the NFL Rozelle Rule Invalid Under the Rule of Reason," 9 Connecticut Law Review 336 (1977).

Comment, "Contractual Rights and Duties of the Professional Athlete--Playing the Game in a Bidding War," 77 Dickinson Law Review 352 (1973).

Comment, "Torts--Participant in Athletic Competition States Cause of Action for Injuries Against Other Participant," 42 Missouri Law Review 347 (1977).

Comment, "True Story of What Happens When the Big Kids Say, 'It's My Football and You'll Either Play By My Rules or You Won't Play at All," 55 Nebraska Law Review 335 (1976).

Comment, "Contract Matters and Disciplinary Procedures in Professional Sport," 39 Saskatchewan Law Review 213 (1974).

Comment, "Legal Aspects of Sports," 24 Record 306 (1969).

Comment, "Sports, Torts, Courts," 12 Trial 21 (1977).

Crime and its Impact--An Assessment, President's Commission on Law Enforcement and the Administration of Justice (1967).

Eastwood, J., "The Effects of Viewing a Film of Professional Hockey on Aggression," 6 Medicine and Science in Sports 158 (1974).

Epstein, R., "The Case Against Artificial Turf," 14 Trial 42 (1978).

Faulkner, R.R., "Making Violence by Doing Work: Selves, Situations, and the World of Professional Hockey," 1 Sociology of Work and Occupations 288 (August, 1974).

Fischler, Stan, "Speaking Out On Hockey," Sporting News 22 (March 1, 1975).

Flakne, Gary W. and Allan H. Caplan, "Sports Violence and the Prosecution," 12 Trial 33 (1977).

Friendly, H., "Some Kind of Hearing," 123 University of Pennsylvania Law Review 1267 (1975).

Gessford, James B., "Arbitration of Professional Athletes' Contracts: An Effective System of Dispute Resolution," 55 Nebraska Law Review 362 (1976).

Gilroy, T.P. and P.J. Madden, "Labor Relations in Professional Sports," 28 Labor Law Journal 768 (1977).

Goldstein, S.M., "Out of Bounds Under the Sherman Act? Player Restraints in Professional Team Sports," 4 Pepperdine Law Review 285 (1977).

Goldstein, Lynn A., "Participants Liability for Injury to a Fellow Participant in an Organized Athletic Event," 53 Chicago-Kent Law Review 97 (1976).

Goode, W.J., "Force and Violence in the Family," Violence in the Family (1975).

Gorla, G., "Decision of the Rota Fiorentina of 1780 on Liability for Damages Caused by the Ball Game," 49 Tulane Law Review 346 (1975).

Halowell, L. and Ronald I. Meshbesher, "Sports Violence and the Criminal Law," 12 Trial 27 (1977).

Hartnagel, Teevan, and McIntyre, "Television Violence and Violent Behavior," 54 Social Forces 341 (1975).

Hechtler, W., "Criminal Law and Violence in Sports," 19 Criminal Law Quarterly 425 (1977).

Hofeld, Al F., "Athletes--Their Rights and Correlative Duties," 19 Trial Lawyer's Guide 383 (1976).

Kaplan and Singer, "Television Violence and Viewer Aggression: A Reexamination of the Evidence," Journal of Social Issues 35 (1976).

Kennedy, "Wanted: An End to Mayhem," Sports Illustrated 18 (November 17, 1975).

Kram, "Their Lives are On the Line," Sports Illustrated 36 (August 18, 1975).

Kuhlmann, Walter, "Violence in Professional Sports," Wisconsin Law Review 771 (1975).

LaFrance, A., "Criminal Defense Systems for the Poor," 50 Notre Dame Lawyer 44 (1974).

Lambert, D.J., "Tort Law and Participant Sports," 4 Journal of Contemporary Law 143 (1978).

Langerman, S. and Noel Fidel, "Responsibility is Also Part of the Game," 12 Trial 23 (1977).

Lee, B.E., "Survey of Professional Team Sport Player Control Mechanisms Under Antitrust and Labor Law Principles: Peace at Last," 11 Valparaiso University Law Review 373 (1977).

Lombardi, Vince and T. Cohane, "Why Pros Play Better Football," 25 Look 107 (October 24, 1961).

Lotter, Aline H., "Keeping the Illusion Alive: The Public Interest in Professional Sports," 12 Suffolk University Law Review 48 (1978).

Love, John J., "Criminal Law: Consent as a Defense to Criminal Battery--the Problem of Athletic Contests," 28 Oklahoma Law Review 840 (1975).

Lowell, C.H., "Collective Bargaining the the Professional Team Sport Industry," 38 Law and Contemporary Problems 201 (1973).

Markus, "Sport Safety: On the Offensive," 8 Trial 12 (1972).

Mashaw, "The Management Side of Due Process: Accuracy, Fairness, and Timeliness in Adjudication of Social Welfare Claims," 59 Cornell Law Review 772 (1974).

Mertens, "Congruence Theory," Crime and Justice American Style (1971).

Miller, D.G., "Some Modest Proposals for Collective Bargaining in Professional Sports," 48 LAB Bulletin 149 (1973).

Morris, John P., "In the Wake of the Flood," 38 Law and Contemporary Problems 85 (1973).

Nelson, S., "Bringing Sports Under Legal Control," 10 Connecticut Law Review 251 (1978).

Note, "Discipline in Professional Sports: The Need for Player Protection," 60 Georgetown Law Journal 771 (1972).

Note, "Torts--Assumption of Risk--A Professional Football Player Assumes the Risk of Receiving a Blow, Delivered Out of Anger and Frustration But Without Specific Intent to Injure, During a Game," 12 Georgia Law Review 380 (1978).

Note, "Antitrust--Professional Football--the Rozelle Rule as an Unreasonable Restraint of Trade, 26 Kansas Law Review 121 (1977).

Note, "Consent in Criminal Law: Violence in Sports," 75 Michigan Law Review 148 (1976).

Partin, Matt, "Tort Liability for Players in Contact Sports," 45 University of Missouri-Kansas City Law Review 119 (1976).

Philo, H.M. and G. Stine, "The Liability Path to Safer Helmets," 12 Trial 38 (1977).

Reed, "Week of Disgrace on the Ice," Sports Illustrated 22 (April 26, 1976).

Schmidt, L., "In Football, It's Arbitration," 13 Trial 38 (1978).

Schneiderman, Michael, "Professional Sport: Involuntary Servitude and the Popular Will," 7 Gonzaga Law Review 63 (1971).

Schuett, Patricia K., "Tort Liability in Professional Sports: Battle in the Sports Arena," 57 Nebraska Law Review 1128 (1978).

Shapiro, D.I., "Professional Athlete: Liberty or Peonage?," 13 Alberta Law Review 212 (1975).

Slusher, "Sport: A Philosophical Perspective," 38 Law and Contemporary Problems 129 (1973).

Smith, Michael, "Social Determinants of Violence in Hockey: A Review," prepared for Canadian Journal of Applied Sport Sciences (December, 1978).

Smith, Michael, "Towards an Explanation of Hockey Violence: A Reference-Other Approach," prepared for Canadian Journal of Sociology (1979).

Stigler, G.J., "The Optimum Enforcement of Laws," Journal of Political Economy 528.

Thibaut, Walker, LaTour, and Holden, "Procedural Justice as Fairness," 26 Stanford Law Review 1271 (1974).

Tutko, T., "Sports Winning Really Isn't Everything," 11 People 29 (1972).

Vaz, E.W. and D. Thomas, "What Price Victory? An Analysis of Minor League Players' Attitudes Towards Winning," 2 International Review of Sport Sociology 47 (1974).

Vaz, E., "The Culture of Young Hockey Players: Some Initial Observations," Sport Sociology: Contemporary Themes 212 (1976).

Vorenberg, James, "Narrowing the Discretion of Criminal Justice Officials," Duke Law Journal 651 (1976).

Wechsler, "The Challenge of a Model Penal Code," 65 Harvard Law Review 1097 (1952).

Weistart, John D., "Athletics. Foreward," 38 Law and Contemporary Problems 171 (1973).

Weistart, John C., "Player Discipline in Professional Sports: the Antitrust Issues," 18 William and Mary Law Review 677 (1977).

Yeager, "The Savage State of Sports," Physician and Sportsmedicine 94 (1977).

## Prosecutorial Surveys

Of the 34 surveys dispatched, the following attorneys responded with survey responses, cover letter explanations, or additional appended material (date received in parentheses):

Bailey, Christopher T. King County Prosecuting Attorney. Seattle, Washington (December 12, 1978).

Cahalan, William L. Wayne County Prosecuting Attorney. Detroit, Michigan (December 6, 1978; December 21, 1978; January 29, 1979).

Caplan, Allan H. Assistant Hennepin County Attorney. Minneapolis, Minnesota (December 4, 1978).

Carey, Bernard. State's Attorney of Cook County. Chicago, Illinois (December 20, 1978).

Colville, Robert E. Allegheny County District Attorney. Pittsburgh, Pennsylvania (December 11, 1978).

County Prosecutor. Bergen County. Hackensack, New Jersey (December 6, 1978).

Dillon, Dennis. Nassau County District Attorney. Mineola, New York (December 12, 1978).

Gentile, Paul T. Bronx County Chief Assistant District Attorney. Bronx, New York (December 7, 1978).

Haas, Harl. Multnomah County District Attorney. Portland, Oregon (December 13, 1978).

Hyder, Charles F. Maricopa County Attorney. Phoenix, Arizona (January 9, 1979).

Jensen, D. Lowell. Alameda County District Attorney. Oakland, California (December 6, 1978).

Miller, Edwin L., Jr. San Diego County District Attorney. San Diego, California (December 26, 1978).

Morgenthau, Robert M. New York County District Attorney. New York, New York (December 11, 1978).

Peach, George A. Circuit Attorney. St. Louis, Missouri (December 4, 1978).

Reno, Janet. State Attorney. Miami, Florida (December 18, 1978).

Salcines, E.J. Hillsborough County State Attorney. Tampa, Florida (March 7, 1979).

Tooley, Dale. Denver District Attorney. Denver, Colorado (December 14, 1978).

Vance, Carol S. Harris County District Attorney. Houston, Texas (December 28, 1978).

Van de Kamp, John K. Los Angeles County District Attorney. Los Angeles, California (December 14, 1978).

Yankelove, Alexander. Associate Deputy State's Attorney of Baltimore City. Baltimore, Maryland (December 18, 1978).

## Appendices

A Ray Fitzgerald, "A Lawyers Playbook."

B Survey sent to professional athletes.

C Cover letter sent to National Hockey League Player Association Representatives

D Letter from William R. McMurtry

E Photographs of Green-Maki incident

F Smith's study of percent of players who agree with statements regarding the utility of violence

G Examples of illegal hitting learned from watching professional hockey

H Questionnaire sent to the 17 NHL General Managers

I Response from Los Angeles Kings General Manager George Maguire

J Standard Canadian Football League Standard Player Contract

K Standard NHL Player Contract

L Major League Baseball Rules of Procedure

M Survey sent to county prosecutors

N Cover letter sent with survey

O Letter from Dennis Dillon, Nassau County (New York) District Attorney

P Letter from Carol Vance, Harris County (Houston) District Attorney

Q Correspondence with Dominick R. Carnovale, Wayne County (Detroit) Chief Assistant Prosecuting Attorney

R Diagram of the Paiement-Polonich stickswinging incident

S Official's Report to League President by game official John McCauley.

T Executive Vice-President O'Neill's Decision in the Paiement-Polonich incident

U    Press Release from Wayne County Prosecuting Attorney's Office

V    Letter to NHLPA Executive Director Alan Eagleson

W    Response from Executive Director Eagleson

X    Constitution of the National Hockey League Players' Association

# APPENDIX B

I am writing a research paper analyzing the way the league deals with unnecessary on the field violence.

I sincerely hope that you will find the time to complete this questionnaire and send it back to me (or give it to your Player Representative if he is collecting them). I realize that some of these issues may be sensitive for some of you. However, please be assured that your answers will be kept strictly confidential. As I am sending surveys to players in all major sports, I hope to get enough responses to enable me to draw some legal conclusions about the system. Please feel free to add any comments you care to. Good luck for the rest of the season.

---

## PART ONE: VIOLENCE DURING THE GAME

While most violent acts are just part of the game, some of the more "unnecessary acts" are dealt with through the league hearing procedures rather than through the courts. I am trying to learn more about this.

1. Have you ever contemplated suing another player for something that happened during a game? If so, please describe the details, being as specific as you want.

2. If such a thought hasn't crossed your mind, but you have heard of someone else thinking about a lawsuit, please describe the details, being as specific as you want.

3. Why do you think there are so few court lawsuits against players for acts which occur during games?

4. Specifically, do you think any of the following are reasons for the fact that there are so few lawsuits? (With each one, please tell me if you have felt any of these pressures yourself):

   A: Provisions in the contract and league rules that require a player to go to the league office before he goes to courts.

B: Pressure by teammates and other players discouraging the harmed player from suing.

C: Difficulty in getting other players, coaches, or management to testify in court.

D: Pressure by team management, coaches, or owners discouraging the harmed player from suing.

E: Monetary pressures discouraging the harmed player from suing. (Fear that filing a lawsuit will hurt later contract negotiations or grievance claims).

F: Are there any other factors that I should know about?

5. Since most punishment is handed out through the league's fine and suspension procedures, would you please comment on your general impression of these procedures. Are they usually fair? How could they be improved? After a player has been fined or suspended in one of these league proceedings, is he treated any differently by teammates, other players, coaches, or management? (If any of these procedures have focused on you, please be as specific as you want).

## APPENDIX C

Dear Player Representative:

As I indicated in the enclosed questionnaires, I am writing a research paper analyzing the way the league deals with unnecessary "during the game" violence.

While most violent acts are just part of the game, some of the more "unnecessary acts" are dealt with through the league hearing procedures rather than through the courts.

I sincerely hope that you will find the time to distribute these questionnaires. If it is inconvenient to collect and return them yourself, please ask the players to do so on their own. Most importantly, I want to emphasize that these surveys will be kept absolutely confidential. As I am sending questionnaires to players in all major sports, I hope to get enough responses to enable me to draw some legal conclusions about the system.

I have received some basic help from the NHLPA in Toronto and the NFLPA in Washington. They also gave me your name and address in the hope that I would be able to distribute this questionnaire.

From an academic perspective, I would be excited about any assistance you could provide. Thank you for your cooperation. Good luck for the rest of the season.

Most sincerely,

Rick Horrow

Rick Horrow

# APPENDIX G

Examples of Illegal Hitting Learned From Watching Professional Hockey

---

I learned spearing and butt-ending.

You sort of go on your side like turning a corner and trip him with a skate.

Charging. You skate towards another guy who doesn't have the puck and knock him down. Or coming up from behind and knocking him down.

Sneaky elbows, little choppy slashes Bobby Clarke style.

Hitting at weak points with the stick, say at the back of the legs.

Coming up from behind and using your stick to hit the back of his skates and trip him.

Butt-end, spearing, slashing, high sticking, elbow in the head.

Put the elbow just a bit up and get him in the gut with your stick.

Along the boards, if a player is coming along you angle him off by starting with your shoulder and then bring up your elbow.

The way you "bug" in front of the net.

Clipping. Taking the guy's feet out by sliding underneath.

Sticking the stick between their legs. Tripping them as they go into the boards.

Ive seen it and use it: when you check a guy, elbow him. If you get in a corner you can hook or spear him without getting caught.

Giving him a shot in the face as he's coming up to you. The ref can't see the butt ends.

How to trip properly.

Like Gordie Howe, butt-ends when the ref isn't looking.

---

Adapted from Smith, Michael, "Social Determinants of Violence in Hockey: A Review," prepared for Canadien Journal of Applied Sport Sciences (December, 1978).

## APPENDIX H

Dear General Manager:

I am writing a research paper analyzing the relationship of the criminal law to professional sports violence. I hope to explore the league procedures for dealing with unusually severe acts of sports violence. Such acts, because of their exceptional nature, may arguably be ripe for criminal prosecution, notwithstanding traditional assumption of risk and consent defenses. While I know the nature of the sport dictates that most such "violent acts" are "just part of the game," it seems clear that the most repugnant acts are dealt with through the league fine and suspension procedures rather than through the criminal courts.

Most specifically, I am interested in the following:

1. Formal and informal pressures which operate to keep such cases out of the criminal courts. For example:

    a. Clauses in the Collective Bargaining Agreement and/or Bylaws which require the pursuit of grievances through the league internal mechanisms first.

    b. Any informal pressure by other players or team management which operates to keep cases out of the criminal courts.

2. An exploration of the methods which are used to "enforce" such prohibitions against going to the criminal courts:

    a. Monetary pressures of some kind.

    b. Possible manipulation of pension funds, Workmens' Compensation claims, or injured players' contract grievances.

    c. Harder line in subsequent contract negotiations.

3. An analysis of the "special charactetistics" of the cases which have been criminally prosecuted; including those which have been investigated by the prosecutor (the recent Paiement case).

4. A detailed exploration of the league fine and suspension hearing procedures, and player and General Manager reaction to those procedures.

If possible, I would like any insights, perceptions and comments you might have about any or all parts of my thesis. I am attempting to seek as many perspectives as I possibly can. I am sending letters and questionnaires to all players and management in all major sports. I hope to get enough responses to enable me to draw some representative conclusions about the system.

Accordingly, from an academic perspective, I would be excited about any assistance you could provide.

Thank you for your consideration.

Most sincerely,

Richard Horrow

Rick Horrow

# APPENDIX L

## RULES OF PROCEDURE

**Formulated by the Commissioner and Announced Pursuant to the Major League Agreement, and the Professional Baseball Agreement.**

(1) NOTICE. Written notice of the time and place of hearings shall be given under the direction of the Commissioner.

(2) APPEARANCE. In all claims and disputes submitted to the Commissioner the persons or organizations concerned shall be entitled to appear and be heard in person, to present witnesses, to cross examine witnesses and to be represented by an attorney. In the case of dispute between a Major League Club and a National Association Club, or other matter involving or concerning a National Association League or National Association Club, a representative designated by the National Association shall be entitled to appear.

(3) PROCEEDINGS. Proceedings before the Commissioner shall be conducted in general like judicial proceedings and with due regard for all the principles of natural justice and fair play, but the Commissioner may proceed informally whenever he deems it desirable.

(4) PROOFS. The Commissioner will in general follow the established rules of evidence but may depart from them in cases in which the ends of justice will in his judgment best be subserved by so doing. He may receive and consider affidavits if, in his judgment, there is good reason for the non-appearance of the affiants.

(5) SUMMONS. In the case of all persons or organizations who have accorded recognition to the office and authority of the Commissioner, a summons by him, by letter or telegram, to appear either as a party or as a witness before him, the Secretary-Treasurer or before any person he may designate, shall be binding upon the person or official to whom directed. Failure to respond to the summons, or to produce the documents or other evidence which it may specify, or to testify and give evidence fully and accurately to the best of his knowledge, and any offering, or attempt to offer, of any false testimony or evidence, or any attempt to induce another to offer or attempt to offer any false testimony or evidence, will be treated by the Commissioner as conduct deemed not to be in the best interests of Baseball and penalties will be imposed by him pursuant to the terms of the Major League Agreement, and/or the Professional Baseball Agreement, as the case may be.

(6) DEPOSITIONS. The Commissioner, when he deems proper, may direct testimony to be taken and evidence to be produced at convenient places before a notary public or other officer, or before the Secretary-Treasurer, and in such cases will proceed substantially as if the testimony had been taken on an open commission in a judicial proceeding.

(7) DEFAULT. If any person, club or league party to any dispute, claim, complaint or charge shall fail to answer fully thereto within fifteen (15) days after notice thereof, or such further time, if any, as the Commissioner may have allowed in writing, the Commissioner shall render judgment or take action, as the case may be, against the party in default.

(8) RECORD. The Secretary-Treasurer will assist the Commissioner in matters pending before him and will preserve all documents entrusted to him. Stenographic reports of hearings may be made at the discretion of the Commissioner. Notification of all action will be given under direction of the Commissioner to all parties in interest, and public statements will be made by him in all cases where, in his judgment, publicity is either necessary or proper.

BOWIE K. KUHN, Commissioner.

## APPENDIX M

### Questionnaire: Prosecution of Sports Violence

I am writing a research paper analyzing the relationship of the criminal law to professional sports "violence." I hope to explore the processes for dealing with unusually severe acts of player violence. Such acts, because of their exceptional nature, may arguably be ripe for criminal prosecution, notwithstanding traditional assumption of risk and consent defenses. While I know the nature of organized sport dictates that most such "violent acts" are "just part of the game," it seems clear that the more repugnant acts are dealt with exclusively through league fine and suspension procedures rather than through the criminal courts.

Among other things, I am most interested in exploring the factors involved in any decision whether or not to prosecute exceptionally severe acts of sports violence.

I understand that this survey may be somewhat of an imposition in light of your office's demanding caseload. I also understand that interests in confidentiality and prosecutorial integrity in decisionmaking may be implicated. Accordingly, I will appreciate any position you take in any of your responses. However, as this area is of extreme interest to me from an academic perspective, I would be excited about any assistance you could provide.

~~||||~~ ~~||||~~ ~~||||~~ ~~||||~~

24 surveys
20 responses

---

I) Please comment upon any "exceptionally severe acts of sports violence" which have come to your attention (through any formal or informal means) within the last five years.

| HAVE | HAVE NOT |
|---|---|
| ~~\|\|\|\|~~ \|\|\| | ~~\|\|\|\|~~ ~~\|\|\|\|~~ \|\| |

a. Please indicate how such acts have "come to your attention." (Through the media?; watching a game?; complaining players, officials, or team or league management?)

attending fans ||
media ~~||||~~
grand jury |
victims |||

b. Have there been any such cases that your office has considered prosecuting? To the extent feasible, please describe these cases.

Please comment on the relative influence of the following factors in the office's decision whether or not to prosecute:

1. Extent of media coverage and public awareness of the event.

| MUCH (↑ influence) | SOME | NONE (NO influence) |
|---|---|---|
| | //// | ~~////~~ / |

2. Availability of players as complainants and/or witnesses (willingness to testify).

| WERE AVAILABLE (no influence) | SOMETIMES | NOT AVAILABLE (↑ influence) |
|---|---|---|
| ~~////~~ /// | / | // |

3. Problems of proof (especially given "consent," "self defense," and "assumption of risk" defenses).

| PROBLEM | SOME | NO PROBLEM |
|---|---|---|
| ~~////~~ // | / | ~~////~~ |

4. Pressure from players, teams, or leagues to "keep cases out of the criminal courts."

| MUCH (↑ influence) | SOME | NONE (NO influence) |
|---|---|---|
| | /// | ~~////~~ /// |

5. Deference to the leagues' internal fine and suspension mechanisms.

| MUCH | SOME | NONE |
|---|---|---|
| // | // | 卌 //// |

6. Willingness to allow injured players to pursue remedies through the civil court system.

| MUCH | SOME | NONE |
|---|---|---|
| | // | 卌 //// |

7. Any other factors deemed significant.

II) Have there been any such cases that your office has actually prosecuted within the last five years?

a. To the extent feasible, please comment upon these cases and their dispositions (including citations, if possible).

b. To what extent were any of the factors described in I(b) involved in these prosecutions.

III) Please comment upon your perceptions of the role of criminal prosecution in controlling exceptionally severe acts of sports violence.

APPENDIX R

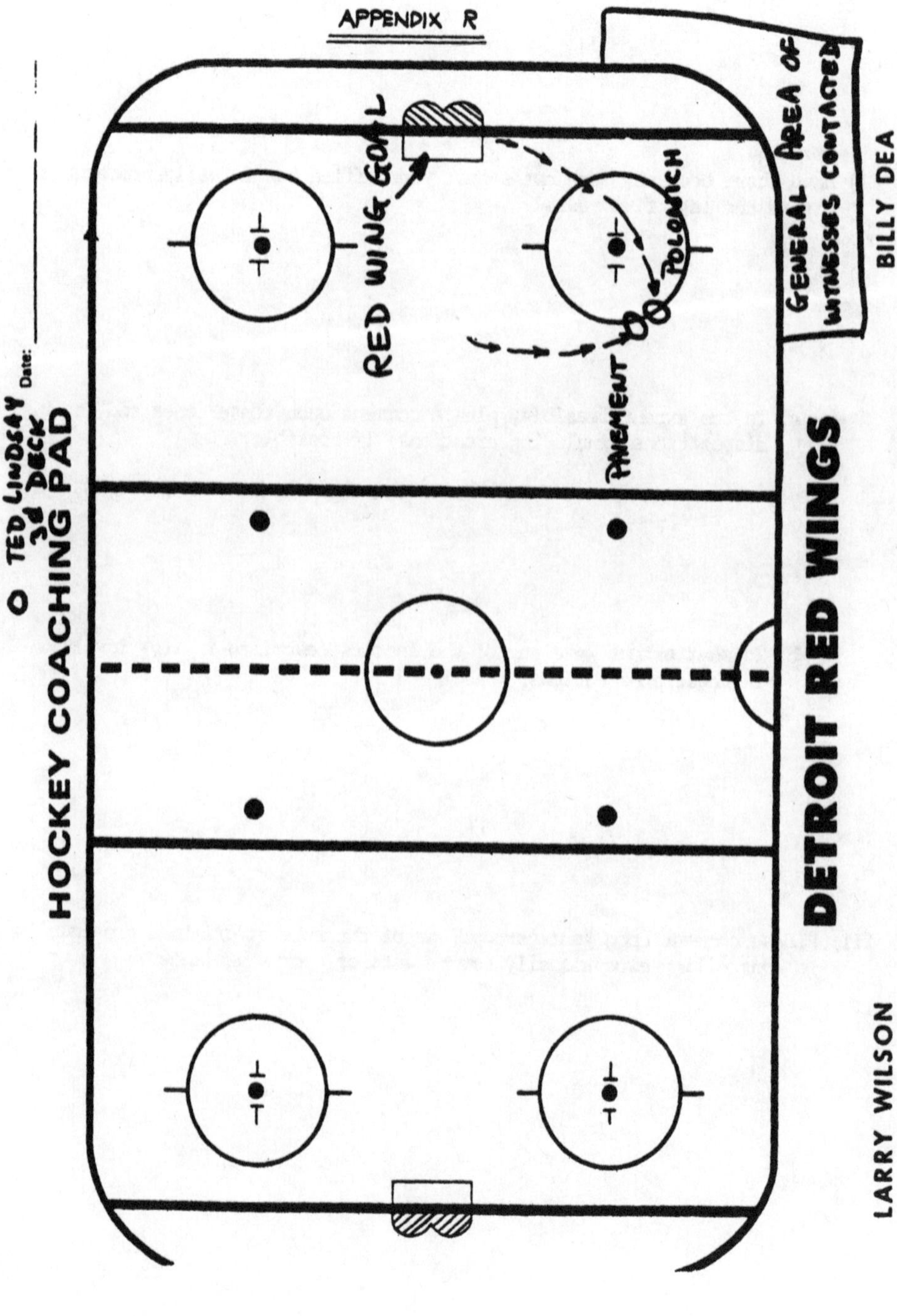

HOCKEY COACHING PAD
O TED LINDSAY 3d DECK
Date:
RED WING GOAL
PAVEMENT
POLONICH
GENERAL AREA OF WITNESSES CONTACTED
BILLY DEA
DETROIT RED WINGS
LARRY WILSON

II) Have there been any such cases that your office has actually prosecuted within the last five years?

a. To the extent feasible, please comment upon these cases and their dispositions (including citations, if possible).

b. To what extent were any of the factors described in I(b) involved in these prosecutions.

III) Please comment upon your perceptions of the role of criminal prosecution in controlling exceptionally severe acts of sports violence.

APPENDIX R

HOCKEY COACHING PAD

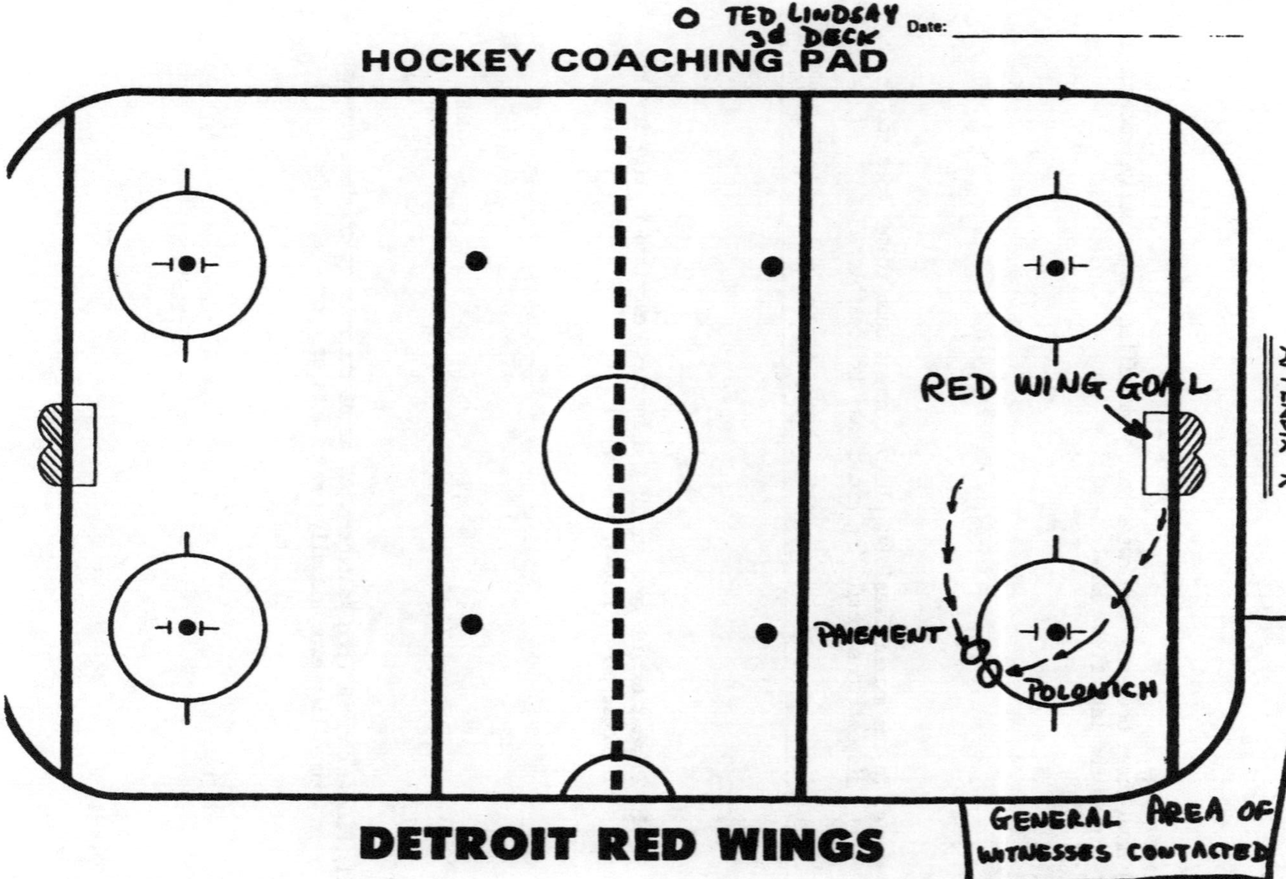


DETROIT RED WINGS

LARRY WILSON

BILLY DEA

# APPENDIX S
# OFFICIAL'S REPORT TO LEAGUE PRESIDENT

LEAGUE ......... NHL ......................... GAME NO.. 58 ........ DATE.. Oct. 25, 1978

TEAMS .... Colorado ........ AT.. Detroit ............ FINAL SCORE Det. 5 Col. 4

REFEREE .... McCauley ....... LINESMEN ....... Pavelich .... ..... Morris ..........

REASON FOR REPORT .... Wilf Paiement, Colorado ..... Match Penalty ............

Was verbal report given to League President (Mr. O'Neill) ( . x ... ) yes ( ..... ) no

When? After Game ( .. X ... ) Following Day ( .. ... )

Time of Incident ..... 10:28 ........... Period ...... 2 .............. . Score Det. 1 Col. 0

Describe in detail events leading up to and including incident on the *reverse side* of this Report including diagrams if necessary. (Use additional sheets if required).

What Penalties (if any) were assessed: Wilf Paiement, Colorado .. 10 mins., match penalty

Denis Polanich, Detroit, major high sticking ...........................

.......................................................................

.......................................................................

General Comments: Polanich had the puck coming out of the corner in his own end zone. After passing it up the ice (an icing situation) he brought his stick up which struck Paiement in the face. Paiement then took a vicious two-handed slash (baseball style swing) striking Polanich across the face sending Polanich to the ice. He lay there, face down, in a pool of blood. Polanich was given a major penalty under Rule 58C, Paiement received a match penalty under Rule 49 deliberate injury to an opponent.

.......................................................................

John McCauley ..........

.......................................................................

.......................................................................

# APPENDIX T

DECISION

WILF PAIEMENT - MATCH PENALTY
GAME #58 - COLORADO AT DETROIT
OCTOBER 25, 1978

In a game between Colorado Rockies and Detroit Red Wings played at Detroit on October 25, 1978 a match penalty under Rule 49 - Deliberate Injury of an Opponent - was assessed to Wilf Paiement of the Colorado Rockies for striking Dennis Polonich of the Detroit Red Wings in the face with his stick. The blow was described by the Referee John McCauley as a "baseball type swing". The injuries sustained by Polonich included a severe nasal fracture, multiple lacerations to the face and a concussion.

For the purpose of reviewing the facts pertaining to this incident two hearings were convened by Brian O'Neill, NHL Executive Vice-President, one on October 27, 1978 and the other on November 6, 1978. In attendance at the first hearing were player Wilf Paiement, Ray Miron - Colorado Rockies General Manager, Referee John McCauley and the Referee-in-Chief - Scotty Morrison.

The second hearing was held in order to review the final medical report and to hear the oral testimony of the injured player Dennis Polonich who was unable to attend the first hearing. In attendance at the second hearing besides Polonich and Paiement were Red Wings General Manager Ted Lindsay, Ray Miron, Armand Pohan and Aldo Guidolin all of the Colorado Rockies, as well as Referee John McCauley and Referee-in-Chief - Scotty Morrison. Also in attendance was Bill Watters, Mr. Paiement's representative.

The facts of the incident as provided by the written reports, oral testimony and video tape are as follows:

## APPENDIX T

At 10:28 of the second period Polonich of Detroit passed the puck from his defensive zone and as he shot the puck his stick came up and struck Paiment in the mouth. In retaliation for this blow Paiement swung his stick at Polonich and struck him in the face with a vicious blow that resulted in the injuries referred to previously. Polonich fell immediately to the ice and was bleeding profusely. Paiement was then escorted from the ice and sent to his dressing room.

In his testimony Paiement stated that he thought that Polonich had deliberately struck him in the mouth with his stick and that he immediately retaliated. The video tape showed Polonich's stick striking Paiement but it cannot be determined whether it was deliberate.

Paiement also disputes that he used the force attributed to him by the Referee although he admits that it was a two-handed swing. It was pointed out, also, in defense of Paiement that he has not received any previous match penalties and that in four seasons in the League has not been noted as a player who uses his stick against his opponent.

For his part Polonich stated that he had no memory of the incident and the attending physician verifies that he had no recollection of events after the first period and for several hours after the injury.

A full report on the physical condition of Dennis Polonich was received on November 6th by attending Physician Dr. John H. Finley of Detroit. The report describes the injury in detail and states that he is recovering satisfactorily. Polonich was discharged

## APPENDIX T

from hospital after three days and following additional tests was given permission to skate on November 2, 1978. The doctor indicated, also, that if there are no delayed abnormalities Polonich could return to play with facial protection sometime between November 8 and November 15, 1978.

It is my decision, therefore, that Wilf Paiement shall be suspended without pay for a total of fifteen (15) games which shall include the six games that he has served already, the next seven games of his Club and the two remaining games against Detroit Red Wings - November 29, 1978 and February 25, 1979. In addition he is fined the maximum amount permitted under the Rules - $500.

This suspension represents approximately 20% of the playing season and is one of the severest disciplinary actions imposed in the League's history for an on-ice altercation. Each player and Club must take note that stick-swinging will bring a forfeiture of the privelege of playing. This is the first incident of a deliberate injury to an opponent in several years and we trust all players will learn that there is not to be another.

Brian O'Neill
Executive Vice-President

NATIONAL HOCKEY LEAGUE

November 7, 1978.

APPENDIX U

WILLIAM L. CAHALAN
PROSECUTING ATTORNEY
DOMINICK R. CARNOVALE
CHIEF ASSISTANT

COUNTY OF WAYNE
OFFICE OF THE PROSECUTING ATTORNEY
DETROIT, MICHIGAN

1200 FRANK MURPHY HALL OF JUSTICE
1441 ST. ANTOINE STREET
DETROIT, MICHIGAN 48226
TEL. 224-5777

PRESS RELEASE

FOR IMMEDIATE RELEASE

DECEMBER 19, 1978

THIS OFFICE HAS COMPLETED AN INVESTIGATION INTO AN INCIDENT WHICH OCCURRED DURING A DETROIT RED WING HOCKEY GAME ON OCTOBER 25, 1978.

THE PURPOSE OF THIS INVESTIGATION WAS TO DETERMINE IF ANY CRIMINAL CHARGES SHOULD BE BROUGHT AGAINST WILF PAIEMENT, A PLAYER FOR THE COLORADO ROCKIES, FOR STRIKING RED WING PLAYER DENNIS POLONICH IN THE FACE WITH A HOCKEY STICK DURING THE GAME.

AFTER A CAREFUL REVIEW OF THIS INVESTIGATION, WE HAVE DECIDED THAT NO CRIMINAL CHARGE WILL BE BROUGHT AGAINST MR. PAIEMENT.

THE INVESTIGATION ITSELF WAS THOROUGH AND COMPLETE. NOT ONLY WAS MR. POLONICH INTERVIEWED, OVER 150 CONTACTS WERE MADE, THEREBY LOCATING A LARGE NUMBER OF EYE WITNESSES WHO ALSO WERE INTERVIEWED AND INTERROGATED. VIDEOTAPES WERE REVIEWED AND THE RECORDS OF THE NATIONAL HOCKEY LEAGUE DISCIPLINARY PROCEEDING AGAINST MR. PAIEMENT WERE OBTAINED AND EVALUATED.

APPENDIX U

THE DECISION WHETHER OR NOT TO PROSECUTE A PLAYER FOR ACTS COMMITTED DURING AN ATHLETIC CONTEST CAN BE A DIFFICULT ONE TO MAKE. A PROSECUTION WHICH IS NOT SOUNDLY BASED IN LAW AND FACT WOULD HAVE NO DETERRENT EFFECT AT ALL, AND MIGHT EVEN ENCOURAGE MORE VIOLENCE IN CONTACT SPORTS SUCH AS HOCKEY.

ON THE OTHER HAND, THE OPERATION OF LAW DOES NOT STOP AT THE TICKET GATES OF ANY SPORTS EVENT IN MY JURISDICTION. EVEN THOUGH THIS SPECIFIC INCIDENT WILL NOT RESULT IN A CRIMINAL PROSECUTION, EVERYONE CONCERNED SHOULD UNDERSTAND THAT CRIMINAL VIOLENCE OCCURRING DURING ANY SPORTING EVENT WILL, IF SUPPORTED BY FACT AND LAW, BE PROSECUTED. NONETHELESS, WE ARE OF THE OPINION THAT THE EVIDENCE HERE WILL NOT SUPPORT A CRIMINAL CHARGE AGAINST MR. PAIEMENT.

APPENDIX X

# Constitution of the National Hockey League Players' Association

## ARTICLE I
### NAME

This Organization shall be known as the National Hockey League Players' Association, hereinafter also referred to as the Association. This document shall be known as the Constitution of the Association.

## ARTICLE II
### OBJECTS

Section 1. The objects and purposes of the Association shall be:

a. To bring together in this organization, regardless of race, creed, colour or nationality, all National League Hockey players.
b. To promote and foster the best interests of hockey.
c. To establish improvements in conditions of employment for National League hockey players.
d. To provide information and assistance to National League hockey players and engage in activities to advance and safeguard their welfare.
e. To develop such projects and enterprises which will bring further benefits to Members as individuals or to the Association as an entity.
f. To take all steps and actions consistent with the Constitution and By-laws of the Association to implement and carry out the objects, rights, activities and responsibilities of this organization.

## ARTICLE III
### MEMBERSHIP

All players who shall hold a signed contract with a club in the National Hockey League shall be eligible for membership in the Association.

## ARTICLE IV
### CLUB PLAYER REPRESENTATIVES

Section 1. The active Members of each National League club shall elect, from among their number, a Club Player Representative and an Alternate Club Player Representative. The election of each shall be by secret ballot vote of a majority of the active Members in good standing voting.

Section 2. The next general election of Club Player Representatives and Alternate Club Player Representatives shall be conducted on or before December 1, 1967, and subsequent general elections shall take place every year thereafter. At least twenty-four (24) hours notice shall be given before each election by notice posted on the dressing room bulletin board. The term of office shall be for one year, except that should such Representative or Alternate Representative resign, cease to remain on the active roster of the Club he represents, or fail to maintain his Association membership in good standing, his office shall be declared vacant.

Vacancies shall be filled for the remainder of the term of office by the holding of another election, as set forth in this Article, within seven (7) days after the vacancy occurs. In the event the office becomes vacant between the end of the playing season and the opening of the next season, the election shall take place within ten (10) days after the beginning of training camp.

Section 3. Each Club Player Representative shall serve as a member of the Executive Board of the Association, as hereinafter set forth, and shall confer regularly with the Members from his Club and represent such Members in the resolution of joint problems at the Club level.

Section 4. Each Alternate Club Player Representative in the absence or disability of the Club Player Representative, shall perform the duties and have the powers of the Club Player Representative.

## ARTICLE V
### OFFICERS OF THE ASSOCIATION

Section 1. A President and Vice-President shall be elected by a majority vote of the Club Player Representatives. The President and Vice-President must be on the active roster of a Club in the National League, and may, but need not be a Club Player Representative. The President and Vice-President shall be from different divisions.

Section 2. The next election of the President and Vice-President shall be conducted at the Executive Board meeting held during the week of the 1968 All-Star Game, and subsequent elections shall take place, every year thereafter. The term of office shall be for one year except that should such President or Vice-President resign, cease to remain on the active roster of a Club in the League, or fail to maintain his Association membership in good standing, his office shall be declared vacant. Vacancies shall be filled for the remainder of the term of office by a majority vote of the Club Player Representatives. Such election may be conducted by telegraphic or mail ballots, and shall be held within fifteen (15) days after the vacancy occurs.

Section 3. The President and Vice-President shall serve as members of the Executive Board of the Association, as hereinafter set forth.

Section 4. The President and Vice-President shall also serve as Co-Treasurers of the Association. As Treasurers, they shall receive and collect all monies due to the Association, oversee the making of such disbursements as are authorized by the Executive Board, cause to be kept an accurate account of all monies received and expended for the use of the Association, and make an annual report of the financial operations of the Association at the meeting of the Executive Board during the week of the League Draft Meetings. The Treasurers, before assuming their duties, shall furnish to the Association surety bonds in a sum designated by the Executive Board to insure the faithful discharge of their duties.

Section 5. The Vice-President, in the absence or disability of the President, shall perform the duties and have the powers of the President.

## ARTICLE VI
### EXECUTIVE BOARD

Section 1. The Executive Board of the Association shall consist of the President, Vice-President and the Club Player Representatives. The President shall serve as Chairman of the Executive Board.

Section 2. The Chairman shall call regular meetings of the Executive Board twice each year, and may call such additional meetings as he deems necessary. The regular meetings shall be held each year during the week of the All-Star Game, and during the week of the League Draft Meetings. All appropriate expenses incurred by members of the Executive Board in attending Executive Board meetings shall be reimbursed by the Association.

Section 3. The Executive Board shall direct the affairs of the Association, consistent with the Constitution and By-Laws, and shall establish policy and appoint such committees as may be necessary to carry out the objects and purposes of the Association.

Section 4. The Executive Board may suspend a Member from the Association for proper cause. If a Member is suspended for reasons other than non-payment of dues, he may petition the Executive Board for a redetermination and shall have the right, at his own expense, to appear before the Executive Board at its next regular meeting and present arguments and witnesses in support of his petition. Within 30 days following such hearing, the Executive Board shall issue its final decision.

## ARTICLE VII
### EXECUTIVE DIRECTOR

Section 1. The Executive Director shall be appointed by the Executive Board to carry out and implement the policies of the Association. The terms and conditions of employment of the Executive Director shall be established by the Executive Board.

Section 2. The Executive Director shall maintain and direct the activities of the permanent office of the Association. He shall be authorized to engage counsel, technical assistance and secretaries and establish salaries or fees and conditions of employment for such persons, subject to an annual budget established by the Executive Board.

Section 3. Between meetings of the Executive Board, the Executive Director shall direct the affairs of the Association and shall function on behalf of the Executive Board, subject to the approval of the Board.

## ARTICLE VIII
### DUES

Section 1. The Executive Board, at its regular meeting during the week of the League Draft Meetings, shall fix for the following year the rate of annual dues for Members of the Association. Special assessments may be levied upon recommendation of the Executive Board and ratification by a majority of the Members in good standing voting.

Section 2. A Member who fails to pay or authorize the payment of his dues shall automatically be suspended from the Association and shall lose all the rights and privileges of membership.

## ARTICLE IX
### EFFECTIVE DATE

This Constitution and By-Laws shall become effective immediately upon its ratification by the Members.

## ARTICLE X
### AMENDMENTS

This Constitution and By-Laws may be amended upon recommendation of the Executive Board and ratification by a majority of the Members in good standing voting.